DOLLY PARTON

100 REMARKABLE MOMENTS IN AN EXTRAORDINARY LIFE

TRACEY E. W. LAIRD

EPIC INK

TO THE CREATIVE SPARK IN EVERY PERSON,

AND TO SSDDL, MY OWN SPARK.

First published in 2023 by Epic Ink, an imprint of The Quarto Group,
142 West 36th Street, 4th Floor, New York, NY 10018, USA
T (212) 779-4972 F (212) 779-6058 www.Quarto.com

Epic Ink titles are also available at discount for retail, wholesale, promotional, and bulk purchase. For details, contact the Special Sales Manager by email at specialsales@quarto.com or by mail at The Quarto Group, Attn: Special Sales Manager, 100 Cummings Center Suite 265D, Beverly, MA 01915 USA.

10 9 8 7 6 5 4 3 2 1

ISBN: 978-0-7603-8296-7

Library of Congress Cataloging-in-Publication Data

Names: Laird, Tracey E. W., author.
Title: Dolly Parton : 100 remarkable moments in an extraordinary life / Tracey Laird.
Description: New York : Epic Ink, 2023. | Series: 100 remarkable moments ;
    2 | Includes bibliographical references and index. | Summary: "Dolly
    Parton: 100 Remarkable Moments in an Extraordinary Life is a beautifully
    illustrated celebration of a timeless icon who has shaped what it means
    to be a superstar"-- Provided by publisher.
Identifiers: LCCN 2023011594 (print) | LCCN 2023011595 (ebook) | ISBN
    9780760382967 (hardcover) | ISBN 9780760382974 (ebook)
Subjects: LCSH: Parton, Dolly | Singers--United States--Biography. |
    Country musicians--United States--Biography. | LCGFT: Biographies.
Classification: LCC ML420.P28 L25 2023 (print) | LCC ML420.P28 (ebook) |
    DDC 782.421642092 [B]--dc23/eng/20230309
LC record available at https://lccn.loc.gov/2023011594
LC ebook record available at https://lccn.loc.gov/2023011595

Group Publisher: Rage Kindelsperger
Creative Director: Laura Drew
Managing Editor: Cara Donaldson
Editor: Katie McGuire
Interior Design: Beth Middleworth
Cover Image: Pictorial Press/Alamy Stock Photo

Printed in China

CONTENTS

INTRODUCTION · 4

BORN TO TELL SONGS · 7
CHILDHOOD THROUGH 1966

BIG DREAMS WITH BIG WINGS · 39
1967–1975

THE TIDE'S GONNA TURN · 69
1976–1980

FIND YOUR PLACE AND SHINE · 101
1981–1990

BACK TO HER ROOTS · 141
1991–2000

A TWENTY-FIRST-CENTURY CULTURAL ICON · 165
2001–2013

STILL ROCKIN' · 207
2014 AND ONWARD

BIOGRAPHICAL NOTES · 252

SOURCES · 254

INDEX · 260

ACKNOWLEDGMENTS · 264

ABOUT THE AUTHOR · 264

IMAGE CREDITS · 264

Introduction
Dolly Once Chased a Butterfly

As a child, Dolly Parton was prone to wander. She loved chasing butterflies, which sometimes led to trouble. As Dolly told Lynn Hirschberg for *W Magazine* during a 2021 interview, "I used to get in trouble with my mom, 'cause they'd have to come find me and I'd be chasing a butterfly from one bush to another." At times, Dolly would become so absorbed in that pursuit that she lost track of both time and space. Perhaps that prefigured her stature today, as Dolly's presence defies both.

As a little girl, Dolly once followed a butterfly to the point that she lost her way and found herself stranded in the woods. She came across the family cow, Bessie, also a regular wanderer, but one who always made her way back to the Parton family home around feeding time. Dolly grabbed onto the collar around the cow's neck and held on until she was delivered, scuffed and bruised, from the ordeal. Her mother's fear and anxiety over her missing child spun on sight into equal parts relief and anger. Ever since, Dolly has maintained her love of butterflies, as well as her instinct for finding a way to stay grounded amidst the unfolding of moment after moment in an extraordinary life.

The image of the butterfly follows Dolly now as she once followed the creatures themselves. The butterfly's shape constitutes the "W" in the logo for her theme park, Dollywood. Butterflies make their way onto every page of a 2019 children's book written about her life, part of a series dedicated to iconic and influential people. It adorns some of her most stunning custom-made clothing and is fashioned in pink crystal on the stopper for a fragrance line launched in 2021 called Dolly: Scent From Above. And butterflies apparently cover parts of her body in the form of pastel-colored tattoos, alongside images of ribbons and bows, that transform scars left on her fair skin from surgical incisions.

In the 2021 *W Magazine* interview, Dolly talked about her feeling for these transforming creatures: "Butterflies don't sting, they don't bite, and they are so beautiful." They also seem tireless, just like her. Now in her late seventies, Dolly's creative energy continues to move her from one project to another, as a butterfly drinks the nectar of many springtime flowers. Her curiosity and sense of compassion keep leading her to unexpected collaborations—musical, medical, and otherwise. And her image is

now recognized and celebrated worldwide. She is known by epithets like the one that journalist Sarah Smarsh gave her in her book *She Come By It Natural*, about Dolly's importance to working-class women: the Great Unifier. She has also been called the Iron Butterfly.

ABOVE: Dolly (standing in the back, on the right side) with family at Christmas in 1960.

BORN TO TELL SONGS

CHILDHOOD THROUGH 1966

"Little kids are my biggest fans. They really sense that fairy tale part of me, the gaudy clothes and silly things I wear. That's what a little kid dreams of. I know I did and I knew I'd have it someday."

—DOLLY TO CANADIAN REPORTER PATRICK SNYDER IN 1978

OPPOSITE: Sunset over the Great Smoky Mountains in Gatlinburg, Tennessee.

In the Good Old Days
A Smoky Mountain Childhood

Certain scenes are hard to shake from the 1968 song "In the Good Old Days (When Times Were Bad)." In her lyrics, Dolly summons up her childhood home with images: snow blowing through cracks in the wall where the newspaper coverings had worn off, her father's hands bleeding from hard labor, the despair of watching a hailstorm destroy the crops all those long, back-breaking hours had nurtured.

Dolly's early life was remarkable both for its hardship and for the loving household her parents maintained despite the difficulties. As Dolly declares in the song's chorus, she would neither trade her childhood memories for anything, nor go back and relive them. By 1973, when the song appeared again on her eleventh solo album, *My Tennessee Mountain Home*, time had tempered those memories to take on more nostalgic shapes: the fireflies evoked in the album's title cut, the taste of sugarcane and gingerbread in "I Remember," and the image of her mom cooking dinner in "Old Black Kettle." Dolly would carry all these memories with her over the course of her legendary career.

Dolly Parton was the fourth of twelve children born to parents Robert Lee Parton ("Lee," to those who knew him) and Avie Lee Owens Parton. During

the earliest years of her childhood, Dolly's family sustained itself via farming, with her father finding other work when and where he could. In 1978, she reflected to Atlanta-based reporter Joseph Litsch, "We had no money at all. Our tobacco crop was our money crop and Daddy sold it once a year around Christmas time and he'd make a couple thousand dollars and that's the only money we had all year and with twelve kids and hospital bills and that sort of thing, you can tell that didn't go far."

The annual influx of cash funded a trip to town when, as she describes in her 1994 memoir *Dolly: My Life and Other Unfinished Business*, Dolly's father carried sticks marked with the length of each child's foot and returned with a clutch of brown leather boots to distribute.

Among her warmest memories, Dolly credits her mother's ingenuity for finding ways to occupy the children and also make them feel special. In a homegrown riff on an ancient folktale about sharing resources, told in one form or another across the world, Avie Lee would send them out to collect stones to make "stone soup." In Avie Lee's case, she aimed more to keep her large brood occupied. When the children returned with their stones, she inspected each offering in order to choose the perfect one.

ABOVE: Dolly and her parents in 1987.

Dolly glowed with a sense of contribution and pride the day hers was chosen, as her mother placed the stone in the bottom of the pot and added vegetables, broth, and other more typical ingredients.

In her songs, as in her memoir, Dolly writes—in her matter-of-fact manner—of the joy and wonder of her early life alongside the genuine hardships her family endured together. They had no running water ("unless you 'run' to get some," Dolly joked). They slept on straw-stuffed mattresses, often four or five to a bed. The youngest children ate standing along an old church pew set against the wall, and forks and knives were shared at mealtimes because there weren't enough for everyone. Among her saddest memories is the death of her infant brother Larry, a loss the young Dolly struggled to accept. Dolly was nine when Larry died, at only four days old. He was to have been "her baby": "That just meant that you got to take extra care of it. You have got to get up with it at night and rock it back and forth." Dolly added,

"So there is a lot of heartache and stuff that goes on with that."

One particularly memorable tale is of Dolly stepping over a fence and coming down on an old plow blade that had been left partially buried in the dirt. Her toes were nearly separated from her foot. Several men gathered to help hold her while her mother poured kerosene on the wound and stitched her foot back together. Dolly credits her mother's wherewithal in that moment with the fact that her foot still works today.

Dolly often describes herself as a deep-feeling person, something stitched within her from the earliest days of her rural Smoky Mountain childhood. As Dolly summed it up in 1978, "We had food to eat and a house to live in. Mama always made our clothes out of scraps and things people would give us. It was really hard times, but we really didn't know there were hard times then."

LITTLE TINY TASSELTOP

The first song Dolly ever wrote was "Little Tiny Tasseltop," about a little corncob doll she'd been given. She was around five when she wrote it, in 1951 or '52, and lyrics include "Cornsilk hair and big brown eyes, how you make me smile." Periodically Dolly performed this sweet little song in public, including on the 1983 TV special *Dolly Parton Meets the Kids*. She revisited the song on a Christmas-themed episode of her variety show, *Dolly*, in 1987. In 2016 she shared it with Gayle King for *CBS This Morning*, recalling how her mother saved the song because she was fascinated that her young daughter could write and rhyme the lyrics so well. "Little Tiny Tasseltop" was the first of what would be more than 3,000 songs penned over the decades. And she's not done yet.

Backwoods Barbie

"I lucked up on an image and I'm glad I did because there's nobody else like me in show business."

Dolly likens herself to a sponge, soaking up bits and pieces from every person and every experience and learning from all the other people she meets. That's what seems to have occurred one day during her childhood, when she went to town with her mother and encountered a woman walking along a street in Sevier County. Dolly had no way of knowing that this woman was "what you call a loose woman, the ones that throw it around a bit, as they say." Dolly saw her short skirt, heavy makeup, and "beautiful skin," and "I remember saying, 'Oh she's so pretty, she's so pretty.' Mom would say, 'Oh she's just trash.' And, so, I thought in my mind, 'That's what I want to be when I grow up—trash.'"

This anonymous woman likely never knew how her clothing and makeup fascinated the young Dolly. Yet Dolly's childhood perception of glamour carried with her into young adulthood, when she found a way to incorporate it into her professional life.

People have been fixated on Dolly's image since early in her career. That same childhood memory surfaces again and again, every time someone asks questions about her iconic, over-the-top clothing, makeup, and store-bought hair. At thirty-two, Dolly told the Atlanta-based reporter Joe Litsch, "I don't want to be ordinary enough to keep up with the styles. I don't want that responsibility because I'm too busy working." This was in 1978. At the time, she had signed a three-movie contract with 20th Century Fox but had

ABOVE: Dolly in one of her now signature hairdos.

yet to make *9 to 5*, the film that would make her a Hollywood star.

She went on to explain to Litsch how she loved the "big fat hairdos" that had come into style when she was in high school, achieved by "backcombing or rattin'." She enjoyed it so much she kept it up even when people began to tell her the style was passé. According to Litsch, at that point in their conversation she sat upright "in mock indignation." Her big hair captured the attention of those who may otherwise have overlooked her. They paid attention long enough to realize "that I did have some talent and there were other qualities about me that are very important." She said, "Then I came up with the idea that as a singer I would use this image. Then I would look different because nobody was doing it then . . . Now they know that I'm not an ignorant person, that I don't do this out of ignorance, but out of intelligence because I lucked up on an image and I'm glad I did because there's nobody else like me in show business. And that's good because who wants to be like somebody else?"

"I feel sexy. I like being a woman. If I'd-a been a man, I'd-a probably been a drag queen."

—DOLLY IN 1983, DURING A UK PRESS CONFERENCE FOR THE TV SPECIAL DOLLY IN LONDON

ABOVE: The winners at the 1968 CMA Awards, including (L to R) Johnny Cash, Jeannie C. Riley (face obscured), Porter, Dolly, Sheb Wooley, Tammy Wynette, Glen Campbell, Bobby Russell, and Chet Atkins.

Singing in Church

A lifelong devotion to faith and community has helped guide Dolly's life

Some of Dolly's earliest musical memories stem from church. It was there she sang in public for the first time around age six. She recalled in a 2013 television interview for the series *Song by Song*, "The first songs I wrote were gospel songs because it was what I felt and knew."

Her family were devout Christians who regularly attended the Pentecostal church, a worship setting characterized by a certain freedom of expression. If people got in the spirit, they could sing or dance or even speak. Dolly told NPR's Terry Gross in 2001 that "we were one of those shouting, healing, holy-roller churches, you know. And it was high-powered, which was great. I really learned to sing in church, I think, really with emotion. And we were a free, you know, it was a free-spirited church, and if you'd wrote a song, a gospel song, of course, you could get up and sing it."

That musicality moved fluidly from church to home. As she told *Interview* in 1989, Dolly was "hearin' my uncles and aunts sittin' around pickin' guitars and banjos and mountain instruments and singin'—that, more than the big stars, was my introduction to music." Dolly no longer attends church—how could she, given her level of fame?—but she does have a private chapel

at every one of her properties. The chapel is an official place to pray, though, as she wrote in the introduction to her cookbook *Dolly's Dixie Fixin's*, "I do my best praying in the kitchen." Her faith stays with her in every room of the house, as it has with every step along her remarkable life's journey.

The experience of a large family shaped her faith. For one thing, the community was so small, everyone at the little church was either a close friend or relative. "And my granddaddy being the preacher, we didn't feel ashamed to sing and play our guitars," Dolly said. "We believed in makin' a joyful noise unto the Lord." Together with her Aunt Dorothy Jo, Dolly wrote a song about Grandpa Jake, who preached for the first time at age seventeen and was eventually ordained. "Daddy Was an Old-Time Preacher Man" became a big duet hit with a lilting country swing for Dolly and Porter Wagoner during the early 1970s.

Fire and brimstone, and the shame and fear that can be woven into those frameworks, never made much sense to Dolly. What stayed with her was the way faith and her community were sources of strength in hard times for her family, as necessary for survival as food. As she reflected in 1987, "I think growing up in a big family with people who really believed there was a higher power helped." The seeds planted there in the little Pentecostal church in the Appalachian hills flowered into a deeply personal experience and understanding of faith that would sustain Dolly through troubles of her own. When asked whether she still attended the Pentecostal church during the 1989 *Interview* piece, she said, "I believe faith is in the heart. I'm not a religious person, but I'm very spiritual. I believe that God is love, and I've always been a firm believer in that thing that is greater than us, that great energy, that great love, and I've used that all my life. I think a lot of my achievements have come from the strength that came from my faith in God."

Dolly released a gospel album in 1971 titled *Golden Streets of Glory*, and mixed the sacred with the patriotic for the 2003 album *For God and Country*. In between those two releases, Dolly's albums consistently included songs referencing faith. In the twenty-first century,

Dolly collaborated with great success with artists in the contemporary Christian space, including the 2019 gospel hit "God Only Knows" with band For King & Country, and "There Was Jesus" with singer and songwriter Zach Williams that same year. Dolly won a 2021 Grammy for Best Contemporary Christian Music Performance/Song and two Gospel Music Association Dove Awards.

The other consistent aspect of Dolly's faith throughout her entire career has been how deeply she absorbed the teachings she heard early on about judgment, acceptance, and love. Speaking with writer Deborah Evans Price for *Billboard* in 2014, Dolly summed up her outlook by saying, "As far as the Christians, if people want to pass judgment, they're already sinning. The sin of judging is just as bad as any other sin they might say somebody else is committing. I try to love everybody."

On the Radio for WIVK

Dolly Performs on Cas Walker Farm and Home Hour

"I was on TV before we owned one."

**—DOLLY TO BILL DEMAIN FOR *PERFORMING SONGWRITER MAGAZINE*,
IN HIS COLLECTION *IN THEIR OWN WORDS***

Apart from church singing, Dolly's first memorable performance before a live audience happened when she was ten years old. Up until then, she typically sang to any siblings she could round up, or maybe a chicken or pig within earshot of the front porch. Sometimes she would wedge a stick between floorboards on the front porch and turn a tin can upside down on the top to fashion a makeshift microphone.

That all changed the day she stood before an actual microphone in front of a relatively small crowd, around sixty people, in the small auditorium at radio station WIVK in Knoxville, Tennessee. At a time when radio still held daily live performances, crowds gathered to see *Cas Walker Farm and Home Hour*, and on this day, they were introduced to a new singer named Dolly Parton. Dolly performed the one song she and her Uncle Bill had prepared, a cover of George Jones's "You Gotta Be My Baby." It was an up-tempo, rollicking honky-tonk number with a lilting melody of the kind made standard by Hank Williams. The enthusiastic reaction for Dolly's rendition prompted an encore, which they had not prepared. So they just repeated the song. The crowd loved it, and as she recalled years later in her memoir, Dolly loved the sound of those cheers. She continued to love that sound for all the decades to come.

Uncle Bill Owens was one of her mother's brothers, a musician who played "his big ol' red Gretsch guitar." He had been an early champion of Dolly's musical ambition and would continue to be as her career later took off. Uncle Bill was also a songwriter whose work was recorded by Loretta Lynn, Porter Wagoner, Kris Kristofferson, and Ricky Skaggs. He would eventually perform regularly at Dollywood, and can be spotted onscreen, along with other family members, playing in the "Wild Possums Band" in Dolly's 1984 movie with Sylvester Stallone, *Rhinestone*. He would also play a dedicated role in environmental efforts to return the American

OPPOSITE: The chapel in Dollywood.

chestnut tree to the Appalachian region, where it had almost completely disappeared.

Uncle Bill had recognized Dolly's talent and encouraged her songwriting. As Bill told a local Knoxville news station, WBIR, decades later about his promotion of his niece's talents, "I ain't a bit bashful." He finagled a way for her to get backstage and meet Cas Walker, a colorful local character and businessman who had built a small empire of local grocery stores. Walker's daily show fit a tradition of small-town Southern business magnates who sponsored radio slots to fill the airwaves with musical entertainment and periodic political rants. He was evidently impressed when, rather than asking for a job, young Dolly said, "Mr. Walker, I want to work for you." Her phrasing "work for" earned her a spot.

Walker's radio show evolved to television, and Dolly continued to perform on the show from age ten until her high school graduation in 1964. Walker's TV show aired Monday, Wednesday, and Thursday nights, so Dolly worked during summer breaks as well as Christmas and other holidays. The five dollars she earned per performance was about equal to the amount a working man like her father would bring home for a full day's labor. Uncle Bill ferried her back and forth to the show, and she often stayed with her Aunt Estelle, her mother's sister, who was married to Uncle Dot Watson.

ABOVE: Dolly, circa 1955.

Along with Dolly's aunt and uncle, others were part of her support system as a young local star. A married couple, Carl and Pearl Butler, fellow performers and musicians on Walker's show, often had Dolly to their house for meals. As years went on, they remained important friends, introducing Dolly to some of their music business connections and also hiring Bill for road performances. Bill, like so many members of Dolly's family, played guitar, and loved to write and sing songs. In a tribute to him after his passing in 2021, Dolly estimated he had written approximately 800 songs over the course of his life.

Puppy Love
Dolly releases her first record

Dolly was thirteen years old when she made her first trip out of Sevier County. Another of her mother's brothers, Uncle Henry, had arranged for her to record for Goldband Records. Uncle Henry was stationed with the Air Force in Lake Charles, Louisiana, where he'd befriended Eddie Shuler. Shuler was part of the post–World War II explosion of small, independent record labels that fueled regional styles and ultimately led to the explosion of rock-and-roll sounds during the mid-1950s.

Shuler, who also repaired television sets for a living, had a passion for music. He started Goldband Records in 1945 and recorded influential Cajun musicians like Iry LeJeune. In 1954, Goldband made history when it released the recording by Boozoo Chavis playing a local style blending rhythm and blues with French Creole music. It turned out to be the first recording ever of the subgenre eventually known as zydeco, a word coined from the lyric in Chavis's song, "*Les haricots sont pas sale,*" or "the beans are not salty." The lyric refers to poverty so dire you can't even flavor your beans.

With the funds Uncle Henry sent, the young teenage Dolly boarded a bus in Sevierville with her Grandma Rena. Dolly had never left the Tennessee hills and Grandma Rena had never traveled alone. Along the way, they got stranded in Alabama, ran out of food, and slept overnight at the bus station, but they eventually made it to Lake Charles. There, Dolly saw her first live oak tree, kissed Eddie Shuler's

---

ABOVE: Dolly, age 14 , from Sevier County High School in 1960.

handsome Cajun son Johnny, and tasted a banana for the first time ever. As she described in her memoir, the trip was transformative—a confirmation that the world she knew had been waiting for her beyond the hills really did hold wonders, as she had suspected all along. The recording, "Puppy Love," penned with Uncle Bill, could have described those "first love" feelings stirred by Johnny Shuler. On the other side was "Girl Left Alone," which Uncle Bill had written with Dolly's Aunt Dorothy Jo.

ON CHASING DREAMS

Dolly once paid a quarter to see a sideshow at the local fair, the "Alligator Girl from the Nile." When she and her friends entered, she recognized the girl as one of her cousins "wearing a swimsuit, and it looked like they had glued green-dyed cornflakes onto her skin to give her that 'crocodile' look." The cousin's father stormed up to the fairgrounds to take her home. But at the next opportunity, the cousin ran off again.

What Dolly learned from the experience was this: "Dreams may be as fragile as soggy cornflakes, but chase them anyway, and store away as many of them as you can in that special place that makes you you. After all, today's alligator girl is tomorrow's storyteller, and both are precious in their own way."

A Little Girl from East Tennessee
Stepping up to the WSM microphone
on the Friday Night Opry

Dolly was thirteen years old when Johnny Cash introduced her as she stepped up to the microphone with the call letters WSM on the historic stage of the *Grand Ole Opry*. This was the *Friday Night Opry*, a live country music show similar in format to Saturday's *Grand Ole Opry*, grandmother of all the "radio barn dance" variety programs once filling radio airwaves across the US. The *Friday Night Opry* began its life in 1948 as an *Opry* spin-off called the *Friday Night Frolics*, hosted by country legend Eddy Arnold. The *Frolics* changed its name when it moved to Nashville's historic Ryman Auditorium.

Actually getting to *be* on that stage was a long shot goal for Dolly and Uncle Bill at the time. The two of them would sometimes hang out in the parking lot near the back entrance to the Ryman, one of their numerous stabs at making headway toward their musical ambitions. Uncle Bill reportedly "dogged country star Chet Atkins outside the *Grand Ole Opry* stage door until he let Dolly sing there."

Dolly's chance at the spotlight was eventually won via sweet-talking, when Louisiana-born country music star Jimmy C. Newman kindly shared his spot for this first performance. She had been asking other performers backstage, knowing that each was slotted for two songs. Jimmy was impressed by her verve. "I promise I'll be good and won't do anything I'm not supposed to," she assured him. Jimmy signaled to Johnny Cash she would go onstage in his stead.

Dolly had already met Johnny Cash once, in the parking lot where she later recalled once blurting out, "Oh, Mr. Cash, I've just got to sing on the *Grand Ole Opry*." Around fourteen years her senior, Johnny had joined the *Opry* as a regular in 1956 and had recorded iconic songs "Folsom Prison Blues" and "I Walk the Line." By this time, he had parted ways with Sun Records in Memphis to record for Columbia.

Not long after her heartfelt plea, there she stood, with Johnny Cash introducing her. Johnny said to the crowd, "Her daddy's listening to the radio at home, and she's gonna be in real trouble if she doesn't sing tonight, so let's bring her out here!'" She walked to the center of the stage at the Ryman, a venue that holds over 2,300 people, approaching the microphone she had so long imagined while listening to *Opry* broadcasts over her family's battery-powered radio. It must have stood about the same height as the stick with a tin can on top.

She again sang George Jones's song "You Gotta Be My Baby." The only other song she recalled having down solidly in her performance repertoire during this early era was Rose Maddox's "Tall Men." In her first interview in 1967, Dolly told *Music City News* writer Everett Corbin that she got three encores. Thirty years later, she mused, "That performance did a lot for my confidence."

ABOVE: The Grand Ole Opry House in 1960.

It's Sure Gonna Hurt

Dolly makes a rockin' record for Mercury

Dolly entered a recording studio for the second time in 1962, at the age of fifteen. As she later described to *Music City News* writer Everett Corbin in 1967—Dolly's first interview, in fact—she "was still in school and couldn't travel. I couldn't leave school. Daddy and Mama were rather strict. They didn't want me out runnin' around at that age. You couldn't blame 'em."

Mercury Records had its origins in Chicago in 1945, recording music that ranged from classical to folk, country to R&B. Some of the company's most celebrated recordings were made with jazz masters of the mid-1950s on a subsidiary label, EmArcy. A collaboration with Starday Records beginning in the late 1950s gradually led to the opening of Mercury Records Nashville in 1961, and the country legends recorded there included George Jones, Jerry Lee Lewis, Roger Miller, and Faron Young. In this era, Mercury also enjoyed hits like "Walk On By" by Leroy Van Dyke and Joe Dowell's pop song "Wooden Heart," both in 1961, and Ray Stevens's novelty tune "Ahab the Arab" in 1962, the same year Dolly recorded.

In 1962, Dolly and Uncle Bill also signed an agreement with Tree Publishing for their songwriting. Tree Publishing had arranged the Mercury session at the behest of William Doyce "Buddy" Killen, who had come to Nashville around 1950 at the age of eighteen, set on playing bass at the *Grand Ole Opry*. He took on a job listening to new songs for Tree and helped build the company into a powerful publishing house known for hits including "Heartbreak Hotel," "Green Green Grass of Home," and "I Fall to Pieces." Buddy eventually became the publishing company's owner.

At the 1962 session, Dolly made two sides for Mercury. The first was a song she wrote with Uncle Bill titled "(It May Not Kill Me but) It's Sure Gonna Hurt." Dolly was clearly channeling Brenda Lee with this record's A-side. Brenda had a country chart hit with "One Step at a Time" in 1957, then recorded the perennial classic "Rockin' Around the Christmas Tree" in 1958. Her career exploded between 1959 and 1964 with a series of pop recordings—about fifty of them—and six R&B crossovers. "A Teenager in Love," a big international success for Dion and the Belmonts in 1959, was clearly another influence. In addition to its predominant early '60s rock-and-roll shuffle, the chord structure of this precedent largely maps "It's Sure Gonna Hurt," though with enough melodic departure to create distinct identity in an era when musical intellectual property was defined by sheet music.

ABOVE: Dolly, age 16, as a high school sophomore in 1962.

Dolly's high soprano is further distinctive. It establishes the song's hook, with vocal background credited to the Merry Melody Singers fleshing out the last three words: "It may not kill me, but it's sure gonna hurt."

A saloon or honky-tonk-style piano tinkles along in the background, the unmistakable flare of the era's influential session pianist Floyd Cramer. Cramer would have known Mercury producer Jerry Kennedy from the *Louisiana Hayride*, the famous radio barn dance that aired from Jerry's hometown of Shreveport, Louisiana, from 1948 to 1960. Jerry's formative years were shaped listening to the *Hayride*'s 50,000-watt clear channel station, KWKH; attending *Hayride* broadcasts from Shreveport's Municipal Auditorium; and eventually playing guitar on its stage. A lineup of future stars performing there—ranging from Rose Maddox to Johnny Cash, from Slim Whitman to Johnny Horton—shaped his musical sensibilities and ear for interconnections across the genre categories.

In the case of this recording, tinkling saloon piano meets the "bubblegum" sound relegated at the time to female singers with a high soprano range. The lyrics are in the second person, musing on heartbreak over being left by a love for another. While the new lovers are "out paintin' the town red," the narrator is "paintin' it blue."

The B-side, "The Love You Gave," penned by Robert Riley and Marie Jones, continues the early rock and-roll feel, with drums emphasizing both halves of every measure's second beat. "The Love You Gave" is about the memory of a lost love. A melodic organ lays out a high countermelody in the first full measure of the instrumental intro, and then a lower register comes in via a saxophone percolating beneath the high vocals.

Neither the recording nor the publishing agreement led anywhere, but they were small tastes of success that Dolly took with her back home to finish high school. In her 2020 book with journalist Robert Oermann, *Dolly Parton, Songteller: My Life in Lyrics*, Dolly includes an image of a check she received from Tree Publishing for $1.02. The caption reads, "I'm surprised that I even made that much, since nothing I wrote in those days was a hit."

LAUGHS AT LINEBAUGH'S

Over the years, Dolly developed a friendship with the legendary guitarist, studio producer, and RCA executive Chet Atkins. Their relationship was playful. He once sent her paperwork for a mock lawsuit over her grabbing his buttocks. In her reply, Dolly quipped that the alleged harassment was more accurately "his-assment." Another funny story features a Nashville institution called Linebaugh's (pronounced "Line Baw's"), famous for their strawberry pie. One of Dolly's earliest business meetings with Chet Atkins took place at Shoney's, a chain restaurant that was also known for its strawberry pie. When the dessert arrived, Dolly declared, "Golly, these strawberries are bigger than Linebaugh's!" which brought peals of laughter from Chet. Her rural Tennessee accent made it sound like "lion's balls."

Hello, Dolly!
Dolly takes one bus to New York, and then another one to Nashville

In her earliest education, Dolly attended a schoolhouse where one teacher taught first through eighth grades, to a room of around a dozen children from the surrounding rural communities. Dolly never liked school but nevertheless persisted. When she earned her high school diploma, she was the first member of her family to do so. Dolly attended Sevier County High School, which had a tradition of each group of seniors making a trip. Their class raised money—selling donuts, seeds, candy, anything—for buses to take them to New York City, by way of Washington, DC.

It was Dolly's second big bus trip (Louisiana had been her first), and her introduction to New York City coincided with two major events: the 1964 World's Fair was being held in Flushing Meadows, and a new Broadway musical was "hot, hot, hot," to quote Dolly years later: *Hello, Dolly!* Billboards and signs for the opening of the now-classic show were plastered everywhere and seemed directed at her. Dolly recalled for the *New Yorker*, when she was back in town to open her own Broadway musical in 2009, "It was all over the cabs, and the signs, and I said, 'They must have been

waitin' for me!'" That trip was the first time Dolly stayed in a hotel, and it marked her first (and last) ride on the New York subway.

After Dolly graduated high school, she set off on her third big Greyhound bus trip the very next day. This time, she was headed to Nashville, with a vision to become a singer-songwriter and a star. Dolly traveled light. She took her guitar, some songs, and "the rest of my belongings in a set of matching luggage—three paper bags from the same grocery store." Some lean times followed, including nights when she scoured hotel hallways for leftover food on room service trays. Some of Dolly's earliest jobs included answering the phone for a sign company owned by the son of a neighbor in her apartment, and refilling condiments at a local diner in exchange for food.

Her 1973 album *My Tennessee Mountain Home* leads off with a recitation titled "The Letter." Dated June 2, 1964, it was the first she wrote home to her folks after leaving. She had gotten a job, she tells them, singing on *The Eddie Hill Show* on TV, and had already gotten feedback from several performers about wanting to sing her songs. She doesn't mention the food.

> *"I suppose if it weren't for naivete and fool-hearted, pigheaded stubbornness, nobody would ever see their dreams through."*
>
> **—DOLLY, REFLECTING ON THIS MOMENT IN *DOLLY: MY LIFE AND OTHER UNFINISHED BUSINESS***

ABOVE: Dolly on the wheel well of a fire engine from Engine Company 7 in Nashville.

Dolly Signs with Fred Foster

"I imagine I'll be doing that until my dying day . . ."

"It's [sic] never has run dry, so it's never once crossed my mind that I wouldn't be able to write.
The only dry spell I hit is when I don't have the time, I never feel I've creatively gone dry,
because everything's a song for me. It's just natural. I imagine I'll be doing that until my dying day,
I've been doing it since I was a little biddy kid."

—DOLLY DURING A 2012 INTERVIEW WITH CAROLINE FROST FOR THE *HUFFINGTON POST UK*

Dolly played a song called "Everything Is Beautiful (In Its Own Way)" for Fred Foster, the man behind her first big break. It was a song she had written before she ever left home.

Foster was impressed enough to sign her to Monument Records, and he also hired Dolly and Uncle Bill as songwriters with his publishing company, Combine. She recorded the song for Monument in 1965, with singer and songwriter Ray Stevens producing. Stevens was best known for a novelty hit "Ahab the Arab," and would go on memorably, and humorously, to record "The Streak." As things go in the music business, however, Dolly's Monument single was not released.

During her first significant interview in 1967 with Everett Corbin for Nashville's *Music City News*, she did not know that. She anticipated the song to soon be released as a single, apart from her forthcoming debut album *Hello, I'm Dolly*. She described "Everything Is Beautiful" to Corbin as "not pop, it's kinda folky/sacred/country/pop." Though Dolly was quick to add that the single would "have a real country song on back of it." She went on to describe in words she very well could have spoken today, over five decades in the future: "It's somethin' different and it's a clean idea. It's somethin' people need. People seem to forget about God and ever'thing when all this stuff is goin' on in the world and they don't really think to look around at the things that really mean anything. So I think it would be a good song to put out now."

"Everything Is Beautiful" describes fields of clover and water flowing from a mountainside. But then it turns to the "clouds that form a black summer windstorm" that destroys the harvest. This verse concludes, "In the midst of such anger, destruction, and danger, / The storm's even beautiful in its own way."

Dolly would also sing this during her audition for *The Porter Wagoner Show*, and the song finally appeared in 1972 on her solo album titled *My Favorite Songwriter, Porter Wagoner*.

Meanwhile, in 1970, Ray Stevens scored a tremendous hit with a very different song, using the same title. When Dolly included her lyrics in the 2020 collection *Songteller*, she mused over Stevens's hit: "I always wondered if he remembered mine." She had been a little more pointed when it came up in her late '90s memoir, reflecting "that gives some idea what a young girl trying to break into the music business at that time could expect."

Dolly would eventually gain success with the song, when in 1982 she recorded it as a duet with Willie Nelson for *The Winning Hand*, an album that was put together to raise money for their old friend and mentor Fred Foster, who had since run into financial trouble. The project included Dolly singing duets with Brenda Lee and Kris Kristofferson, other legends who had also benefited from Foster's guidance and friendship earlier in their careers.

DOLLY PARTON

ABOVE: Publicity photo of Dolly released by Monument Records.

Dolly and Carl Dean

"He's my anchor and I'm his excitement."

"Carl's never wanted to be in the limelight, so I didn't put him there. He wants to be left alone and be a homebody and then hear about what I've been up to when I get back. He's my anchor and I'm his excitement."

—DOLLY, QUOTED IN AN AUGUST 2011 PIECE FOR THE *GUARDIAN* BY HADLEY FREEMAN

Dolly was standing outside the Wishy Washy Laundromat the day after she arrived in Nashville in 1964, dirty clothes in tow. Her attire, she recalled, was a "red ruffled rib-tickler outfit with tight bell-bottomed pants." A car rolled slowly by, and a man commented out his window that she could get a sunburn in that. Fresh from the country, Dolly waved and quipped back some friendly response.

The man got out to chat and they kept talking as Dolly went back inside to tend her load of clothes. "I was surprised and delighted that while he talked to me, he looked at my face (a rare thing for me)," Dolly said later. "He seemed to be genuinely interested in finding out who I was and what I was about. What I was about at that moment was of course being interested in him. He was so different from the men I had known back home."

This was Dolly's first introduction to Carl Dean. Carl was a Nashville native, a few years older than Dolly, who was learning the family business when they met. He kept coming around to visit, sitting outside at Dolly's aunt and uncle's house while she babysat her nephews.

He eventually invited her to dinner, which turned out to be at his mother's house.

They married two years later, on Memorial Day in 1966, in the small town of Ringgold, Georgia, with her mother in attendance. Dolly was twenty years old. They held the quiet ceremony outside Tennessee because Dolly had been advised to postpone marriage in light of the traction her career was gaining and she didn't want word getting out. Besides her mother, only the preacher, Don Duvall, and his wife witnessed the vows. Dolly wanted to marry in a church rather than a courthouse, and Pastor Duvall was willing to perform the ceremony in the small Baptist church in town. Dolly wore a short, knee-length, white, sleeveless wedding dress with a veil on top of her piled-up hair. Carl wore a dark suit and tie.

Dolly's career traction included a 1966 Broadcast Music, Inc. (BMI) Song of the Year Award for "Put It Off Until Tomorrow." Dolly asked Carl to attend the ceremony with her and Uncle Bill, her cowriter. As Dolly tells it, Carl didn't so much attend the event as endure it. He began removing his shirt and

ABOVE: Dolly, circa 1966.

uncomfortable rented tuxedo tie as soon as they hit the car and drove home wearing just his shoes, pants, and suspenders. "Finally he turned to me and said calmly, 'Honey, I love you and I will support you in your career any way that I can. I know it's a big part of you and you wouldn't be the same person if you didn't do it. But the limelight's just not for me. I'll be there at home waiting for you, but I am not going to any more of these wingdings.' He has been a wingdingless man of his word ever since."

For someone so famous, Dolly's private life with her husband has remained consistently private. They like to rent an RV, maybe pick up fast food from a drive-through window. Dolly likes to fish and cook. She told Jay Scott for the *Globe and Mail* in 1982, "We like to camp out and stay in cheap hotels. I like to go out and see *anything*."

British journalist Lesley Adamson wrote a piece in 1977 for the *Guardian* that enumerates Dolly's successes: in songwriting, in recording, and in her marriage, which, Adamson wrote, "qualified for the Nashville version of the Dunmow Flitch." That reference goes as far back as the fourteenth century and Chaucer's *Canterbury Tales*, where there's a passing reference in the prologue for "The Wife of Bath's Tale" to a tradition that continues in the small community of Great Dunmow, in Essex. Every four years, the Dunmow Flitch Trials are a kind of marriage competition. Couples married for at least a year and a day must convince a panel of judges—six unmarried males and six unmarried females—that they have never wished they hadn't married, not even for a day. The winning couple is awarded a "flitch" of bacon and are carried through town on a raised bench. Adamson's point, in short, was that Dolly and Carl's marriage appears solid. In 2022, they celebrated their fifty-sixth wedding anniversary.

MY MISTAKES ARE NO WORSE THAN YOURS

At some point during their first year of marriage, Carl asked if Dolly had ever been intimate with another man. Her response was not the one Carl had anticipated and he was hurt, but he eventually recovered and never brought it up again. In the manner she would repeat again and again, Dolly turned this painful, passing moment of human experience into one of her most iconic songs centered on female experience: "Just Because I'm a Woman."

The song was held up by the journalist Sarah Smarsh for how it "illuminated the sexual double standards that encouraged men to be playboys but morally incriminated the women who slept with them. The song follows a traditional country-guitar strum, but the ideas Parton pushed through Nashville in the lyrics were as revolutionary as the feminist publications coming out of academic and radical small presses." While it was banned on some US radio stations, the song became a hit in South Africa.

A Doorway to Country

Who's that singing harmony?

The line that kicks off Bill Phillips's "Put It Off Until Tomorrow" returns again and again, the glue holding the tune together: "Put it off until tomorrow, you've hurt me enough today." In between, the lyrics are typical, all about heartbreak over the impending departure of a lover, and the music bears all the "countrypolitan" indicators of Nashville's Music Row in 1966.

Recorded for Decca, the session was produced by Owen Bradley, one of the visionaries who fashioned the era's characteristic fusion of country sounds with greater pop sensibilities. Background harmony vocals are an essential element of that "Nashville Sound," and something about them stands out on "Put It Off Until Tomorrow."

Dolly was the unacknowledged harmony vocalist on the recording. She was also the cowriter of the song, along with her Uncle Bill Owens, and joined the final recording session to help maintain the feel of the demo. "Put It Off" was the first hit for Dolly and her uncle, with whom she had been writing songs since she was a child. The song climbed to the top ten in country music *Billboard* charts and earned a songwriting award from BMI.

Even more significantly, the success of the song gained Dolly the leverage to push for making her own country music recordings. When the song premiered, Dolly was already recording with Monument Records, led by Fred Foster, whom she would always value as an early mentor. Foster, however, envisioned Dolly as a pop singer, due to the high-pitched voice he felt was better suited to that style of music.

The first pop record Dolly "tried to do anything with" was "I Wasted My Tears," also co-written with her uncle. The flip side was another family affair, "What Do You Think About Lovin'?" written with Bill and another uncle, Robert Owens. She had put out a song titled "Happy, Happy Birthday, Baby," too, which brought little notice.

But things began to change when disc jockeys inquired about that background voice in Philips's latest hit. The doors to country music recording opened. Dolly and Bill wrote an answer to "Put It Off" that they titled "You're Known by the Company You Keep," and paired it with another of their songs, "The Little Things." They were gaining momentum.

ABOVE: Dolly in Nashville in 1965.

Dolly's First Album

The singer proves she's nobody's fool

In retrospect, it seems a little surprising that Dolly's first hit was written by someone else, given the reputation she would build for her songwriting. But the buzz around her background vocals on Bill Phillips's hit "Put It Off" finally convinced Fred Foster at Monument to let her try country music, and it's fitting that the song "Dumb Blonde" captures something about her that would linger throughout her public life. Dolly conveys the sense of knowing full well the range of observations and assumptions her personal appearance might inspire, and then takes full command of the direction in which the conversation goes from there.

The song's composer, Curly Putman, had already scored hits with tunes like "Green, Green Grass of Home," recorded in 1965 by first Johnny Darrell and then Porter Wagoner, and then by Tom Jones, who gained a broad audience for it in 1967.

"My Elusive Dreams," another Putman creation, was a 1967 duet hit for Tammy Wynette and David Houston. Putman went on to cowrite some of country music's most enduring songs, including George Jones's "He Stopped Loving Her Today." Fred Foster found Putman's song "Dumb Blonde," and thought it would suit Dolly. She told music writer Jack Hurst in 1970 that Fred "figured it would make people forget about whether my voice was any good or not and just listen to the song." Putman's song led off her debut album on Monument, the simply titled *Hello, I'm Dolly*. It marked her biggest success to date, with the single peaking at number twenty-four on the *Billboard* country chart and the album reaching number eleven for country albums.

Besides expressing an essential quality about her that would pervade her professional future, "Dumb Blonde" greased the wheels of success.

ABOVE: Cover of *Hello, I'm Dolly*, Dolly's first album, from 1967.

Up until then, Dolly had slowly been making headway, shilling her songs all over town. She was appearing on the underfunded Nashville-based program *The Eddie Hill Show* on WLAC-TV, where Hill paid her out of his own pocket. When interviewed by Everett Corbin for *Music City News* in 1967, "Something Fishy," the second single off the album (and one she wrote), had just come out and was also doing well.

And Dolly continued writing. Earlier in 1967, Hank Williams, Jr. had recorded the Dolly-penned song "I'm in No Condition." Skeeter Davis had recorded one she cowrote with Uncle Bill titled "Fuel to a Flame." Five years later, in 1972, Skeeter would do an entire album of Dolly's songs, *Skeeter Sings Dolly*. Jan Howard had recorded, but not yet released, Dolly's "Your Ole Handy Man," and

Dolly was anticipating the upcoming release of Kitty Wells's "More Love Than Sense." It wouldn't be long before Dolly, nobody's fool ever, would start a new publishing company with Uncle Bill to copyright the growing catalog of material.

ABOVE: Dolly on the cover of *Music City News* in 1967.

The Business of Songwriting
Dolly forms Owe-Par Publishing with Uncle Bill

Among other things, Dolly is famous for her business acumen, which she established early in her career. Since moving to Nashville in 1964, Dolly had been struggling in the city, despite some live spots on *The Ralph Emery Show* and on an early morning radio program *The Eddie Hill Show*. Her first big break came when Fred Foster signed both her and Uncle Bill to contracts with both of his companies, Combine Music and Monument Records. Fred thought Dolly should sing rockabilly, the more countrified regional take on rock-and-roll associated with Elvis's earliest recordings in 1954 on Sun Records in Memphis, along with other members of the Sun roster like Carl Perkins and Jerry Lee Lewis. She had, after all, once appeared on *American Bandstand*, and in another universe her high soprano might have found a home in some Phil Spector–style girl-group arrangements. But that was not Dolly's vision.

When their Combine contract expired, twenty-year-old Dolly and Uncle Bill started Owe-Par Publishing Company, combining portions of their last names. This meant they could copyright their own music, a decision that would be a significant income strategy when songs like "Joshua" and "Coat of Many Colors" became hits a few years down the road. This decision also stands out as a moment of clarity in terms of Dolly maintaining artistic control of her career and her songs. Keeping it in the family, the pair brought in Bill's brother, Uncle Louis Owens, to manage the business.

Eventually, Porter Wagoner would purchase half the company as his interest in Dolly's professional success grew. She and Porter also jointly owned a recording studio. Several years down the road when she departed his TV show, she would likewise shed these financial entanglements with Porter and start a new publishing entity in 1974, Velvet Apple Music.

These publishing companies anticipated Dolly's future record labels, first Blue Eye and then Dolly Records. This same business savvy would likewise manifest in television and film production through the company Sandollar Productions, which Dolly began with Sandy Gallin, her manager for twenty-five years.

From there, Dolly's sense of possibility expanded in multiple directions. Dollywood, her theme park, arguably best represents her ability to recognize the ways in which her creative life and productivity filter through the lens of her public persona to create a larger-than-life picture—what scholar Leigh Edwards calls Dolly's mastery of "transmedia storytelling." It's a phenomenon that has only heightened in recent decades, when ways for fans to connect with Dolly are generated on multiple levels of experience all at once.

Publishing her own songs through Owe-Par was where Dolly's business insights first took root. And their expansive directions over the decades since are matched only by Dolly's own creative and musical journey.

ABOVE: Dolly and her Uncle Bill in 2013.

ABOVE: Dolly with (L to R) singer-songwriter Johnny Russell, Uncle Bill, and producer Fred Foster at Tootsie's Orchid Lounge in Nashville.

BIG DREAMS
WITH BIG WINGS

1967–1975

*"I'm glad I pinned my wig on good because
I would hate to flip it in front of all these bigwigs."*

**—DOLLY, SPEAKING BETWEEN SONGS DURING AN OUTDOOR PERFORMANCE
ON AN EVIDENTLY WINDY DAY IN CARTHAGE, TENNESSEE,
REPORTED IN THE *TENNESSEAN* ON OCTOBER 14, 1973**

OPPOSITE: Dolly and Porter Wagoner.

Pretty Miss Dolly Parton

Porter Wagoner hires "one of the finest little gals that I've ever met"

On September 5, 1967, Porter Wagoner began his introduction of Dolly's debut on his popular television show with, "Right now, I want you to meet the little lady on our show." He explained that Miss Norma Jean, Dolly's predecessor, needed time at home for her personal life after many years with the show. "Here's a little gal that I know you're going to really learn to love," Porter continues, "because she's a fine singer and one of the finest little gals that I've ever met."

And then "Pretty Miss Dolly Parton" began the song for which she was most famous at the time, "Dumb Blonde." She wore a sleeveless magenta dress that matched Porter's jacket. The introduction (and the matching outfits) told viewers how Porter saw Dolly's role: his sidekick, the "girl singer" to add a little variety to *The Porter Wagoner Show*.

At the time, Porter hosted the longest-running country music syndicated variety show in history. He took the combination of country music, easygoing banter, corny humor, and conversational advertising handed down from a long history of the radio barn dance, itself the offspring of vaudeville, and successfully delivered it to living-room TV sets beginning in 1961. Porter had been directly influenced by Red Foley, who hosted the *Ozark Jubilee*, which began televised broadcasts from Porter's home turf of Springfield, Missouri. Porter had been a frequent guest there and absorbed the lessons that sustained his own show for two decades.

At the end of Dolly's first episode of *The Porter Wagoner Show*, she returned to sing "Something Fishy," her second-best-known song at the time. As she sang, Porter stepped up beside her and interrupted; it was the close of the show and they were out of time. When Jad Abumrad, host of the 2019 podcast *Dolly Parton's America*, comments that the exchange sure appears to be about the power dynamic between Dolly and Porter, Dolly's answer is that "it's more complicated than that." Porter's show had already been a long success and "he didn't need me to have his hit show." But Dolly brought more to the table than Porter anticipated for his "girl singer," a revelation that would eventually

ABOVE: Dolly and Porter Wagoner performing in Nashvilla, circa 1967.

drive tensions in the love-hate relationship the two would navigate over the next seven years working together. Dolly put it this way in 2019: "He wasn't expecting me to be all that I was either. When he hired me as a singer, he was just hiring what he thought was a right pretty little girl. But I was a serious writer. He didn't know that. I was a serious entertainer. He didn't know that. I mean, he didn't know how many dreams I had."

When Dolly received the initial message back in 1967 that Porter wanted to meet and she should bring her guitar, she assumed it was for her songs. She had been sending him—along with many other people in town—songs she hoped he and Norma Jean would use. But during the meeting, Porter told her that his current girl singer, Norma Jean, was marrying and moving to Oklahoma. Porter wanted Dolly to replace her. The $60,000 per year salary was a boon—and, she later speculated, likely more money than her daddy had seen during his whole life.

Dolly gained two essential gifts from the experience. One was exposure. Thanks to Porter's immensely popular show, millions of people across the United States learned the name and songs of this talented twenty-one-year-old. The other was professional chops. Porter shared his knowledge of the Nashville music business and introduced Dolly to RCA Records, with whom she would record for the next two decades. He also modeled an unfailing graciousness when fans formed lines after a performance to get his autograph, never losing sight that they were the reason behind his success.

At the same time, Dolly later likened those seven years on *The Porter Wagoner Show* to both the terms of indentured servitude and the biblical story of Jacob working seven years for the hand of Rachel, only to be tricked into marrying her older sister Leah and working seven more. Across the seven years, which was two more than their original agreement, their relationship shifted. Dolly's success gained momentum and she came into her own as a songwriter and performer. They produced a string of hit duet recordings, but Porter became controlling, possessive, and manipulative as Dolly's star rose.

LEFT: Award winners (L to R) Roy Clark, Merle Haggard, Dolly, and Porter at the 1970 Country Music Association Awards.

Just Between You and Me

Dolly records her first duet album with Porter Wagoner

Early on in their partnership, Porter pushed Dolly to leave Monument Records for a contract with RCA. According to her '90s memoir, Porter personally went to bat for her at RCA. Dolly writes that Porter "is telling the truth when he says that he made RCA a guarantee to get them to sign me. Porter told them he would pay them every cent they ever lost on me out of his own pocket. He never had to pay a dime."

Their early RCA recordings were duets, due to Dolly's remaining obligations as a soloist for Monument. The first duet album, *Just Between You and Me*, tread the fairly typical Nashville Music Row recording paths of the day, with top-shelf studio musicians adding color and drive to the felicitous blend of singing that produced thirteen duet albums from Dolly and Porter before all was said and done. A group of harmony backup singers remained on hand to fill out the vocal sound, often as the end of a song approached. The album's producer, Bob Ferguson, would go on to work with Dolly numerous times in the coming years, on both duet and solo releases.

Of the twelve cuts on *Just Between You and Me*, five were heartbreaker songs about lovers parting ways, including the album's only single "The Last Thing on My Mind," written by Tom Paxton. Another

heartbreaker titled "Sorrow's Tearing Down the House (That Happiness Once Built)" begins the album's B-side, flipping from Side A's final joyful tune, "Four O'Thirty Three," co-written by Dolly's Uncle Bill and Earl Montgomery.

Two cheating songs, one suspicion-of-cheating song, and one maudlin story called "Mommie, Ain't That Daddy" constitute the remainder of the album. The last was written by Dolly and stands out for its evocative detail; in contrast, a number of the other songs dwell in general language about leaving, longing, and regret. "Mommie" establishes a tragic scene, with children's footprints in the snow, on their way to the thrift store to buy some clothes. The children catch sight of a man begging, and we learn through an extended voiceover by Porter that the man has dissipated himself with alcohol, unrecognizable as the loving husband and father he once was. The album ends with a re-recording of "Put It Off Until Tomorrow," from Dolly's first solo release for Monument, the same song that scored a 1966 hit for Bill Phillips. Its inclusion highlights the slicker production values RCA brought to country music recording during the late 1960s. Dolly's more pronounced vocal cry—a technique geared toward emotional intensity often associated with country as well as mariachi singing—may evince RCA's vision for how a female country singer should sound.

But perhaps one of the more interesting tunes from the album is "Two Sides to Every Story," also written by Dolly and Uncle Bill. It unfolds as an up-tempo, two-step conversation, with two parties questioning one another regarding their whereabouts the night before. In the amicable blend of their voices and the rapport that comes through in the recording, as on TV, it is apparent why audiences speculated that Dolly and Porter's relationship extended beyond their music-making. During her seven-year tenure on Porter's show, the duo would record nine more albums. A song called "Holding on to Nothing" appeared on *Porter 'n' Dolly*, the first album recorded after her departure. The lyrics describe two people holding on to a relationship, even when little emotional attachment remains, and describes feeling "guilty when they envy me and you." In hindsight, the song, which was a hit for the duo, would take on relevance for Dolly regarding the relationship she had with Porter.

ABOVE: Dolly and Porter pose for a portrait with their backup band, "The Wagonmasters," circa 1968.

Whatever She Says

Dolly scores recognition with a country classic, "Mule Skinner Blues (Blue Yodel No. 8)"

Dolly credits Porter with the idea for her to record "Mule Skinner Blues," and it was her most successful recording to that point. It likewise indicated that she no longer needed Porter to convince audiences to embrace Dolly; she was coming into her own.

Porter Wagoner's television career started when representatives from the Chattem Drug & Chemical Company got a notion to hire a country music performer to sell home remedies to rural-minded consumers. Founded in Chattanooga in 1879, Chattem sold laxatives like the once-popular Thedford's Black Draught, which had been around since 1840. The company's reps visited the *Grand Ole Opry*, looking for someone who might fit the bill, and found Porter.

Somewhere between eighteen and twenty stations ran *The Porter Wagoner Show* during its early days. By the time Dolly joined, the show aired on over 100 TV stations, reaching between four and five million viewers.

When *Tennessean* reporter Jack Hurst interviewed Dolly on September 27, 1970, her recording of "Mule Skinner Blues (Blue Yodel No. 8)" was at number three on the *Billboard* charts for country music and number one on *Record World* charts. Another song of hers, "Daddy Was an Old Time Preacher Man," was number eight. That same year, "Dolly Parton Day" was declared in Sevierville, Tennessee. Shortly after, she recorded a live album at the Sevier County High School and set up a scholarship fund for students there.

Dolly had been working for Porter for just over three years by the time of the interview, which took place in the office of Owe-Par Music. Hurst describes being greeted by one of Dolly's uncles, Louis Owens, whose desk sat beneath several BMI awards hanging on the wall. Hurst was unconvinced, even back then, that Dolly had been riding Porter's coattails. He notes in the finished piece that "she writes nearly all of her own recordings, many of Wagoner's, and most of their duets. Thus, it is much more than her beauty that makes Miss Dolly valuable to *The Porter Wagoner Show*, the longest-running and most successful of Nashville syndicated country music television shows."

Beneath the straightforward observations, Hurst employs the detail-oriented new journalism approach of the day to convey something of the atmosphere and curious power dynamics that would eventually push Dolly to move on. Given Dolly's own consistent restraint, gratitude, and graciousness about the topic, Hurst's observations fill in some gaps. He types out a phone exchange that occurred after the interview, thirty minutes after he got home. Uncle Louis Owens called and said, "Uh, Dolly left me a note here to call you." He said, "She wanted me to—well, here's what the note says. 'Ask him to please be sure and put in that any success I've achieved in the last few years I owe to Porter Wagoner, who is a fine man and everything he appears to be.'"

"All right," Hurst replied. "Whatever she says."

"Mule Skinner Blues" became a throughline from her musical heritage to her musical future, a throughline she could not have seen clearly at the time. Originally written and recorded by the "Father of Country Music," Jimmie Rodgers, the song's treatment by Bill Monroe in the 1940s defined a new genre: bluegrass. Dolly's version picks it up from there. Not only was it her first top ten hit, but her rousing rendition also became a consistent part of her concerts, and a touchstone when she returned to a more traditional Appalachian-grounded sound around the turn of the twenty-first century.

ABOVE: On the set of *The Porter Wagoner Show.*

Sad-Ass Songs

"Down from Dover" tackles hardship in its fictional protagonist's life

Dolly was riding on a tour bus, on the road with Porter Wagoner and the Wagonmasters, when she passed through the small town of Dover, Tennessee. From the window, she saw a shadow falling slowly across a field. "It wasn't clover but it rhymed with Dover . . . And I sang, 'And the sun behind the cloud just cast a crawling shadow over the fields of clover.'" Her next thought turned to populating this fictional place forming in her mind: *What kind of person might live in a small place named Dover?* The story about a girl began to take shape from there.

A young woman finds herself pregnant out of wedlock but anticipates the father's promised return from Dover. Unfolding ballad-style, in AABA form, each verse lands on the title phrase. The "B" line adds an element of contrast each time. The one about the shadows on the clover field establishes this tale's certain doom from verse one. Its poetic subtlety continues in how the lyrics mark the passing of time: the deep snow when he left gives way first to spring and summer and then the browning of leaves. The next verse describes being shamed and rejected

by her family. The song's biggest musical change happens via a stepwise modulation at the verse recounting the love she felt and her disbelief that he abandoned her. Loneliness and despair come in the final verse, when the child arrives, stillborn. The song's last line is shattering: "And dying was her way of telling me he wasn't coming down from Dover."

The song was banned from the radio when it first appeared on Dolly's 1970 album *The Fairest of Them All*. Dolly later reflected, "They wouldn't play it because it was so suggestive and it was about a pregnant girl and it was so against what country radio was at that time." This was a very active period of songwriting for her and a time when, as she told podcast host Jad Abumrad for *Dolly Parton's America*, "I used to write a lot of sad-ass songs."

Sad-ass songs are part of Dolly's heritage. More than once, she has reflected (as she did in the 2019 documentary *Dolly Parton: Here I Am*) that "as a little child my mother used to sing all those songs that really told about tragedies." These were staples of Appalachian ballad singing, a practice with roots in even older traditions in the British Isles. Stories are delivered in frightening or sad detail, unfolding relentlessly via the repetitive ballad structure toward a grim, gory, or otherwise sorrowful conclusion, as heard in "Down from Dover." Part of the emotional power of these songs comes with the relative lack of emotion in the delivery itself. Later country music tends to add a "cry in the voice" or other more modern stylistic elements for emotional effect.

Some of these modern contemporary touches were more present when Dolly re-recorded "Down from Dover" for the album *Little Sparrow* (2001). It opens with the sound of panpipes, and there are audible shifts on the metal guitar strings that convey a sense of intimacy. A mournful fiddle wails in the background, and harmony underscores certain lines. Everything gets quiet on the verse when the delivery happens. This version also adds a verse that fills in the gaps between the protagonist's rejection by her family and the tragic birth. It describes finding "a place to stay on the farm taking care of that old lady" and sending the address to her mom to pass on "when he came down from Dover." That same attention to exquisite detail keeps the new verse seamless with the original ones.

LITTLE MOVIES

"The Bridge" is another sad-ass song, cut from the same devastating cloth as "Down from Dover." Dolly wrote this one as a teenager and gave it about the most arresting ending a song could have. As the lyrics relate the hopeless situation of the protagonist, the song builds to her approach on the bridge railing, resolved to suffer no more. The music's abrupt ending makes clear what happened next.

Dolly spoke about writing such harrowing tales as "The Bridge" and "Down from Dover" in the 2019 documentary *Here I Am*. "Back when I grew up we didn't have the movies," she explained. "We didn't even have television for many years of my life. So I used to write songs so my family could enjoy seeing these little stories. So every song I'd write, I'd run home and I'd sing 'em to the family. You know, whatever I was doing. So it was kind of entertainment. But it really is like a little movie when I write songs."

ABOVE: Dolly (center) on the cover of *Music City News* in 1969.

Joshua

Dolly finds her first number one solo hit

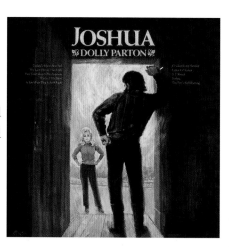

"Joshua" was the name of both Dolly's first number one solo hit and a full album of original material. *Joshua* the album included the outlaw love/murder ballad "J. J. Sneed"; the song "Chicken Every Sunday," about pride in the face of class discrimination; and the maudlin, over-the-top weeper about an orphan child's death, "Letter to Heaven." During a 1971 interview for the Atlanta-based underground newspaper *The Great Speckled Bird*, writer Gene Guerrero asked Dolly if "Joshua" was a signal of new directions for her songwriting. Dolly said, "I just think every song I write is an individual and I think the music on it will be fitting for that."

"Joshua" is the tale of a mountain recluse living "a good ways down the railroad tracks," who is feared by all the locals. It's the epitome of country music's story song tradition, unfolding in the first person. The protagonist decides to go investigate this mysterious hermit, not believing anyone could be as mean as people say he is.

At key points in the tale, the rim-shot train beat rhythm drives the song's momentum. At one of these moments of high tension, the narrator approaches the rundown shack. She introduces herself and she and Joshua talk on the porch. As the first chorus asks Joshua, "Ain't you got nobody to call your own?" the harmony moves up a step and the two of them continue to talk all night. A harmonica joins in the layers, adding a lively and upbeat feel. By the song's end, the protagonist and Joshua have fallen in love, and Dolly's yodeling conveys their carefree sense of abandon and happiness in the backwoods shack by the railroad track.

The song "Joshua" earned Dolly her first Grammy nomination. It also earned her one of two BMI Awards that year—the other for "Daddy Was an Old Time Preacher Man." With the success of "Joshua," Dolly's power as both a performer and a creative and versatile songwriter were revealed beyond question.

ABOVE: Cover of the album *Joshua*, released in 1971.

It Looked All Right to Me

A childhood memory becomes one of Dolly's most enduring songs

"I like ballads. Real strong, pitiful, sad, cryin' ballads."

—DOLLY IN 1967, IN AN INTERVIEW WITH EVERETT CORBIN FOR *MUSIC CITY NEWS*

Dolly was about two years into her stint with *The Porter Wagoner Show* when she wrote a song about her childhood that would become one of her most enduring, the song she always names as her favorite. Written in 1969, five years after she left home for Nashville, "Coat of Many Colors" was grounded in a personal memory of Dolly's mother once making her a coat out of pieces of discarded fabric. Time had swaddled the memory in feelings of love, warmth, and gratitude, but the song also conveyed feelings of shame, as well as defiance in the face of unkindness.

The song is "simply complicated," as Dolly once described her own songwriting approach, aiming for "enough depth to be appreciated and enough simplicity to be understood." Its wedding of deeply personal and universal in part accounts for the song's journey and its staying power across five decades (and counting). It is one of those songs people go to when they need a good cry, making a list of "36 sad songs that make us cry every time we hear 'em" on *It's a Southern Thing* in 2020. Its emotional wallop comes

not only from its lyrics, but also the music, which imbues the song with an arresting and appealing quality.

Musicologist Lydia Hamessley categorizes "Coat of Many Colors" as one of Dolly's autobiographical songs, in which she draws from her past to craft a "memory palace—a place to store her memories in lyrics and melodies that evoke people, feelings, places, and events, bringing them to life whenever she sings one of her songs." Both the melody and the harmony are relatively static at the beginning, with the first significant move to the dominant harmony happening with the lyrics "way down in the fall." This static opening draws the listener into the setting, and then the chord change propels the unfolding drama forward. The shift sets up the moral of the story to carry more punch, with the song's narrator feeling "I was rich as I could be," prideful of her mother's handiwork.

Porter recognized a well-crafted tune when he heard one and recorded "Coat of Many Colors" twice before Dolly's version appeared on her 1971 album, titled for the song. Despite her presence on backup vocals, his jaunty version misses the song's gravitas and emotional force.

Yet it's not just the song; no matter how she varies her own specific performances of it, something authentic comes through that makes people feel connected to Dolly. Over the years, her performances have evolved so that she typically speaks rather than sings the key verse beginning with the words, "I couldn't understand it because I felt that I was rich . . ."

"Coat of Many Colors" has twice been made into a children's book: first in 1994, with illustrations by Judith Sutton, and then in 2016, with illustrations by Brooke Boynton-Hughes. Dolly dedicated the 1994 *Coat of Many Colors* to her mother. By 2016, the song and the story it tells had taken on an explicit anti-bullying message, and Dolly released a new kid-specific song, "Makin' Fun Ain't Funny," to go with it.

"Coat of Many Colors" was added to the Library of Congress National Recording Registry in 2011 and made into a TV movie on NBC in 2015, with singer Jennifer Nettles in the role of Avie Lee, Dolly's mother. That movie was successful enough to inspire a follow-up the next year, *Christmas of Many Colors*. In 2019, "Coat of Many Colors" was added to the Grammy Hall of Fame.

ABOVE: Dolly performs on the shore of the Cumberland River in Carthage, Tennessee, in 1973.

"Jolene"

A little girl, a flirtatious bank teller,
and a song that won't quit

During her 2009 *Live From London* performance, captured as a PBS special and also released on DVD, Dolly said to the crowd, "Some of you probably go back with me a long ways, and you probably remember me singing about an ol' red-headed gal by the name of Jolene." Then she shouts to kick off the song, "Well, let's sing about her again!"

Dolly's original 1973 recording of "Jolene" works on multiple levels at once. A looping guitar lick starts it off, percolating and bubbling throughout. The title name gets repeated in increasingly higher registers, building the sense of pleading that characterizes the song overall. Each verse line ends on the same name, first lauding Jolene's physical charms before the speaker makes her case: "Please don't take my man." The song is a concert staple and crowds from London to Los Angeles join in to beg Jolene to choose compassion; after all, Jolene, "you could have your choice of men."

The inspirations for the hit might surprise some fans. When Dolly first joined *The Porter Wagoner Show*, the performers would linger after the broadcast to sign autographs for fans gathered to watch it live. They did the same after concerts on the road, and Dolly has long credited Porter with modeling a gracious attitude toward audiences. At a performance during the late 1960s, Dolly "was onstage, and there was this beautiful little girl—she was probably eight years old at the time." The girl approached Dolly for her autograph. "And she had this beautiful red hair, this beautiful skin, these beautiful green eyes." Struck

---

ABOVE: Cover of the album *Jolene*, released in 1974.

---

by how pretty she was, Dolly asked her name. *Jolene.* Dolly had never heard the name before, but liked and remembered it.

In talking about the song "Jolene," Dolly also cites a time her husband was flirting with a bank teller and she felt slight stirrings of jealously. Over the years, this part of the story has sometimes been embellished from stage or during interviews. Sometimes, Dolly adds intimations that she fought the woman for her man. Other times, she muses wryly that, gazing at her spouse of many decades snoring in his easy chair, she wishes Jolene had taken him.

UCLA-based musicologist Mitchell Morris wrote about Dolly's "crossover" era in the late 1970s, after "Jolene" became a hit, and her ability to occupy space as both the authentic product of a poor, rural Appalachian childhood and a sophisticated performer very much in control of her image and her music. Both of these images still resonate, as Morris illustrates with the story of Dolly's performance at the Los Angeles House of Blues in 2002. A handful of drag queens, doing their best Dolly, were close to the stage, and after some banter with these fans, Dolly started to sing "Jolene" but "repeatedly sang 'drag queen' instead of 'Jolene' in the song, to uproarious approval by the audience."

"Jolene" is a vignette-in-a-song. It's a character one can put on—like a mask on Halloween or a costume at Mardi Gras—and then take off when the song is over. For that reason, and maybe also because it's fun to sing, the song is a karaoke chestnut, and one that's been covered by a range of artists. The White Stripes, for example, brought a stripped-down, drum-heavy sense of defiance to the chorus. Most recently, Lil Nas X brought his distinctive sense of gender and genre fluidity to the song. In his version, the focus is on the singer's voice, fully present and at the edge of the mix, and punctuated at first with sparse, reverberating chords on the electric guitar. His version conveys a sense of defeat, in contrast to the earnestness marking the original.

When the song was dramatized in the 2019 Netflix series *Dolly Parton's Heartstrings*, Dolly introduced the episode—the first in the series—by reflecting on the song's lingering popularity. Everyone has felt insecure, she suggested, or like they didn't measure up at one time or another. So "Jolene" is a chance to put on those feelings for two minutes and forty-one seconds, and then take them off again and continue forward.

"I'm careful never to get caught up in the Dolly image, other than to develop and protect it, because if you start believing the public persona is you, you get frustrated and mixed up. Like, I suppose I am a sex symbol, but that idea is funny to me because I see Dolly as a cartoon. She's fat, wears a wig and so on. Oh, sure, I feel sexy, and to some people I come across as extremely sexy, but Dolly's as big a joke to me as she is to others."

**—DOLLY IN A 1982 INTERVIEW WITH CLIFF JAHR FOR *LADIES' HOME JOURNAL*,
COLLECTED IN RANDY SCHMIDT, *DOLLY ON DOLLY***

Moving On

Dolly's departure from
The Porter Wagoner Show *causes heartache*

"I'm able to put the hurting things into my songs and then it don't hurt me any more. I get the world to share my hurt. It's better than a psychiatrist."

—DOLLY, TO *NEW YORK TIMES* MUSIC WRITER JOHN ROCKWELL IN 1975

Dolly had tried to talk with Porter numerous times. She was ready for new directions for her music and her career, and after seven years, it was time for a change. She had never intended to spend her entire career as someone else's "girl singer." Her vision was to become a star in her own right. Porter refused to even have the conversation. So, Dolly did what Dolly does best: she wrote a song. "Everybody can understand a song," she said later. "There were so many things I wanted to say, there was so much emotion, feeling, and heartache on his part and on my part. Once I started it, the song seemed to pour out."

"I Will Always Love You" was her quiet, reflective parting sentiment to Porter. She finished singing it, and Porter was crying. He told her it was the best song she'd ever written. He also relented, agreeing to release her from the TV show—on the condition that he continue producing her records. (Porter predicted that RCA would not want to keep her as a soloist. He

was wrong on that count, and Dolly continued making records for RCA until 1986.)

In the second episode of the 2019 podcast *Dolly Parton's America*, the topic of Dolly's relationship with Porter Wagoner came up. The show's host Jad Abumrad mentioned all the story's regular touchstones: Dolly had begun to feel stifled, realizing that the only way she would be able to pursue her ultimate vision for her own music and career was to break away from Porter. This part of Dolly's story, when told by others, often includes dark intimations regarding Porter's controlling ways: his cutting Uncle Bill from his role as a core professional consultant and partner, his bullying with regard to production decisions for Dolly's recordings, his growing sense of ownership over her success, and so on. But when Jad asked Dolly how she found a way to forgive Porter, she paused, then said simply, "Forgiveness is all there is."

Although Dolly had signed only a five-year contract with *The Porter Wagoner Show*, by the early 1970s, Porter

seemed unwilling to believe her success would have occurred or could continue without him. Never mind the years she and Uncle Bill had knocked on doors, handed out songs, recorded for Monument, and built the reputation that brought her to Porter's attention in the first place. By the time she joined Porter, Dolly wrote two decades later, "I had three chart records of my own and had cowritten a 'country song of the year' with

Uncle Bill. I had a band and had traveled around the country by then. I had appeared on national television shows, including *American Bandstand.*"

By the mid-1970s Porter was in denial about who by that time was riding whose coattails. As Dolly's star shone brighter, he sunk deeper into feelings of resentment and bitterness. Several years after her departure, Porter sued Dolly, claiming a

ABOVE: Dolly and Porter in Nashville, circa 1968.

share of future earnings for the rest of her life, based on his sense of singular responsibility for her success.

Dolly settled with Porter out of court, agreeing to pay him a million dollars. In the 2019 podcast, Dolly reported that eventually "we made up." Later, Porter told Dolly that suing her, "was the worst thing I ever done. I'm so sorry I did that.' He told me that. He said, 'I just was hurt and angry.'"

Eventually, Porter's long run of success—one that began during the early 1960s, when his TV show proved a mainstay on the emerging medium—petered out. He had been dropped from his label in 1981, but was still writing songs, and experiencing financial trouble. To help him out, Dolly bought his publishing company and then gave it right back to him, "because I wanted his kids to have it." She said, "It was the least I could do. I was glad to do it. It made me feel better about everything else."

"That was one of my gifts, for thanking him, too," Dolly said on *Dolly Parton's America*. "'Cause, see, I never knew. How do you ever know how to thank somebody or what you owe somebody? Because, who knows, had it not been for Porter, I may not be sitting right here in this chair right now . . . I'd like to believe I would have made it. But because I felt bad that I had to go, but I knew I had to go or I'd have stifled . . . If I had stayed forever, I might have missed my chance. And God was telling me to go. That spirit of mine was saying 'go, you've got to go.'"

ABOVE: A poster for a 1971 performance by Porter, Dolly, and the Wagonmasters in North Carolina.

Dolly Says No to Elvis

Her first tough business decision turns out to be a doozy

"I wanted to protect my copyright because it was an investment for my family. I've always thought that my songs are like my children—I expect them to support me when I'm old."

—DOLLY, SPEAKING TO SINÉAD GLEESON FOR DUBLIN'S *IRISH TIMES* IN 2011

Not long after "I Will Always Love You" became a hit, Dolly received word that Elvis Presley wanted to record the song. He was in Nashville for a studio project, and plans were in the works for the two of them to get together. Dolly was thrilled. The night before the session, however, she received a call from Colonel Tom Parker, Elvis's notorious manager, who mentioned—almost in passing—that Elvis always got the publishing rights, or at least half, when he recorded a song that was not already a standard.

Though it grieved her mightily, Dolly said no.

She later remembered it as one of the first tough business calls she made in her career. "I said, 'Well, I'm really sorry, but I don't give my publishing to nobody. Not half of it, not ten percent of it, not any of it,'" Dolly recalled years later, in an interview with longtime music writer Bill DeMain. "I had just started my own publishing company, and I said, 'If he loves the song and the song is that good, then he'll record it anyway, and if he don't, well, just say that I'm flattered with the thought.'" When it came up in the BBC documentary *Here I Am* in 2019, Dolly said, "It broke my heart, because Elvis didn't get to sing it, but I had to hold onto it."

Though, at the time, people told her she was crazy, Dolly stood firm. Session musician Lloyd Green added perspective in *Here I Am*, musing, "That was one of the great career decisions Dolly Parton made in her life, 'cause Elvis was Elvis, for God's sake. And she said no, and that demonstrated her astuteness as a businesswoman. That was a great chess move."

Dolly understood the importance of publishing rights almost from the get-go, at least as early as the day she and Uncle Bill formed Owe-Par Publishing. Over the years, Porter Wagoner purchased half the company, so when she parted ways with his television show in 1974, Dolly created a new company called Velvet Apple Music and transferred

---

OPPOSITE: A portrait of Dolly taken at Centennial Park in Nashville.

her songs there. Dolly has controlled her music ever since.

In the case of this particular song, "I Will Always Love You" emerged from so deeply personal and painful an experience for Dolly that the idea of handing over a portion of the song was unfathomable: "If I'd given up half the publishing then I would've made half the money, plus I would've lost half the pride in it. It's the fact that I wrote the song by myself and published it myself just made the whole thing more special. It was not something you had to share."

In one way, this moment signifies the personal nature of Dolly's songwriting; how songwriting lives at the core of her artistic identity. She once characterized songwriting as her way of working through life's pain and making right that which was wrong: "Just the feeling of having it come out, to be able to vocalize that, it kind of permeates every little cell in your body and somehow it kind of works it all out, and I don't feel near as bad after I've written it." Songwriting is her consistent answer when asked, as has happened a lot over her career, to name the one professional activity she would continue were she to give up all the rest.

In another way, her no to Elvis also demonstrates Dolly's stone-cold savviness. Dolly never met Elvis in person. She later said, "There were many times I could have [met him]. I don't know why I didn't. I think I just wanted him to always be the way he was in my mind. I had met some people that I wish I hadn't, you know what I mean? Not that you wish you hadn't, but he was just so special, he was so spiritual and out there anyway. I didn't want nothing to blow the image." She joked years later that, after Whitney Houston's sensational hit recording of the song, she could have bought Graceland with the royalty income.

WHAT INTEGRITY

British musician Mark E. Nevin released an EP in 2018 titled *Dolly Said No to Elvis*. At a time when streaming services threaten to devalue musicians and songwriters by minimizing their profits, Dolly's story stood as inspiration to new generations of musicians. "What integrity it took to turn down what would have been a surefire truck load of money and huge prestige," Nevin reflected in a 2018 interview with the *Yorkshire Post*. "The celebrity culture of our time has meant that the song and songwriter have been devalued, it is partly why it is so rare to hear really great songs these days."

Satin Wings
Dolly records Love Is Like a Butterfly

The title states a simple and pure simile about the feeling of being in love. The *Love Is Like a Butterfly* album cover features a mottled, impressionistic blue-green background, with a multicolored image of a butterfly that spans the entire foreground. Dolly poses in the middle of the butterfly wings, where the insect's body would be, heavily styled with her signature blonde coiffure. Outlined in black, the wings are filled in with blues, greens, yellows, and reds, with the same red color picked up by Dolly's dress. There's a subtle sequined butterfly on her sleeve.

In the song of the same name, all the complex feelings that accompany loving someone are compared to the patterns of a butterfly's "satin wings." The central metaphor is the relationship of butterflies to daffodils: the beloved becomes the nectar that feeds the butterfly's flight. Musically, the melody skips and dips down and then back up, akin to a butterfly's motion in the air. A light chorus fills in open spaces between Dolly's notes and, at one point, takes the first melody lines of the chorus as Dolly layers the title line, slowed down so that the notes coincide. A pulsating repeated guitar chord and cascading piano fills burst forth from the instrumental setting. The overall effect is playful

and joyous, qualities that may have fueled the song's rise to the top of the country music charts.

The rest of the album canvases the range of Dolly's songwriting. It includes several slow, lovelorn laments. "If I Cross Your Mind" is the only non-original cut, written by Porter Wagoner, and included as the B-side of the lead single. "My Eyes Can Only See You" and "Once Upon a Memory" are both slow waltzes, with steel guitar prominent in the former and strings in the latter. Both also use the background harmony singers in more heavy-handed ways than the first song, including a moment during "Once Upon a Memory" when they alone sing a couple of lines. It's hard not to hear these instances as lingering weights Dolly had recently shrugged off—the tiresome preconceived molds of what female country singers should sound like. At the very least, they bear witness to a production aesthetic that simply didn't stand the test of time.

"Blackie, Kentucky" and "You're the One That Taught Me How to Swing" are both character songs, told via the subjectivity of a person in a troubled situation. The first one follows a woman looking to escape the poverty of her coal-mining community by marrying wealth. She finds herself alienated from the husband who cuts her off from family, and from the rich surroundings that have her trapped. The song ends tragically—in suicide—and a note left behind instructing that she be buried back in her beloved home, the only way she could find to return. The second song addresses the impossibility of return to the protagonist's simpler country ways despite the wishes of her lover. It was he, after all, who introduced her to life's more dangerous and daring pleasures in the first place.

"Gettin' Happy" and "Highway Headin' South" shift the mood and musical feel toward a country rocking Texas blues, the type of funky tune Dolly's old friend Charlie Daniels might have made at the time. The first one celebrates finding someone to love, set with a groove that builds via rim shots toward a drum break in the middle, followed by layers of tasty electric guitar licks and rollicking piano. "Highway Headin' South" gets down as well, with a driving beat that fuels a song about someone long stuck in chilly climes of North Dakota and Montana, who plans to return South where she can shed her "goose-down underwear."

"Take Me Back" falls into the Dolly tradition of nostalgic reminiscence. Despite the return of the heavy-handed background vocals, Dolly sings compellingly about childhood memories of her mother and father, who enjoyed simple pleasures of being parents to their children and loving spouses to one another. The album's closing song, "Sacred Memories," similarly meditates on formative experiences, in this case worship in a country church. This song stands out particularly for how it weaves in titles and excerpts from well-known southern evangelical hymns like the Carter Family classic "I Can't Feel At Home In This World Anymore" and "Amazing Grace." When she mentions "If We Never Meet Again," her favorite, the song's otherwise driving beat gets interrupted by a quotation from the hymn at slow tempo, with a full chorus backing her. The driving beat picks up again, leading to another quote, this one from "Power in the Blood," during which Dolly recalls her mama singing loud and strong. The title phrase, "sacred memories," ends the song, with the sound of chords from the organ brought front and center in the mix.

"But there was so much I wanted to do, and he heard it so differently that we just couldn't agree on so many things. It just took away the joy of recordin' the song at all, because then it wasn't what I created it to be. It took on somebody else's personality. And that would be hard to explain if you were not a writer."

—DOLLY DURING A 1977 INTERVIEW WITH MUSIC WRITER ALANNA NASH, TALKING ABOUT PORTER'S ROLE IN PRODUCING HER RECORDINGS SEVERAL YEARS AFTER SHE LEFT THE TV SHOW

ABOVE: Dolly and biographer Alanna Nash (left) rest against an old Cadillac hearse in 1978.

"The Bargain Store"

The "too clever, too complicated" first song off Dolly's new album becomes a hit

"I've worked hard to put wings on my dreams. I've got big dreams. They've got big wings."

—DOLLY REFLECTS ON HER SUCCESS TO MARY CAMPBELL, WRITING FOR THE *AUSTIN AMERICAN-STATESMAN*, IN 1975

Dolly's first hit after striking out on her own post-*Porter Wagoner Show* was the title cut from the 1975 album *The Bargain Store*. Dolly had written the song several years earlier, but had not recorded it because she thought it sounded, in her words, "too odd." She told Jack Hurst for a 1975 news piece, "I thought it was too clever, too complicated, to be commercial."

The song had come to her while in an antique shop, where she was looking at old furniture with the idea of refurbishing pieces for her home. Its opening line floated into her mind: "My life is likened to a bargain store." The rest of the song unfolded from there, a song about a person with a past, someone who has known some rough patches and bruises. As Hurst described it, "She thought of the many ways a person's life could resemble a second-hand merchandise operation—the 'broken dreams, broken plans, the broken heart' that could be serviceable again if a prospective purchaser did not insist upon shiny newness."

The song itself was coproduced by Porter Wagoner and Bob Ferguson. Ferguson had worked with Dolly numerous times before, but "The Bargain Store" was the last RCA recording they did together, as Dolly took her sounds in new directions for subsequent projects.

ABOVE: Dolly performing in Los Angeles, circa 1975.

Some country music radio stations wouldn't play the song because they thought it was about a sex worker. Despite, or maybe because of, the controversy, "The Bargain Store" climbed to the top of the country charts, Dolly's fifth number one in a very short span of time. Australian freelance music critic Matthew Hocter, writing for the independent music journalism website *Albumism* on the album's forty-fifth anniversary, places it in historical context: "Smack bang in the heart of the disco era, the musical *The Wiz*, then just a few months old, moved from Baltimore to New York's Majestic Theatre on Broadway, John Lennon & Yoko Ono became parents to baby Sean, and Parton released her fifteenth studio album." That same year, Dolly would be named the Country Music Association's Female Vocalist of the Year for the first—but not the last—time.

Dolly has said that the song's sexual misinterpretations took her by surprise, though. "Every man I know thinks it's dirty," she explained in *Songteller*. "All I was thinking of was the heart: 'If you don't mind the merchandise is slightly used, with a little mending it can be good as new.' I was saying that you'll be surprised at how good this broken heart is. Just take it. You'll never be sorry that you did. The words just meant that I've had relationships: I've been through stuff; I'm not new at this."

Aside from its past waves, "The Bargain Store" was also Dolly's first hit with the band she formed post-Porter, the Travelin' Family Band. This was more than a catchy name, because its members included her brother Randy on bass; a cousin, Dwight Puckett, on drums; and another cousin,

Sidney Spiva, on steel guitar. In fact, only guitarist Bill Rehrig was not an actual member of her family.

Dolly's family had always made music. Grandfather Jake had been a preacher and gospel songwriter. One song, "Singing His Praise," was recorded by Kitty Wells, and Dolly included another, "Book of Life," on the 1971 album *The Golden Streets of Glory*. In addition to Uncle Bill, Dolly had also cowritten songs with her Aunt Dorothy Jo (Owens) Hope, including "Daddy Was an Old Time Preacher Man," a Porter and Dolly hit duet.

Surrounding herself with family musicians made sense but ultimately proved unsustainable. Ten years of experience had heightened Dolly's level of professionalism, along with a sense that her own music was heading down a new path. She soon put together a new band, Gypsy Fever, to accompany her there. In a 1979 interview with Larry Grobel for *Newsday*, she recollected changes over the preceding several years:

> *I was 30 years old and I thought, if you don't get on with your dreams and if you're going to see your dreams come true and not turn into nightmares, you better get on. My family was the ones who understood the most. In fact, all of my brothers and sisters are very musical, they all wanted their own careers; they were helping me as much as anything. So I told them what I had decided to do, that I was going to get a band that had a lot of studio experience and they were glad to see that I was at last trying to do something to make it easier for me if I was going to work like that in the business.*

Dolly Rocks a Nudie Suit

Bringing some glamour and sparkle to a new RCA album

"Look at me! If I got any charm at all, it's that I look totally phony, but I am totally real. That's my magic."

—DOLLY DURING A 1990 INTERVIEW WITH KAREN JAEHNE FOR *CINEASTE*

On the front cover of the RCA collection *Best of Dolly Parton, Vol. 2*, there is an image of Dolly in close-up, standing in front of what looks to be a tall, wooden-slat fence. She wears large hoop earrings and a big friendly smile. Photographed from the elbows up, she is dressed in a relaxed, loose-fitting shirt, red with black-and-white patterns of checkered squares and small paisleys.

On the album's flip side, Dolly stands in a floor-length yellow jumpsuit adorned with rhinestone-encrusted flowers. The red, white, orange, and darker yellow flowers run along the forearms, down the middle, around the knee area, and at the ankles. The suit covers her from neck to floor, where only the toes of one gold-strapped high heel peek from beneath the gracious mid-1970s bell-bottomed legs.

If the front of the album embodies Dolly the downhome country girl from the Appalachian hills, the back is the sexy, curvaceous, glamorous star of music and television—a star who, despite her small

stature, fills up the album cover in the same way she does a stage or screen. The 1975 jumpsuit was designed by the famous tailor Nudie Cohen, whose combination of glitz and kitsch first came into public consciousness in the early 1950s, via Hollywood cowfolk like Roy Rogers and Dale Evans and, in country music, the concert clothing of Western swing stylist Tex Williams.

Nudie, not unlike Dolly, bridged worlds. Beginning in 1950, his designs first came to typify decades of country music stars. Hank Williams, Lefty Frizzell, Hank Snow, and Webb Pierce were early enthusiasts of the Nudie suit, as they came to be called. Porter Wagoner wore them regularly on his TV show, often adorned with images of wagons and wheels in homage to his own and his band's name, The Wagonmasters. Johnny Cash, himself a bridge across musical audiences, sometimes wore them in black.

Nudie's reach and appeal extended beyond genre bounds, as artists from outside country music came to appreciate his work. Liberace wore them to play piano in his flashy manner. Elvis Presley famously sported a gold lame Nudie suit, commissioned by his manager, Colonel Tom Parker. Gram Parsons wore a suit with symbols—like marijuana leaves—to represent sin and a large cross on the back to represent salvation, a look that *Guardian* critic John Robinson called "the Sistine Chapel ceiling of cowboy attire." The rest of Parson's Flying Burrito Brothers band donned them for their album *The Gilded Palace of Sin*, and a rock lineage was established for Nudie suits. Eventually, Nudie clients ranged from Elton John to Sonny and Cher, from John Lennon to Sly Stone, from ZZ Top to Aretha Franklin.

For Dolly, the outrageous sartorial edge navigated by the Nudie suits fit her own outsize sense of fashion, which she continued to embrace in her own way long after this cover image was taken. As she told a British journalist for the *Guardian* in 1977, "I knew some things about me were going to be noticed. I was so extreme in every way so I decided to dress accordingly. I knew it would be an attention-getter. Now the gaudy appearance, flashy clothes, and teased hair is my trademark. Don't think I dress like this out of ignorance: it's because I'm smart enough to do something out of the ordinary. Not everybody could do this."

ABOVE: (L to R) Emmylou Harris, Nudie Cohn, and Dolly in the 1970s.

THE TIDE'S GONNA TURN

1976–1980

"Every now and then I get lucky and I'll write a love song that other people like and want to sing."
**—DOLLY, INTRODUCING "I WILL ALWAYS LOVE YOU"
DURING HER 2001 PERFORMANCE ON *AUSTIN CITY LIMITS***

OPPOSITE: Dolly performs at the Ivanhoe Theater in Chicago, Illinois, in 1977.

A Change in Management

Dolly hires Sandy Gallin, the manager who would help her break into the mainstream

By the mid-1970s, Dolly was at a bit of a crossroads in terms of directions for her career. She was experiencing success with her songwriting in a period of some of her most enduring and iconic songs, but she wasn't earning very much money. Country music audiences were relatively small at that time, so a number one song in the country market, like "Jolene," only sold about 60,000 records. Additionally, Dolly was experiencing the challenges that came with being bandleader for siblings and cousins, and the line between boss and family member. And on top of that, the tour experience was rife with frustrations, including "poor lighting, poor sound, poor management, poor everything."

As she told music writer Alanna Nash during a 1977 interview, "I happened to see Mac the day I decided I was going to totally change everything." "Mac" was her friend Mac Davis, who began his career as a songwriter famous for tunes recorded by Elvis, including "In the Ghetto" and "A Little Less Conversation." By the 1970s, Mac was singing his own songs as well on hits like "I Believe In Music," "Baby, Don't Get Hooked On Me," and the tongue-in-cheek "It's Hard to Be Humble." He would go on to act in movies, but during the mid-1970s, he hosted *The Mac Davis Show*, a variety show where Dolly once performed a memorable gospel medley with a motley group made up of her, Mac, Tom Jones, and Donna Summer.

After a guest appearance on his variety show, Mac suggested Dolly meet with his manager Sandy Gallin, a partner in the Los Angeles–based management agency Katz-Gallin-Cleary, because he thought the two might hit it off. Mac was right. Dolly and Sandy hit it off right away, sharing an instinct that Dolly's success could extend beyond the boundaries of Nashville. They began a partnership that would last twenty-five years, until Sandy retired. Dolly told a reporter for the *Globe and Mail* in 1978 that Sandy "saw in me all the things I saw in myself."

Dolly brought an already-established persona to work with, what '70s music scholar Mitchell Morris

---

OPPOSITE: Dolly performs at the Day on the Green concert at Oakland Coliseum on May 28, 1978. Sandy Gallin is visible in the background, in sunglasses.

called her "self-cartooning—confecting an image of the ultimate glamour-puss as seen by a naïve farm girl." Dolly presented an element of playfulness about her appearance. She dabbled in stereotypes of Appalachia and Southern identity that extended at least as far back as the character Daisy Mae in Lil' Abner comic strips. Sandy told *Newsday* in 1976 that changing Dolly's image was not part of their plan: "We only intend to supervise her career—the phases of TV, recording and personal appearances."

From the beginning, Dolly was clear about the reasons for her choices: she recognized that Sandy had knowledge and connections to bring her before audiences she otherwise would never have encountered. Gallin's sphere ranged far outside country music, as he'd worked with Cher, Tony Orlando, and Olivia Newton-John. *Brady Bunch* star Florence Henderson and the Osmonds were also among the performers affiliated with the firm. As Dolly told Alanna Nash in 1977, "I changed management because I didn't have what I needed for the things I wanted to do, or the places I wanted to go." It was Sandy who would see her booked on *The Tonight Show* and on the celebrity game show *Hollywood Squares*.

At the time Dolly's shift in artistic direction and management was a source of controversy and cries of betrayal from some in her country audience. Dolly told the *New York Times* in 1976, "A lot of country people feel I'm leaving the country, that I'm not proud of Nashville, which is the biggest lie there is. I don't want to leave the country, but to take the country with me wherever I go. The truth is, I am country. I am Dolly Parton from the mountains, that's what I'll remain." Music writer Lee Walburn published a 1977 piece for the *Atlanta Constitution* titled, "Please, Dolly, Don't Sacrifice The Pure Sound."

Sandy was able to bring Dolly into entirely new professional arenas. He helped guide her toward new production decisions, including producing her own album for the first time and, eventually, bringing West Coast producers into the studio to broaden the appeal of her sound. Working with Sandy would lead to the movie deal that included *9 to 5* and subsequent projects, TV variety shows, and a tour with the Eagles, Linda Ronstadt, Emmylou Harris, and Seals and Crofts.

Dolly said in 1977, "I just had big plans, and I just had big dreams, and I just didn't see any reason why a county line should keep me from goin' where I wanted to go. Every country girl wants to go to the city, and every city girl wants to go to the country. But a person that is free to go where they please can go to the country and the city. And that's exactly what I'm doin'."

"I think Dolly likes to move on. She only likes to chew her tobacco once."

—SANDY GALLIN, INTERVIEWED FOR *HERE I AM*

Dolly!

A variety of entertainment—and top-notch performers —on Dolly's network TV show

Each episode of the short-lived, thirty-minute variety show *Dolly!*, whose pilot aired in February 1976, started the same way. Dolly descended to the stage on a high rope swing to the sound of "Love Is Like a Butterfly." The legendary voice of radio announcer Ralph Emery introduced her, and she launched into an opening song. Sometimes these songs were ones viewers might expect, but just as often they were not. In one episode, she stepped from the swing wearing a floor-length, mint-green chiffon gown, subtle sequins and lace adorning the V-shaped neckline, and burst into a compelling rendition of the Doobie Brothers' hit "China Grove." She also covered Jim Croce's "Bad Bad Leroy Brown," Joni Mitchell's "Circle Game," and, perhaps closer to the sphere she occupied, "Rhinestone Cowboy," made famous by countrypolitan singer Glen Campbell.

At the time her show debuted, Dolly was the only female country music performer to have a syndicated live show—ever. According to reporter Chris Chase, who wrote a *New York Times* feature

on Dolly in 1976, Bill Graham of Show Biz Inc., the company that had produced Porter's TV show for years, started pursuing the idea in 1975. *Dolly!* exemplified the title star's enjoyment of interacting with people, while making both music and conversation. It left her with a desire to pursue further television projects in the future.

The show also brought Dolly into contact with musicians with whom she would later create some of the most enduring musical collaborations of her career. During another unexpected opener ("Knock Three Times" by Tony Orlando and Dawn), Kenny Rogers made a gimmicky entrance from inside a delivery crate, from which he'd been knocking at the appropriate moments in the song. The two bantered a bit in the way that typified the show, but their chemistry both as musicians and stage performers came through clearly. Dolly later wrote in her memoir about their success as collaborators, which she thought "was because Kenny has a kind of cool energy that is a perfect complement to my hot energy. Whatever it was, people just instantly began to think of us as a couple." They would eventually release one of Dolly's most recognized recordings, the duet "Islands in the Stream."

On another episode, Dolly stepped from the swing dressed conservatively in a cream-colored blouse with slits along the sleeves from wrist to elbow and a light orange floral-print skirt. She began singing "Silver Threads" and was joined mid-song by Linda Ronstadt, who had recorded the song with success as a soloist. Then out came Emmylou Harris, and the three finished the song in close harmony. Their voices blended with ease, in a way that seemed to signal the *Trio* collaborations coming in the 1980s and 1990s.

On one of the most precious episodes, Dolly was joined by her mother, father, and seven of her siblings, including Willadeene, Stella, Cassie, Randy, Floyd, Freida, and Rachel. If sequences with music superstars pointed to her future, this episode celebrated Dolly's roots and the heritage that shaped her as a musician and a person. Dolly often recalled her mama singing in a loud, strong voice. In this episode, viewers got to hear it, as Avie Lee sang a few lines of the classic tune "In the Pines." All the Partons joined in for the last two lines, filling out the harmonies.

ABOVE: From Dolly's self-titled variety show, circa 1976.

Dolly and Dancing Bear
Dolly visits Captain Kangaroo and friends

Dolly arrives at Captain Kangaroo's door for a visit, but also to invite the Captain's friend, Dancing Bear, to be in her show. She enters wearing what look to be blue denim pants and a cream-colored blouse paneled in pastel-pink stripes with blue bursts that may be flower petals at the cross points. Dolly's hair is fashioned high, parted off-center, with the rest cascading into curls surrounding her face and covering the front her shoulders. She looks relaxed and casual. Mr. Moose, a hand puppet and another of the Captain's friends, had spoken to her on the phone earlier and announced her upcoming visit.

The Captain is dressed in his typical red blazer with white trim, with his light blond hair fashioned in the usual bangs trimmed straight across and long sideburns framing his face. He can't believe his good fortune, to see both the "little marching band" and Dolly Parton all in the same day. The little marching band was a recurring special-effects miracle in miniature—a three-person ensemble that occasionally passed through the scene—and though we the viewers share these sightings, everyone else in the Captain's world apparently thinks the little marching band is make-believe. Dolly breezes in with a similarly delightful air, as larger-than-life as they are small.

Dolly exchanges gifts with shy Bunny Rabbit, another puppet friend of Captain Kangaroo's: she receives a "Dolly doll" and offers a carrot. She autographs Mr. Moose's ping-pong ball. Learning that Dancing Bear is on vacation in Spain, a quick cut leads to a scene of Dancing Bear doing a sarabande with a rag doll.

The highlight of Dolly's 1976 visit with Captain Kangaroo comes when he asks her to share a song. He pulls a guitar from his large trunk of musical instruments and Dolly sings "Cracker Jack," a story song about a beloved dog. In the song, a girl finds a dog in the woods, takes him in, and he becomes "the best friend that [she] ever had."

At one point in the show, Dolly is left alone and hears but does not see the little marching band. She thinks the music is coming from an old radio, which the Captain later shows her was unplugged the whole time. This exchange winds its way to another segment, in which Dolly reads aloud *The Teeny Tiny Woman*. This segment anticipates Dolly's future commitment to getting books into the hands of young children with her Imagination Library. When

the COVID-19 pandemic shut down the world, she posted an Internet series of bedtime stories, reading children's books aloud.

Mr. Bainter the painter shows up and Captain Kangaroo enlists his help to look for something missing that's "about this big," and "mostly red and they're marching." Mr. Bainter misunderstands that as "bread and margarine," so the Captain just tells him to look for anything unusual. He returns to the basement, where Dolly has been reading, to help her get a stool for her show. When he returns, Mr. Bainter is vacuuming, much to the concern of the Captain, who worries that the band has been sucked up by the machine.

Dolly reappears just as Dancing Bear returns from vacation, and she departs with him—and the stool—to perform. The members of the little marching band emerge from the vacuum, unharmed, though Dolly never did catch sight of them.

ABOVE: Dolly and Captain Kangaroo in 1976.

Stepping Out, Away, and Into the "Light of a Clear Blue Morning"

Dolly channels intense emotions in another album

"Light of a Clear Blue Morning" sprung from a painful transition now several years in Dolly's rearview mirror. When the time had finally come to end her seven-year stint with *The Porter Wagoner Show*, the moment was fraught. Leaving had been a painful but also a clear decision; it was time to move on to the next phase of her life. She'd cried as the cab carried her home to figure out what was next.

What would become the lead song for her record *New Harvest . . . First Gathering* seemed to settle on her, like a dove descending. "Light of a Clear Blue Morning" conveys the sense of freedom and release a person feels when they realize they've been trapped but have now struck out on their own—the joy of emerging from the shadows of a difficult time.

The song follows a verse-chorus structure. Quieter, more reflective images unfold in the lower-register verses, leading up to the high anthemic, empowering chorus that declares "everything's going to be all right." It's the kind of song you crank up to lift your spirits when you need a boost. As the song builds, the chorus returns, first adding a steady tambourine beat and backup singers, then a cappella, with choral ornaments snaking around the melody and a more subdued tambourine. This all leads to an ecstatic series of chorus repetitions—"everything's going to be all right"—punctuated by a piano that is more Elton John than honky-tonk.

Perhaps it was a combination of transcendent lyrics and the unusual choral ornamentation that inspired the Austin-based professional chorus Conspirare, founded and directed by Craig Hella Johnson, to include an arrangement of the song on their 2009 Grammy-nominated album, *A Company of Voices*, for the label Harmonia Mundi. By that time, it was obvious that Dolly's songwriting legacy occupied a place of continuity within a musical tapestry that includes traditional spirituals, Andrew Lloyd Webber, Roy Orbison, Samuel Barber, and Ennio Morricone—all represented on this choral release.

At the time of the song's initial release, however, critics and reviewers weren't sure what to make of Dolly's embrace of a more pop-oriented sound. Never mind that the Nashville Sound so dominant when she first surfaced as an artist was itself a deliberate bid

toward greater pop appeal. Jay Scott for Canada's *Globe and Mail*, in calling her the first country artist since Johnny Cash to cross over to a popular music audience, suggests Dolly has "shucked her country corn." But then he fixates on her looks, seeming to miss the very next song on the album, a banjo-forward tune called "Applejack" that includes country legends Kitty Wells and Johnny Wright, Roy Acuff, Chet Atkins, Grandpa and Ramona Jones, Ernest Tubb, Carl and Pearl Butler, as well as her own parents. After evoking comparisons to Mae West and Marilyn Monroe, Scott writes: "[Dolly] looks like Jayne Mansfield. Or the early Diana Dors. Or a drag queen. Like a parody of the way women looked in the fifties." After somewhat cynically (and incompletely) boiling her music down to six themes, he also notes that Dolly "is writing the most direct come-on songs being written by a woman in any branch of popular music."

Other writers wring their hands over issues of "purity," which seem to plague country musicians more than any others. Writing for the *Atlanta Constitution* (prior to its merger with the *Atlanta Journal*), Lee Walburn worries that Dolly is approaching "that innocent-looking pit called 'crossover music.'" To his credit, he then acknowledges that she knows what she's about. Critic John Rockwell for the *New York Times* dismisses "Light of a Clear Blue Morning" as "too kitschy." He goes on to sniff that "the inflated, bathetic rhetoric of the arrangements will appeal to the Barry Manilow crowd, and to reject them (or him)

somehow brands one antidemocratic." Though even he can't help but give props to the fact that "Miss Parton's uncontroversial gifts are so apparent" that the album holds promise, despite its "excesses."

You can't help but wonder whether Dolly read these sorts of reviews. And then you probably can't help but imagine her shrugging, confident that this recording, the first album she produced herself, marked more than a move away from Porter. It was a move toward broadening the audience for her music. More than that, it was a move toward that sense of command and confidence to shape her own destiny that makes Dolly such an inspiration almost five decades later.

New Harvest . . . First Gathering represents other changes in her career. It was the first album after parting ways with her Travelin' Family Band, which included some of her siblings and at least one cousin. Her new band, Gypsy Fever, would make two follow-up albums, *Here You Come Again* and *Heartbreaker*, which brought in producer Gary Klein, already famous for his work with Barbra Streisand. During this time, Dolly would appear on a Cher television special in 1978 titled *Cher . . . Special*. She had already replaced her Uncle Louis Owens as her manager, first with the legendary steel guitar player Don Warden, who followed her from Porter Wagoner's organization. Warden, who also had a sharp mind for the music business, stayed on as what Dolly referred to as "Mr. Everything" for close to five decades after she signed in 1976 with Sandy Gallin.

OPPOSITE: Dolly performs at Georgia Tech's Alexander Memorial Coliseum in October 1977.

A Universal Star

Dolly is interviewed by Barbara Walters

"I wanted more than to just be a farmer's daughter, even though I'm proud to be."

—DOLLY, RESPONDING TO BARBARA'S QUESTION ABOUT DOLLY ALWAYS FEELING THAT SHE WAS DIFFERENT

During their televised interview, Barbara Walters sets up a fairy tale for Dolly to finish. "Once upon a time there was a little girl," Barbara begins. "Her name was Dolly Parton and . . ." Dolly picks up the trailing thread:

She lived in a small town in the mountains, which she loved because it was a comfort, because she knew there was love and security there in her family. But she was a child very curious. And she wanted all the things that she had always been impressed with, like the fairy tales or the Mother Goose stories, and the Cinderellas and the lost slipper. Well, I guess she kinda wanted to find the other slipper. So she worked hard and she dreamed a lot and one day it came true. She was a fairy princess and she lived happily ever after.

Their conversation canvassed Dolly's childhood, Dolly's identity in relation to "hillbilly" stereotypes of white Appalachian communities, Dolly's physique and her style of dress, and her marriage to spotlight-averse Carl Dean. Barbara appeared concerned over Dolly's

"extreme" appearance, as though trying to convince her that her wig and flashy clothes were unnecessary. Dolly assured her that her choices were intentional, that "I don't like to be like everybody else."

"Show business is a money-making joke," Dolly added, "and I've just always liked telling jokes."

At one point, Barbara asked, "Dolly, where I come from, would I have called you a hillbilly?" Dolly replied that that may have come naturally, but "I would have probably kicked your shins or something." Barbara kept at it: "But when I think of hillbillies, am I thinking of your kind of people?"

"I think you probably are," Dolly replied. She explained that, Lil' Abner and Daisy Mae associations aside, the Appalachian people were characterized by their pride and their class. "It was country class," she said, "but it was a great deal of class."

Barbara visited the tour bus, where Dolly highlighted the couch that converts to a bed and the cabinet that neatly houses several wigs on mannequin heads. She described the three closets, opening the one that holds her glittery stage clothes. "All of these clothes are hand-washable," Dolly told Barbara. "I just

put them in a sink in a motel room. I just rinse them out, they're wrinkle-free, I don't have to iron them, 'cause that works out really good for me."

Barbara questioned Dolly about her goals, particularly following changes like her departure from *The Porter Wagoner Show* and, more recently, the hiring of new management and replacement of the Travelin' Family Band. Barbara asked if people close to Dolly were worried that she had changed, maybe "gone Hollywood." Dolly explained—in the same measured and kind way with which she had responded to Barbara's dubious feelings about her looks—"I'm not making a crossover from country to pop, I'm trying to be accepted in the pop field as well as the country field.

I feel my music is its own music, just like I'm my own person." She added, "And as a businessperson, I like to think that there's more money to be made than the money I've been making. I've been working too hard, too long, for too little."

With a clarity of vision remarkable in retrospect, given how her intentions came to life, Dolly described to Barbara Walters a vision of her professional and artistic directions: "I want to be a star. A universal star. I would like to be a superstar. I guess all people dream of that. So in order to be a superstar, you can't be just a superstar in one area. That means you have to appeal to a majority of people. And that's what I'm trying to do."

ABOVE: Dolly with Barbara Walters in 1977.

A Year's Pay

Dolly makes her first appearance on

The Tonight Show Starring Johnny Carson

The moment that lingers in the collective public memory from Dolly's first appearance on *The Tonight Show Starring Johnny Carson* is brief. Johnny addresses Dolly's figure, asking if she's "always been rather zaftig." They banter affably about how people in Tennessee would phrase the question ("bosomy," she suggests), and Dolly tells him people always ask if her breasts are real. Johnny jumps in to say he would never do so. He says, "I have certain guidelines on this show"—a significant pause here—"but I would give about a year's pay to peek under there." Johnny continues, "I cannot tell you how tacky I feel right now for saying that, but I had to get it out." He trails off, seeming a little embarrassed at his own unguarded remark. Dolly laughs the whole time.

Up until this moment, they had been talking about jokes, specifically the ubiquity of jokes about Dolly's wigs, clothes, and boobs. In her good-natured way, she shared a couple of examples. One begins, "What's worse than a giraffe with a sore throat?" The answer: "Dolly Parton with a chest cold." Then she shares a joke that country singer Mel Tillis made during a performance. She knew Tillis from her days working on *The Porter Wagoner Show*, where he was regularly featured. Between

songs at a recent performance, Mel reportedly said, "Oh, I see we have Dolly Parton in the audience." People began looking around, clapping, trying to locate her, at which point Mel said, "Oh, I'm sorry, that's two bald-headed men sitting together."

Dolly's conclusion to Johnny was that after you hear jokes about yourself "so raw as that, you kind of get used to it and, then, you know, you kind of make your own jokes." That captures what has consistently been Dolly's attitude when it comes to her breasts. In 1989, she told the *Washington Post* critic Rita Kempley, "I mean if I was going to be offended, why don't I cover 'em up? You can set and talk with me for five minutes and know that there's a little more to me than tits, I'd like to think."

That first visit to *The Tonight Show* established a rapport between Johnny and Dolly that maintained itself through her numerous appearances in the years to come. A significant event in her professional life would prompt a promotional visit to Johnny's show, and their conversations were inevitably entertaining. In 1980, she told him she learned the whole script for *9 to 5* by heart, not realizing she only needed to know a handful of lines each day (and also only her own part). It was her first movie, and she hadn't realized scenes are filmed

out of sequence. She returned in 1982 to talk about *The Best Little Whorehouse in Texas* and her album *Heartbreak Express*, and Johnny commented on Dolly's switch from playing a secretary in the previous film. Dolly replied, "I made a better whore than I did a secretary." During the ensuing laughter, she makes corrections until finally settling on the statement she intended: "I played a better madam . . ."

In 1984, she visited to talk about the film *Rhinestone*, co-starring Sylvester Stallone, and performed "Tennessee Homesick Blues," a song that includes lyrics about longing for grits and gravy with country ham, as well as the memorable line about it

being "hard to be a diamond in a rhinestone world." When she sat down to chat, Johnny alluded to a moment backstage when apparently he passed her in a relative state of disassembly, somewhere between shower and dressing room. He apologized for any awkwardness. Dolly, not missing beat, completed a seven-year-old circle when she said, "I'd give a year's salary to get in that shower with you."

By the end of this appearance, Dolly had rallied Johnny and the entire audience to sing "He's Got the Whole World In His Hands." You could say that it appeared she had the whole audience in her own.

ABOVE: Dolly on *The Tonight Show Starring Johnny Carson*.

Crossing Over

Here You Come Again *helps Dolly find her footing beyond the country scene*

*"That's such a good song a monkey could have made it a hit.
Well, you're looking at a million-dollar monkey."*

**—DOLLY TO LAWRENCE GROBEL DURING A 1978 *PLAYBOY* INTERVIEW,
REFLECTING ON HER INITIAL WORRY THAT THE SONG WAS TOO SLICK**

Here You Come Again, the larger album as well as its lead song, took shape as a result of Dolly's partnership with manager Sandy Gallin. With Dolly, Sandy dreamed of ways to expand her audience. Her previous album, *New Harvest . . . First Gathering*, had been a start. It featured her new band Gypsy Fever, all accomplished studio musicians with wide-ranging experience. She had hired Gregg Perry to lead the band and found his musical vision inspiring. Dolly had also produced *New Harvest* herself and, when all was said and done, it sounded more like the music she was hearing in her head than anything that had come before. It was true to her personal artistic trajectory. That said, it missed the target when it came to sales figures.

The disappointing sales for *New Harvest* convinced Dolly to turn production duties on the next project over to Gary Klein. Klein had established his reputation on the West Coast via phenomenal recording successes with diva Barbra Streisand and blazer-wearing countrypolitan Glen Campbell. Speaking with Canadian journalist Patrick Snyder the following year, Dolly admitted she'd never heard of Klein before their work together began, and speculated the reverse was true as well. "This was something I agreed to do because

ABOVE: Cover of the album *Here You Come Again*, released in 1977.

I hadn't been able to make that change to pop by myself," she added.

California connections provided a spark to Dolly's musical sensibility in other ways. For one, Barry Mann and Cynthia Weil wrote the lead single, "Here You Come Again." These veteran songwriters were a married team who had been active since the early 1960s, with major hits including "On Broadway," "You've Lost That Lovin' Feelin'," and "Saturday Night at the Movies." "Here You Come Again" turned out to be the first million-selling record Dolly made, bringing the album to platinum status. As the *Atlanta Constitution* reported at the time, it was "the first album by a woman country singer to even come near that mark."

Dolly's aim was to build a bigger audience and this album succeeded, although it also drew some pushback in the name of "country purity." Still, as her old friend and fellow musician Mac Davis said during an interview for *Here I Am*, "Crossing over to pop was an ultimate goal, but it also was destiny. It was bound to happen. Dolly is one of those people that breaks that line. As hillbilly as she might sound, people understand that she's bright, and she's beautiful inside and out, and that just automatically drips off of Dolly."

ABOVE: Dolly greets fans and leaves her handprints at an instore appearance at Peaches Records on May 3, 1977, in Atlanta, Georgia.

Entertainer of the Year
Dolly receives the CMA's highest honor (and experiences a wardrobe malfunction)

Right before Dolly's name was announced from the stage as the winner of the Country Music Association's top honor for 1978, she had a problem. The pink and white dress she wore to the occasion was made of thin material. In her words, "I busted it all the way down the front—wide open." Due to this "wardrobe malfunction," she took the podium to accept CMA's Entertainer of the Year award wearing a borrowed overcoat to cover the torn dress. As apparently undaunted as ever, Dolly joked, "I guess it's like daddy said—you shouldn't try to put fifty pounds of mud in a five-pound sack."

The Entertainer of the Year award is determined by votes among members of the CMA. At the time of Dolly's win, that constituted around five thousand people, a mix of songwriters, singers, instrumentalists, and executives. When Dolly won for the first time in 1978, she was only the second woman ever to do so, preceded by the late Loretta Lynn. Dolly was also nominated for top female vocalist, for top single with "Here You Come Again," and for album of the year for the larger project.

United Press International reporter Mark Schwed, writing in 1978, noted that Dolly had been up for the award two years before, but not chosen. Her win was read as a sign that the Nashville-centered static over abandoning country music had calmed down. After the show, Dolly's eye remained on the future. She commented, "Now that I've received this compliment, the criticism is over, but I'm free to do whatever I want. I will be doing a couple of movies but that's not until next year."

The same year Dolly was named Entertainer of the Year, a writer named James Otis published a book for Quick Fox press titled *Dolly Parton: A Personal Portrait*. In a five-part series, reprinted for the *Atlanta Constitution* after Dolly's CMA accolade, Otis highlighted her mid-1970s career moves, and the tremors that subsequently rippled through settled musical waters along Nashville's Music Row. Otis named Dolly "the first woman to cross over the boundaries of country and western music and make a solid bid for pop superstardom."

Later that year, in November 1978, singer R.W. Blackwood, Jr., whose "Sunday Afternoon Boat Ride in the Park on the Lake" had gained notice in 1977, recorded a tribute song. Simply titled "Dolly," the song was written by Buzz Cason and Austin Roberts. Cason had known Dolly from her early Nashville days with Monument Records and had even co-written her first single, "Don't Drop Out," back when Monument still thought Dolly should do girl-group-inspired rock-and-roll.

"Dolly" the song describes in straightforward terms the highlights of the titular performer's journey from the Smoky Mountains to the present day, with a sweet and gentle chorus—"Dolly, sweet songbird in your flight"—and projects her path "soon to be a star so bright." The narrative song ends with Dolly in Hollywood, and names her "gold records," "Here You Come Again" and "Two Doors Down," from her most recent album release. Co-writer Cason explained that he aimed "to make it traditional sounding and like a Tennessee song. I wanted to make it a tribute—not a ripoff." The following year, the Tennessee legislature named a stretch of US Highway 411 passing through Sevier County "The Dolly Parton Parkway."

ABOVE: Dolly poses for a portrait backstage at the Day on the Green concert at Oakland Coliseum in California in 1978.

"Two Doors Down"

Dolly channels a fear of missing out into a new hit

"Two Doors Down" became the second major hit from Dolly's crossover album *Here You Come Again*. Unlike the title cut, Dolly wrote this song, one of four self-penned tunes on the project. The lyrics establish a vignette where a lonely person listens to the festivities unfolding "two doors down," then decides to put heartache aside and join the party; in the final verse, that person has returned home—along with a new love interest—for a party of their own.

The song sounds funky, bringing to mind the disco era during which it was written. The chorus is built on a low, thick drum kick that comes on strong every other downbeat, with rounded bass licks and a syncopated electric guitar riff. Gospel-style background singers bring an uplifting feel to the overall sound.

Amid this musical variety, Dolly's voice as a songwriter remains strong and recognizable. Put simply, it still sounds like Dolly. When she spoke with reporter Larry Grobel for *Newsday* in 1979, she talked about musical categories:

I don't think labels are necessarily necessary. I want my music to be Dolly Parton music. It's country, it's pop, it's folky, it's different. It is ordinary and extraordinary at the same time. But if I am going to be labeled I would rather it be country, because that is a more fitting label for me. I'm a country person and country people, I know they are for real, which I can't say for a lot of people I know in the other business.

Dolly wrote "Two Doors Down" while following a restrictive diet after a period of unwelcome weight gain. She sat at a table in a Howard Johnson's with some friends who were enjoying fried clams. "I'll never forget sitting there with all of that glorious fried fat filling my nostrils and feeling completely left out," Dolly recalled. "I went home and wrote one of my biggest hits, 'Two Doors Down.' I also went off my diet and had some fried clams."

ABOVE: Dolly in 1978.

Imitation Is the Sincerest Form of Flattery

Dolly loses a Dolly Parton lookalike contest

"One of my favorite sayings that I say about myself, that I made up, is that my desire to do something has always been greater than my fear of it."

—DOLLY TO RUPAUL IN *MARIE CLAIRE*, OCTOBER 2021

By the late 1970s, Dolly Parton lookalike contests crept up in all kinds of places and for all kinds of purposes. At Mickey Gilley's famous urban-cowboy honky-tonk, there were thirty-two contestants for a 1979 contest included among *Texas Monthly*'s annual New Year's Day Bum Steer Awards. The *Miami Herald* reported on that city's contest in July 1982, part of a promotional event for *The Best Little Whorehouse in Texas*, with contestants that included a three-year-old girl. The male mayor of Midwest City, Oklahoma, announced on January 31, 1983, that he planned to dress up as Dolly for an annual fundraiser—the Rag Time Follies—aimed toward buying equipment for the local hospital.

Sometime in the late '70s, Dolly herself got in on the fun. Dolly and Cher were common inspirations for contestants at drag shows, so Dolly leaned into her image, amping up every part of her signature look. She got in line to walk across the stage, and nobody seemed to recognize her. "That's what was funny," Dolly said in a 2012 *Nightline* interview, "'cause all these other beautiful drag queens had worked for months and weeks getting their clothes and all that . . . and they just thought I was some little short gay guy, and I got the least applause but I was just dying laughing inside. I say it's a good thing I was a girl or I'd be a drag queen."

Dolly has always communicated a sense of fun or playfulness when it comes to her appearance. She told *Washington Post* reporter Rita Kempley in 1989 that "it's all fun for me anyway. It's like a dress-up doll. I've often said in joking, but it's the truth, that I pattern the way I look after what they called the trash in our town. I love to paint and pamper and primp. I can't imagine me trying to be plain. I feel real plain as a person. I love people and they seem to sense it and I can be got close to. And I do care. By the same token, I don't feel like just walking around in a dark suit or a flat hairdo."

That sense of fun has carried through her entire career, and it is infectious. It is also enduring. On March 1, 2022, a local culture and events website based in Brooklyn, New York, called *Greenpointers* reported on the "triumphant return" of a Dolly Parton lookalike contest at a barbecue joint following "a long, pandemic-related absence." The reporter describes the winning edge Dolly #5 brought to the Q&A portion of the competition at Mable's Smokehouse. The winning Dolly focused on the real Dolly's contributions to COVID-19 vaccine funding, saying, "It's good to feel normal for the first time in a long time and we have Dolly to thank for that."

ABOVE: Dolly and Dolly impersonator Jason CoZmo arrive at the *Dumplin'* premiere at the Chinese Theater in Los Angeles in 2018.

Bunny Ears and a Bow Tie
Dolly poses for the cover of Playboy

"I may look fake but I'm real where it counts."

—DOLLY SPEAKING TO HADLEY FREEMAN FOR A 2011 *GUARDIAN* INTERVIEW

Dolly Parton appeared on the cover of the October 1978 issue of *Playboy* magazine. The image features Dolly in a black, sleeveless bustier, showing off a generous amount of cleavage, and the signature Playboy bunny ears poking out of her wavy blonde wig. She wears pink sequined wristbands that match the choker around her neck, adorned with a white sequined bow tie. Her hands are positioned as though she is straightening the tie, and her smile is direct. She looks like she's having fun.

The photo shoot happened in Los Angeles with Hollywood photographer Harry Langdon, whose shots canvas people in entertainment ranging from Tina Turner to George Clooney. Between the photo shoot and the publication of the October issue, Dolly reportedly told the press on one occasion that "if I approve the picture, I'm gonna be on the cover. If I don't, I'll still have the article in the magazine. I have to see how fat I look, I guess."

The lengthy feature inside resulted from extensive recorded interviews taking place in multiple locations. Dolly's career was on the move:

Here You Come Again had propelled her toward TV late-night appearances and specials, offers to publish her writing, and movie deals, and Sandy Gallin and her management team were strategizing toward broader awareness of Dolly's many talents and assets. In that rush of activity and exposure, the *Playboy* interview stood out. Dolly later recalled she had opened up to the press with rare candor during the conversation.

Dolly first met freelance writer Lawrence Grobel at a Los Angeles apartment she was renting. They talked for five hours. Lawrence would note the sparse furnishings of the apartment, a detail conveying her packed schedule—he called her one of the busiest people he had ever met. The apartment appeared to be little more than a crash pad to sleep before the next appointment. Lawrence then met up with Dolly at the Apple Blossom Festival in Virginia and joined her for part of a six-month tour.

As for the picture, Dolly must have approved of it. Apparently, so did Carl. On July 20, 2021, Dolly recreated the magazine cover as a birthday surprise for her husband. She posted a message on social media about his gift: a framed image of the 1978 original cover and the updated image with Dolly once again donning the notorious costume, side by side. Dolly commented, "He still thinks I'm a hot chick after 57 years and I'm not gonna try to talk him out of that."

ABOVE: Dolly poses for *Playboy* in 1978.

Carol and Dolly in Nashville

The Queen of Comedy meets the Queen of Country

The camera swept the audience seated at the Grand Ole Opry House at Nashville's Opryland, as the orchestra kicked off a medley including short bits of "The Tennessee Waltz," "Wabash Cannonball," and "I Can't Stop Loving You."

"Ladies and gentlemen," the announcer's voice boomed, "Ms. Dolly Parton and Ms. Carol Burnett." The camera focused on a screen, lit bright pink from the back, against which two silhouettes stood back-to-back. The extreme contrast between their figures brought chuckles from the audience.

So began the hourlong comedy special, starring the incomparable Carol Burnett and Dolly Parton, that aired on CBS on Valentine's Day 1979. It was the first TV special Carol had taped since her groundbreaking variety show ended its eleven-year run almost a year earlier. According to Atlanta-based reporter Joe Litsch, writing in 1979, the idea had formed during one of the audience Q&A sessions Carol typically held before every episode of *The Carol Burnett Show*. Someone in the audience asked about post-retirement goals and Carol named working with

Dolly Parton as one of them. "We were never able to have her on our show because of her schedule, but I would love to do a special with her," she said. She would later describe seeing Dolly on late-night television: "I saw a warmth and honesty about Dolly and I just knew we'd hit it off."

The onstage rapport between the two legendary women suggests that Carol was correct. The show's opening song featured them both in long, flowing chiffon—Carol in bright orange and Dolly in pink—singing the other's praises in a song titled "What Am I Doing Up Here?" Both were seated on pedestals that rose to humorous heights as each extolled the other's virtues. They moved from calling one another Ms. Parton and Ms. Burnett to being on a first-name basis (and an irresistible "Hello, Dolly") by the song's end.

The sketches and musical numbers continued, including the memorable "No One Picks Like a Nashville Picker Picks." Dolly and Carol started off by singing "Orange Blossom Special," which led to a funny moment with Carol and her bad banjo playing. Then came an extended instrumental segment,

OPPOSITE: Dolly with Carol Burnett.

mentioned overtly, the special did include an extended medley of songs with the word "heart" in them. Other segments included a gospel presentation and a sketch about growing up that featured the song "Turn Around (Where Are You Going, My Little One?)," first made popular during the early 1960s. Carol had worked with other women, including an album with comedian Martha Raye, two television specials with Julie Andrews (1962 and 1972), and another with opera singer Beverly Sills titled "Sills and Burnett at the Met" in 1976. She had fun with all these collaborators, but she and Dolly had a particular charm together.

Ahead of the comedy special, the two stars gave a press conference to a room of forty reporters at the *Grand Ole Opry* TV studio. Someone asked what they had in common. Carol joked about how it would be difficult to tell them apart onstage. But Dolly got serious. "I would like to think that I'm a person similar to you," she said. "What I see in you is warmth and kindness and love toward other people and a love for life, your work and other people, and I would like to think those are qualities I possess. I feel from Carol a lot of the things I feel in myself . . ."

carried by well-known Nashville pickers planted in the Opry House audience. The highlight was six-year-old Lewis Philips, child prodigy of the Lewis Family band of bluegrass musicians, who took Carol's banjo and demonstrated his chops. This idea circled back around near the special's end, with a dance number, featuring the Joe Layton Dancers, called "No One Kicks Like a Nashville Kicker Kicks."

The show's timing coincided with promotional efforts for Dolly's latest album at the time, *Heartbreaker.* Although the album didn't get

---

ABOVE: Dolly and Carol Burnett in their 1979 special.

---

9 to 5

Dolly takes part in an iconic film and crafts an anthem for the ages

"I think we each fancied we were lighting up the room. I used to say, 'We each one of us thought we were the one in the middle.' Jane was so political, so active. I was a lesbian. And so Dolly naturally thought she was in the middle."

—LILY TOMLIN TALKING ABOUT *9 TO 5* FOR THE 2019 BBC DOCUMENTARY *HERE I AM*

It's easy to picture the moment: Dolly sits on the set of *9 to 5*, waiting for the next scene to begin, her mind wandering in the open space created by long stretches of downtime and the inevitable boredom that comes with movie-making. She drums her fingers on the table, her acrylic nails making a rhythmic tapping sound. It's like a typewriter—the kind Doralee, her movie character, might use during the office workday, typing memos and letters for her insufferable, chauvinistic boss as she dodges his unwelcome advances and demeaning comments.

Dolly's imagination undoubtedly took flight, as it had since childhood, sparked like flint and stone: a musical idea meeting head-on a compelling human scenario. The song "9 to 5" came to her in bits and snatches. So abundantly did music and lyrics pour forth, she would later say in the 2019 documentary *Here I Am*, that there were a hundred verses that never made it to the final song.

In her 1994 memoir, Dolly recalled that "any time I started working on [the song], the women on the set would just naturally gather around to listen." She describes her hairdresser "clacking her brushes together in time to the rhythm I had set up. The script supervisor would chime in, slapping her clipboard in time. Before long, I had created a whole section of backup singers made up of all the working women around me. Because of what the song had to say, I thought that was especially appropriate. It was also a heap of fun. That helped inspire me in writing the lyrics and made the song as special as it is."

The movie was both a comedy and a commentary on the harassment and mistreatment women regularly faced in the workplace. *9 to 5* tells the story of three women (Jane Fonda, Lily Tomlin, and Dolly) who work for the same intolerable boss, Mr. Hart (played by Dabney Coleman). At first, the others ostracize Dolly's character, Doralee, due to the insinuations and rumors—circulated, it turns out, by their boss—of

a workplace affair between her and Mr. Hart. When Doralee discovers this, she threatens Mr. Hart mightily. In one of Dolly's most memorable screen moments, she backs him into a chair, gets right up in his face, and assures him she will not hesitate to turn him from a rooster into a hen. Then she joins forces with Jane and Lily's characters to get revenge on him for all his misdeeds.

Jane had been a major force behind bringing the movie to screen, and she was the one who suggested Dolly for the part of Doralee. Dolly agreed to be in the film on the condition that she write its theme song. Along with Lily, the three made a powerful on-screen trio. Off screen, they got together, including for overnight slumber parties, to build the camaraderie and rapport that so clearly shines through in the film. Despite never seeing Dolly "without her regalia," in Jane's words years later, even during the sleepovers, the three built a friendship that has lasted. During an interview for the documentary *Here I Am*, Jane said, "You cannot finish a day with Dolly without laughing so hard that you have to cross your legs." The movie

ABOVE: (L to R) Lily Tomlin, Dolly, and Jane Fonda in *9 to 5* (1980).

remains a classic, for its humor and for the travails it depicts through its three central characters. "Those same woes affect women today and will do so for generations to come," noted journalist Sarah Smarsh in *She Come By It Natural*, her book on Dolly's significance for working-class women in America. "But *9 to 5* represents a specific moment of tension in feminism's evolution: The Equal Rights Amendment hadn't yet been squashed, middle-class women were power-walking to work (as poor women had been doing all along), and popular culture revealed a deep collective crisis about gender."

As for the song, its distinctive and infectious power was apparent from the get-go. It reached the top position on the country and Hot 100 charts, and earned a Grammy for Best Country Song, the first penned by a woman without cowriters. But its resonance was clear long before it received an official accolade. Jane Fonda said that the first time Dolly sang it for her and Lily, she got chills: "And we knew this is not just a movie song. This is an anthem."

SOME HISTORY ON DOLLY'S "REGALIA"

During their courtship days, Carl joined the National Guard and completed boot camp near Savannah, Georgia, at Fort Stewart. In her autobiography, Dolly recalled going to visit him, taking along several younger siblings as well as her lifelong best friend, Judy Ogle. Even then, Dolly, who always loved to tease her hair up high, appreciated the convenience of putting on a wig when time ran short for backcombing.

"It took me a while to find Carl," she writes. "When I did I ran up and threw myself into his arms. He is about six feet two inches tall. When I hugged him so hard, his chin grazed the top of my head, sending my wig flying. Carl never missed a beat. He caught my wig in one hand while he continued to hold me with the other."

ABOVE: The poster for *9 to 5* (1980).

FIND YOUR PLACE
AND SHINE

1981–1990

"I'm the kind of person you can ask anything. I'll give you my opinion, and whether it's right or not you gotta decide. If people ask me something that I feel is too personal, rather than tell a lie or talk around it, I tell 'em it's none of their business and change the subject."

—DOLLY DURING A 1990 INTERVIEW WITH KAREN JAEHNE FOR *CINEASTE*

OPPOSITE: Dolly sings and plays banjo for a crowd in 1981.

Polly Darton on *Sesame Street*
A trip to the Grand Ol' Sesame Street Opray

"Children have always responded to me because I have that cartoon-character look."

—DOLLY DURING A 2009 INTERVIEW FOR *TIME MAGAZINE*

Season 12 of *Sesame Street* included an episode, aired on January 2, 1981 (sponsored by the letters H and T, along with number 9), that introduced a new character. Near the episode's end, a dark blue Muppet with a green nose, wearing a red checkered shirt with matching kerchief tied Western-style around his neck, appeared on a Muppet stage. He greeted "country-western fans" in a New York approximation of a Southern drawl, welcomed them to the "Grand Ol' *Sesame Street* Opray," and, adding a Mel Tillis–style stutter, introduced the world to "Sesame Street's country music sweetheart, Ms. P-p-polly Darton!"

The screen curtain rose on the Muppet of the hour, whose flowing blonde locks confirmed the unambiguous tribute. Polly was light purple, also with a green nose, and wore a shiny pink dress with a lacy collar. "Right proud to be here," she said, then introduced the song "Wavin' Goodbye to You With My Heart." A (Muppet) dog joined her onstage and she opened this "parting ways" country tune (complete with prominent banjo and fiddle) with the line, "Oh, I'm so sorry to see that you're leavin'." As the verses

continued, it turned out the song was also about body parts. Polly waved goodbye with her ear, her hair, and, finally, her nose.

Polly Darton would continue to make appearances, including performing the memorable parody "Counting 1 to 5" in Season 14 (April 15, 1983). The song kicked off with an unmistakable cadence and kept the overall shape of its inspiration right to the anthem-like chorus: "Counting 1 to 5, it's so great that I can do it." In December that same year, another Muppet character, Forgetful Jones, was anticipating the visit to *Sesame Street* of his favorite country singer, and the entire episode was written around Polly Darton. She remained an occasional regular, her enduring charm in Muppet form mirroring Dolly's own in human form.

Hadley Freeman, columnist and feature writer for the *Guardian* in Great Britain, wrote in 2011 how she couldn't help herself from asking Dolly first thing during their interview how it felt to be "honored in Muppet form." Dolly responded, "Well, I was so excited! Who wouldn't be? I love that show.

PHOTOGRAPHER/© ABC/GETTY IMAGES.

That was just a hoot! People your age still ask me about that—well, every week."

Dolly herself never appeared on *Sesame Street*, although Miss Piggy and Kermit each visited her TV variety show. She clearly had a ball singing "I'm a Hog for You" with Miss Piggy in the late 1980s. Dolly shares with the Muppets a universal appeal, a certain magical mix of that which is obviously unreal and that which is sincere and kind in very real ways—and all with a welcome dose of humor, to boot.

ABOVE: Dolly with Miss Piggy on *The Dolly Show* in 1988.

The Best Little Whorehouse in Texas
"The only way I would do another picture was if I could have control of it."

There is a scene near the end of *The Best Little Whorehouse in Texas* when Burt Reynolds's character, Sheriff Ed Earl, takes Dolly's Miss Mona into his arms, whisks her across the yard of her former business establishment, and deposits her into the passenger seat of his truck. Miss Mona is the madam of the Chicken Ranch, the nickname for a house of ill repute with a long history in the local community, now shutting down on account of the performative moral outrage of a Houston-based reporter looking to grow his following.

One wouldn't know watching the movie how difficult making it actually was. Dolly looked back on this as a period of struggle; her weight, her broader health, and some important personal relationships were fraught with difficulties all at once. By all accounts, the project was the opposite in most ways of the fun and exhilaration Dolly had had during *9 to 5*, which was her only other experience on a movie set up to that point. In Dolly's telling, "I was still relatively green in the movie business and didn't know that by the time

I got involved, there was already what they call 'a lot of blood on the project.' The people who created the original Broadway show had been weeded out of the mix by the movie studio, and other principles had been fired." At one point, a bumper sticker circulated around Hollywood's streets that read, "Honk if you've been fired from 'Best Little Whorehouse.'" In a final, crushing blow, the film's director, Colin Higgins, died of AIDS shortly after the project's completion.

The film adapted what had been a successful Broadway musical four years earlier, part of the New York "Texas chic" trend of the time. Musicologist Jason Mellard explores that phenomenon in his 2013 book *Progressive Country*. Texas chic arguably peaked with the film *Urban Cowboy*, though other notable examples include writings by native Texan Larry L. King. In 1973, King wrote a piece for *Playboy* about the closing of the real-life Chicken Ranch in the small town of La Grange, Texas. Things took off from there.

The musical's success and the resulting "blood" that spilled when Universal Studios took on the task

OPPOSITE: Dolly and the cast on the poster of *The Best Little Whorehouse in Texas* (1982).

of translating it to film was recounted in bitter detail by King in his book *The Whorehouse Papers*, published in 1982, the same year the movie premiered. *Newsday* printed a three-part series of book excerpts that described the original vision for the film (which included Willie Nelson as Sheriff Ed Earl), Dolly's initial rejection of the part due to reservations about the material's potential harm to her reputation, and the unceremonious removal of the musical's original directors from the film.

Dolly consulted with her family before finally agreeing to the role. She told Jay Scott of the *Globe and Mail* in 1982, "I was afraid it might offend my people: my grand-daddy is a preacher. I read the script to my grand-daddy and my mom and they both laughed a lot. My grand-daddy said, 'If God can forgive you, so can I.'"

Dolly's portrayal is consistent with her other appearances on the big screen: she is sadder but wiser, simultaneously free-spirited and maternal in relation to "her girls," sexy but with an air of freshness, almost innocence.

But even before filming was over, Dolly had indicated to *Boston Globe* journalist Bob Thomas that the compromises of the movie industry were too much. It was an early indicator of the visions for artistic control that eventually came to distinguish her not only as an artist and entertainer but also as a savvy businesswoman. She said in 1981, "The only way I would do another picture was if I could have control of it. That way, I could be sure of workin' with people I wanted to work with."

Critics did not appreciate *The Best Little Whorehouse*. It was generally panned for a lack of convincing chemistry between Dolly and her paramour; an absence of either sexiness or bawdiness, despite the brothel setting, not to mention the lack of Texas flavor; and, in general, a lack of commitment to a single directorial vision. Audiences, on the other hand, embraced the film, and its popularity drove Dolly's signature song, "I Will Always Love You," to become a hit for a second time.

ABOVE: Dolly as Miss Mona in *The Best Little Whorehouse in Texas* (1982).

The Dr. Robert F. Thomas Foundation

Dolly gives back in the name of the "Angel of the Smoky Mountains"

Dolly's 1973 album *My Tennessee Mountain Home* includes a song simply called "Dr. Robert F. Thomas," a straightforward country number with a truck driver gear change modulation halfway through to keep the momentum going. A layer of harmonica adds a tinge of nostalgia during verses Dolly wrote about the dedication and compassion of Dr. Thomas.

Robert F. Thomas first arrived at the Pittman Center Methodist Mission in Sevier County in 1926, along with his wife Eva and son Bobbie. He had been assigned there after his medical training at Syracuse University. By the time he got to East Tennessee, Dr. Thomas was an ordained minister and had also served as a missionary in Malaysia. The Thomas family intended to stay one year in the Great Smoky Mountains. That turned into more than five decades. Among the families Dr. Thomas tended were the Partons, and among the many babies he delivered was Dolly.

After Dr. Thomas died in 1980, local leaders wanted to honor and continue the compassionate medical care he'd established in a region without adequate facilities or personnel. In 1983, they formed the Dr. Robert F. Thomas Foundation. Its original aim was to save the Sevier County Hospital, but over the years they also outfitted ambulances with defibrillators, developed wellness programs, and funded a local clinic for people lacking health insurance. Around the same time the dream of Dollywood was being realized, Dolly began meeting with foundation leaders. Their mission resonated with Dolly's own vision for improving the lives of people in her home region by creating jobs and improving education and healthcare. In 1987, she became the foundation's honorary chairperson.

Dr. Thomas was reported to make a thousand house calls every year, many on foot or horseback. As often as not, he bartered in exchange for medical services, receiving chickens, vegetables, and other agricultural products. He was highly educated in a community where many people, in Dolly's words, "couldn't read and write, and couldn't even read what was on the newspaper." This expanded Dr. Thomas's importance to the community across decades that saw the Great Depression, World War II, and rapid technological change. Dolly said, "So he was actually in every way our connection to the bigger world and also that center in the small world that we lived in."

In a sense, those roles are now reversed. Dolly connects the spirit of generosity and medical care Dr. Thomas brought to the Great Smoky Mountains with the entire world. In 1990, she told an interviewer for *Cineaste* magazine, "His dream was to have the Mayo Clinic of the South; and in his hospital now, we have a great burn center and poison center and all kinds of research going on." In 2007, she raised $500,000 for the Fort Sanders Sevier Medical Center by hosting a benefit concert. At one point, she thanked everyone in the crowd for spending the money, saying, "I ain't worth it, but the folks in Sevier County are." In other years, she has auctioned off a king-size bed located in an apartment she kept on the grounds of Dollywood, right over Apple Jack's restaurant; a date with Dolly; a stay at the DreamMore Resort; and, on two occasions, a "Backwoods Barbie-Q," where the winners got to stay at the guest cottage near her restored childhood home and wake to breakfast prepared by Dolly herself.

In 2008, the Dr. Robert F. Thomas Foundation pledged to raise $10 million in support of the LeConte Medical Center, which would replace the Fort Sanders facility and include a hospital, a cancer survivor center, and the Dolly Parton Center for Women's Services. The new facility opened its doors on February 14, 2010.

ABOVE: Dolly performing in London in 1983.

"Islands in the Stream"

Dolly collaborates with Kenny Rogers for a Bee Gees–penned hit

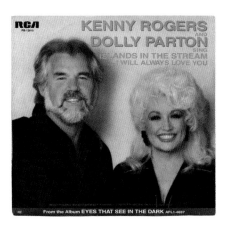

In 1983, Barry Gibb produced a song he had written with his brothers Robin and Maurice Gibb, the trio known collectively as the Bee Gees. They titled the song for the Ernest Hemingway novel *Islands in the Stream*, which was published posthumously in 1970. They originally intended it to be an R&B number for Diana Ross. After the spectacular demise of disco, a genre the Bee Gees owned for a time, the brothers Gibb had successfully shifted their focus back to songwriting, going on to write albums for Diana Ross and Barbra Streisand.

In addition to songwriting, Barry was also producing. He was in the studio with Kenny Rogers, producing *Eyes That See in the Dark*, when Kenny asked him for a couple of songs. Barry offered Kenny "Islands in the Stream," which they worked on for

several days, but Kenny struggled to connect with it. Then the idea for a duet surfaced. Dolly popped into Barry's head as an ideal singing partner, perhaps for the way she trod the line between country and pop, not unlike Kenny. By coincidence, Kenny's manager, who overheard the exchange, just so happened to have seen Dolly working in another part of the building. Kenny sent him downstairs to bring her back. "Once she came in," he would remember later, "that song was never the same. She lit it up and we became good friends from that point on."

Once you learn that the song was written by the Bee Gees, it's plain to hear. "Islands in the Stream" falls in line with the musical vision and songwriting craft of the brothers Gibb, two of whom (Barry and Maurice) play on Kenny and Dolly's 1983 recording. The disco legacy is audible. Yet the song lives in a

ABOVE: The cover art for the single featuring "Islands in the Stream."

different space, where musical barriers—which only ever seemed rigid in the confines of music store record bins or format radio stations—suddenly appeared fluid. They were fluid in the way Dolly had envisioned years before, when she said she wanted to make "Dolly Parton music." This was the era when Eddie Van Halen contributed a guitar solo to Michael Jackson's *Thriller* and Prince discarded all those genre categories to create *Purple Rain*. Dolly already bumped against the borders distinguishing country from pop, and when this duet with Kenny peaked on both charts, she added "adult contemporary" to her roster.

"Islands in the Stream" is built in a way that brings to mind the songwriting style of Paul McCartney, on a series of hooks, at least four. It starts out at a low-temperature simmer with a verse repeated twice, the words establishing that two parties have "something going on." A less memorable, less well-crafted song might go directly to the chorus. "Islands in the Stream" takes it to a contrasting section, maintaining the low, roiling boil. Dolly and Kenny's voices share a light, diaphanous, and flexible quality, as well as a knack for adding just the right amount of husky rasp at the right moment of emphasis. The melodic lines change direction and turn up at this part of the song, as the lyrics dig deeper into the singular nature of love. The iconic "ah-hah" is echoed throughout with different lyrics: an agreement, an understanding, the specific words matter less than the feel. Ah-hah!

In both the recording and live performances, the chemistry between Dolly and Kenny is palpable, a vibe that was notable even during his appearance on her variety show back in 1976, when the duo first met and sang together. Their rapport as musicians and friends grew over time and multiple collaborations, including a successful 1984 Christmas album and a follow-up duet, "Real Love."

Kenny performed for the last time at a Nashville arena concert in 2017. Dolly joined him onstage for their famous duet, by then recognized and beloved all over the world. In an interview that same year, Dolly described their relationship as "almost like brother and sister." She added, "And we're so much alike. We know the same people. We laugh at the same kind of jokes." Their musical collaborations were something Dolly was proud of, but she cherished their friendship as well.

For the Bee Gees' part, "Islands in the Stream" sealed their reputation as song crafters. They had, after all, created music before riding the spectacular meteor that was disco and continued writing afterward. Looking back on songwriting with his brothers for a 2014 piece in *Rolling Stone*, Barry Gibb said, "That's what we loved doing: writing a song that people liked and that would be remembered."

Barry brought Dolly back into the recording studio for another duet in 2021, this time for an album of collaborations with different artists reinterpreting songs from the Bee Gees catalog. *Greenfields: The Gibb Brothers Songbook, Vol. 1,* includes Dolly singing a duet with Barry on the song "Words."

Dolly Chats with Andy Warhol

Kindred spirits meet at Studio 54, then sit down
together for an interview

"I love everybody, and I go right through the bullshit and
I go right to the core of every person because we are all one, we are all the same."

—DOLLY IN HER 1984 INTERVIEW WITH ANDY WARHOL

In 1977, after Dolly performed in Greenwich Village, she made her way to the famous New York disco, Studio 54, where she met and hit it off with Andy Warhol. There was a stretch of time when Dolly and Andy met with some regularity at the club to sit on the couch and talk, amidst all the buzz and excitement. Occasionally, Dolly's manager, Sandy Gallin, would convince her to dance.

Dolly and Andy shared a certain extreme quality in their appearance and an air of bemusement regarding the trappings of their own success. In their own ways, both conveyed a deep interest in people. Warhol's led him to feature artists, musicians, designers, and other culture bearers for decades in *Interview* magazine, which he founded in 1969. Dolly's shines through in her songs.

So they sat down on St. Patrick's Day 1984. The interview's publication in July was timed for the release of the movie *Rhinestone*, in which Dolly plays a country singer who takes a bet about how quickly she can teach Sylvester Stallone's character to sing convincing country music. She wrote twenty new

songs for the project and was still busy with post-wrap duties as the film's musical supervisor at the time of the interview.

But *Rhinestone* wasn't the only topic Dolly covered with Andy. They talked about her business acumen, including investments in farm equipment, real estate, livestock, hardware stores, and macadamia nuts, and Dolly expressed particular pride in her publishing house for her own songs. They talked about her health, and the period overlapping the filming of *The Best Little Whorehouse in Texas* when she began to experience debilitating symptoms that dragged her down physically and mentally for more than eighteen months. She told Andy, "When I was flat on my back I realized that I could never retire, that I hated it, that I would never get myself in that place again." She discussed her weight loss and her enduring love of junk food, and a book title she could see taking shape from this recent past: *Life After Success*.

When the interview turned to religion, Dolly spoke of how often she prayed, and described the journey of her religious sensibility. She'd come to

ABOVE: Dolly and Andy Warhol in the late 1970s.

value the positive aspects of God's presence in her life and made a conscious decision to discard the "hellfire and brimstone" messages that had frightened her as a child. Those fear-based messages didn't jibe with her personal experiences of God or of other people. She said, "I just thought, 'I can't deal with this shit. There cannot be a God that is that mean and cruel, and if there is then I'm too afraid to deal with Him anyway.' So I had to decide who I was, and what God meant to me. I feel that sin and evil are the negative part of you, and I think it's like a battery: you've got to have the negative and the positive in order to be a complete person. I used to punish myself a lot for things I felt, and then I'd just say, 'Well, if it's wrong for me to feel this why do I feel it?'"

About a year after this interview, Andy delivered on a commission for five paintings of Dolly that Sandy Gallin had envisioned for his living room wall. But Sandy hated the paintings. In her memoir, Dolly wrote about the awkward moment that transpired: "We had expected them to look something like the ones of Marilyn Monroe, but these were in a different style and looked harsh and severe. These looked more like Bill Monroe!"

In 2001, Dolly remembered Andy Warhol in another conversation for *Interview*. "He was the only person I've ever met who's weirder than me, that dressed worse and looked stranger—and didn't care: just like me," she said. "I would always ask him: 'What do you look like under that wig?' and he'd reply: 'What do you look like under that one?' I'd say: 'Well you'll never know,' and he'd say: 'Well you'll never know either.'"

ABOVE: Andy Warhol's paintings of Dolly.

"I'm a big star now!"

Dolly gets a star on the Hollywood Walk of Fame

Dolly's name appears on the pink star outlined in bronze, just above a circular disc intersected by a record player arm, the symbol that indicates a recording artist. This was the first of Dolly's two stars on Hollywood's Walk of Fame, a stretch of sidewalk along Hollywood Boulevard dedicated to marking achievements in entertainment, from TV and movie stars to radio icons.

The path to getting a star is surprisingly simple. In Dolly's case, someone nominated her—perhaps a fan club member or a close associate, since nominations can come from all over—and Dolly accepted the nomination, agreeing to appear in person at the ceremony were she to be selected. A handful of representatives from the industries denoted on the Walk of Fame then met to determine the winners, putting together a list of around thirty awardees sent to the Los Angeles Board of Public Works, as they do each June. The criteria for selecting winners includes time in the industry (at least five years), charitable contributions, and professional achievements, awards, and honors.

Shortly after winning the recognition, Dolly appeared on *The Tonight Show*, where her delight was obvious. When Johnny Carson brought it up, Dolly said she felt like a kid when she won. "I'm a big star now!" she said, echoing the little girl inside who always dreamed of a world far larger than the Tennessee mountain hollow she called home.

The star neighboring hers was Sylvester Stallone's, with whom she had recently completed the movie *Rhinestone*. That movie marked a turning point for Dolly, as she shared during a 2003 interview with Jancee Dunn for *Rolling Stone*. She was coming out of a bleak period, including surgery in 1982 and a period of dark depression. "Even though the movie didn't do that well, that was one of my greatest projects," she told Dunn. "Because Stallone was so full of life, and so crazy and so funny and he made me laugh a lot, which was real healthy for me. That movie got me back on track."

If you take this walk in Hollywood, you will find a second star etched with Dolly's name, this one laid in summer 2018. Seven other artists share the honor of having two stars in the same category: Diana Ross, Michael Jackson, Smokey Robinson, John Lennon, Paul McCartney, George Harrison, and Ringo Starr. Dolly shares her second Walk of Fame star with Linda Ronstadt and Emmylou Harris for the *Trio* album project they recorded together, first released 1987 with a follow-up, *Trio II*, in 1999. In 2016, *The Complete Trio Collection* included alternate takes and previously unreleased tracks.

These legendary recording projects involved bumps along the way, but time had smoothed those by the time of the 2018 Walk of Fame announcement, and Dolly was excited to share a star with two of her closest friends. In reaction to the news, she posted on social media: "Now, they tell me that I'm the first person this century, the first woman, to have two stars." Then she added, "But of course, that's natural. I like to do things in pairs, if you know what I mean."

ABOVE: Dolly receiving her star on the Hollywood Walk of Fame in 1984.

Dollywood

Dolly opens a theme park

You're only as big as your biggest dream.

—SIGN ON DISPLAY IN THE MUSEUM AT DOLLYWOOD

Opening Dollywood theme park in 1986 turned out to be the most lucrative business decision Dolly ever made. Few would have predicted it when the doors first opened—including Dolly herself. Back in 1982, during her second televised interview with Barbara Walters, Dolly described her dream of "building a center or a city" somewhere around Gatlinburg, in the part of Tennessee where she grew up. Dolly imagined it would be "a fantasy city, sort of like Disneyland, but where it's like a mountain Disneyland, like a Smoky Mountain fairy land."

Where Dollywood stands today, a tourist attraction already existed. Silver Dollar City in Tennessee was owned by Herschend Family Entertainment (HFE), whose original theme park outside Branson, Missouri, had already proven successful. The Herschends had purchased the land formerly known as Goldrush Junction during the 1970s and rebranded it. The Herschends have a knack for this kind of thing. Their successful operations—like Stone Mountain Park in Atlanta—tend to foreground nostalgia for romanticized notions of the American Old West or rural life. Other themed family attractions include Wild Adventures in Georgia, and Kentucky Kingdom; aquariums in Kentucky, New Jersey, and Vancouver, Canada; along with water parks, dinner theaters, and even the Harlem Globetrotters. They heard Dolly's dream and wisely offered to partner with her, rather than compete. Thus began the process of reimagining Silver Dollar City, Tennessee, as Dollywood.

Visitors to Dollywood find thrill rides as well as a replica of her "Tennessee Mountain Home," a "rags to riches" museum containing artifacts from Dolly's life, and a functioning chapel named for Dr. Robert F. Thomas that holds weddings and Sunday services. Artisan craftspeople from the region also demonstrate skills like blacksmithing, glassblowing, and woodworking. Dolly told a writer for *National Geographic Traveler* in 2009, "I wanted people working there who were connected with the land and the local culture. They made it real, not phony. It made me feel comfortable. And I guess I thought it would make the visitors feel that way, too."

Dollywood in some ways exhibits the competing impulses that comprise Dolly herself: the allure of the mirage, the dream, the fantasy on one hand

and, on the other, a sense of the real, the authentic, the downhome.

Shaded paths and natural elements enhance the beauty of the place, and performances on the Back Porch Theater include members of Dolly's own family and other musicians. Dollywood performances provide another channel for both Dolly's own creative energy and her philanthropic efforts. For example, in 2009, she wrote eight songs for a stage show titled *Sha-Kon-O-Hey! (Land of Blue Smoke)*, a reference to the Cherokee word for the Smokies. Dolly wanted to honor "the people who first loved this place." A CD of the show was sold only at Dollywood and proceeds the first year went to the organization Friends of the Smokies to mark the Great Smoky Mountains National Park's seventy-fifth anniversary. "We worry more about keeping trash away from the bears than we do about the history and environmental quality of the park itself," Dolly said.

Dollywood also houses the nonprofit American Eagle Foundation, which rehabilitates injured birds and provides sanctuary for bald eagles and other birds of prey unable to return to the wild. The park does good for its home region by creating jobs at the park itself and in the supporting businesses, as well as through its philanthropic arm, the Dollywood Foundation, which emphasizes education, funding scholarships for high school graduates to attend college. Around the time Dollywood opened, processes related to economic globalization saw long-standing employers in the region relocating outside the US for cheaper labor. Dollywood helped to fill the gap, though wages for working people in service and hospitality industries typically fall below the income levels for manufacturing jobs they replace.

The nearby Great Smoky Mountains is the most visited national park in the country, drawing more than 10 million people each year, so the idea to bring a portion of those visitors to Dollywood in nearby Pigeon Forge was a sound business decision. But as crowds increase, so too do concerns over the impact on land, air, and water resources. Talking to *National Geographic* in 2009, Dolly said that "quite frankly, all I can really do is help people to care," and then hope that concern translates into actions by policy makers with the power to protect and preserve fragile resources.

Dollywood helps fans diffuse their love for Dolly beyond her as a singular individual. They can play in what she represents. To visit Dollywood is to visit the "Dollyverse" and all it presents as a physical space. To adapt words from the essayist Tressie McMillan Cottom, writing about "the Dolly moment" in February 2021, to visit Dollywood is to dwell in a space "embodying enough contradictions to sustain those we project onto her." For Dolly's part, she sometimes sees Dollywood as a place for her fans to play: "'Cause they feel like it's all me. It's under that Dolly umbrella. And I feel good that I've been able to give them something. An extension of myself, so to speak."

ABOVE: Dolly poses for a portrait at Dollywood in 1988.

A Christmas Movie and a New Company

Dolly founds Sandollar Productions with Sandy Gallin

"I don't feel like there are any mistakes as long as a person grows from the experiences they've had."

—DOLLY TO A WRITER FOR THE *ST. LOUIS POST-DISPATCH* IN 1987

There's a moment during the made-for-television movie *A Smoky Mountain Christmas* when Dolly's character Lorna Davis helps little Cindy "hang a room" by draping a quilt over a suspended rope stretched between two walls of a mountain cabin. Lorna remembers how her father did the same for her when she was coming of age. Then she grabs a guitar to sing "Pretty Is As Pretty Does," a song only found in the movie and not on any album, about how true beauty comes from within. It is a small, heartwarming domestic moment, perhaps distilled from Dolly's memories of her own childhood. It is likewise a chance to study how Dolly plays guitar so well while wearing acrylic nails of extraordinary length.

The movie follows Dolly's character, Lorna, through a sort of holiday-themed fairy tale. Lorna is a country singer who longs to return to her mountain roots, tired of the shallow, big city surroundings to which her success has brought her. She reaches the old family cabin to find it occupied by seven orphan children, hiding there to avoid returning to the cruel children's home from which they escaped. The children warn Lorna about a mountain man with a reputation for catching and eating children. He turns out to be Lee Majors, who, despite the rumors, is kind and caring and ultimately instrumental in rescuing the children. For Dolly fans of a certain generation, there's a peculiar delight in a TV Christmas special directed by The Fonz (Henry Winkler) and starring both the Six Million Dollar Man (Lee Majors) and Jack Tripper (John Ritter) from *Three's Company*. The tale abounds with other strange charms: A witch. A poisoned apple pie. A magic kiss. And a happy ending, when Dolly and the Six Million Dollar Man decide to marry and adopt all seven children.

A Smoky Mountain Christmas was the first project undertaken by Sandollar Productions, the company Dolly co-founded with her manager Sandy Gallin in

1986. By 1989, *Interview* magazine writer William Stadiem commented to Dolly that Sandollar had become a powerful Hollywood presence. Dolly told him, "I like being involved in the business."

Sandollar was one stop along a long and fruitful partnership that she enjoyed with Sandy, one that lasted twenty-five years, until his retirement. Across that long stretch, they sparked and fueled one another's creative energy and founded businesses that include movie and TV production companies,

among others. Dolly told the *St. Louis Post-Dispatch* in 1987, "[Sandy] has many other people that he manages—and big ones, big names—but he doesn't do that with any other client."

Dolly and Sandy shared a special friendship and trust. "We work together every day, we have a great time, and that's why we've gone into business together," she said of the partnership. They also shared a quality of unflappability. They rode out the ups and downs of the entertainment industry

ABOVE: Dolly in *A Smoky Mountain Christmas* (1986).

together, including a second stab at a TV variety show during the late 1980s. Though the show wasn't successful, the business of it was, because it included a guaranteed payout despite its cancellation. And when an idea didn't quite work, they simply moved on to the next. Huge successes came during the 1990s, first with the *Father of the Bride* movies starring Steve Martin and then with 1992's *Buffy the Vampire Slayer*, which became the iconic television series starring Sarah Michelle Gellar from 1997 to 2003.

In this era, industry executive Gail Berman worked for Sandollar, helping to produce both films and series. Dolly once invited Gail to lunch, during which Dolly learned that Gail's share in the *Buffy* royalties had been significantly smaller than those of her male colleagues. Dolly reached across the table with a check made out to Gail, making up the difference. Gail would go on to rise in the industry; at one point she was the only woman to head both a broadcast and a movie company. Along the way, she often found herself the only woman in the room, so male-dominated has the industry remained. She has not forgotten Dolly's example of one woman going out of her way to help another.

When Sandy retired, Dolly kept a hand in production, starting with the short-lived Dolly Parton's Southern Light Productions during the late '90s. Its first project was a TV movie titled *Blue Valley Songbird*, about a Nashville-based performer whose past comes to haunt her. Dixie Pixie Productions, formed in 2015, found greater success in partnerships responsible for the *Coat of Many Colors* movie series and Netflix's *Heartstrings*.

In 2003, *Rolling Stone* writer Jancee Dunn talked with Dolly about her reputation for business savviness. Dolly reflected, "I think that if I am smart in business, it's just that I'm smart about who I am . . . I know what I can, can't, will and won't do, and if I have to be strict about that, I will."

A CHRISTIAN ORGANIZATION

It's natural to assume that Sandollar derives from merging the names Sandy and Dolly, and that explanation appears in print more than once. In her 1994 memoir, however, Dolly points to the sand dollar, a creature she holds dear. She suggests a spiritual significance, its roundness symbolizing "eternity" and the "intricate etching on the side of this simple creature," evoking Christian symbols of peace doves, Easter lilies, and dogwood petals. She adds (with a wink of devilish humor apparently directed at Sandy, who was Jewish), "So, Sandollar was actually a name I sort of 'slipped by' Sandy Gallin. All these years he never knew he was working for a Christian organization."

Feminist in Practice

Dolly is named a Ms. Woman of the Year

Dolly was named one of *Ms.* magazine's thirteen women of the year in January 1987. Given her hyper-feminine, made-up, and exaggerated anatomy, the choice surprised some, coming from a publication whose founder Gloria Steinem once said that "bras, panties, bathing suits, and other stereotypical gear are visual reminders of a commercial, idealized feminine image that our real and diverse female bodies can't possibly fit." "Stereotypical gear"—donned to the max degree—is, after all, Dolly's signature stock-in-trade.

Dolly does not apologize for her love of makeup and glamorous clothing. Never has. She grew up fascinated with makeup and yearning to wear it. She would apply mercurochrome or Merthiolate from the family medicine supplies to color her lips and cheeks, unconcerned that it would take days to wash off. She didn't *want* it washed off. It made her feel beautiful. Growing up in a strict religious household, Dolly's father would punish her when he discovered her sinful excesses, "but the whippin' was worth it for a few days with a red mouth."

Years before the award, *Ms.* had noted Dolly's professional choices and directions during the era she was emerging as a popular as well as a country entertainer. In a 1979 *Ms.* piece, journalist and Columbia professor Margo Jefferson suggested, "Isn't it pleasant to be reminded that ruffles, pleats, drapes, sequins, curls, lashes, hoops, spangles, powders, and paints can be simply toys—entertainment and sports for women quite apart from their value in the game of sexual barter and exchange?"

Dolly turned forty the year before her *Ms.* award, and the magazine highlighted her again in that year's July issue. Dolly saw her fortieth as a significant milestone and paused to take pride in her accomplishments and express gratitude for people who helped her along the way. At the same time, she looked ahead to the next forty and her "big, big plans." "I feel like now I'm comfortable enough, but still hungry enough to work hard on a lot of the dreams that have not [yet] come true," Dolly said. "And that's excitement; I love that! I love to work."

In 1987, *Ms.* founder Gloria Steinem cited her reasons for naming Dolly among the *Ms.* awardees: "for creating popular songs about real women, for turning feminine style into humor and power, and for bringing jobs and understanding to the mountain people of Tennessee." Honoring Dolly asserted an authentic feminism more about agency and self-determination than about anyone's choice of outerwear. In his 2019 series *Dolly Parton's America*, host Jad Abumrad dubbed it "feminists in practice" versus "feminists in theory." Dolly's reaction to his statement seemed to indicate agreement: "I think that's a good way of saying it. I live it. I work it. And I think there's power in it for me."

Dolly loves being a woman. She loves working with women. These are sentiments she has communicated on more than one occasion over the decades. Likewise, she believes that all people everywhere should have the same opportunities to do what they love and be paid for it. As noncontroversial a statement as that is, Dolly's instinct has been to avoid pointed politics. Her work is entertainment, she'll say, treating the word "feminism" carefully, wary of any potential trigger associations with man-hating.

"I don't care if you're Black, white, straight, gay, women, men, whatever," Dolly said on CNN in 2015. "I think everybody that has something to offer should be allowed to give it and be paid for it. But, no, I don't consider myself a feminist, not in the term that some people do, because I—I just think we all should be treated with respect." One reason Dolly remains uncompromisingly beloved in a nation, and even a world, so deeply divided may be that it hardly matters what you call her or what she does. Dolly continues to do her thing, no permission requested.

ABOVE: The Ms. Women of the Year 1987: (L to R) Dolly, actresses Sharon Gless and Tyne Daly, and Senator Barbara Mikulski.

And Dolly Makes Three

Dolly records Trio *with Emmylou Harris and Linda Ronstadt, three women "bound together at the song"*

The closing song on *Trio*, the album that Dolly Parton released with fellow music stars Emmylou Harris and Linda Ronstadt in January 1987, is the old evangelical Protestant hymn "Farther Along." Its expression of both Christian lament and Christian hope is taken at slow tempo, the kind you might hear at a funeral. Each member of the trio takes a turn singing lead, with Dolly opening the song. Her high soprano, flexible and light, gently ornaments the lines of the standard hymn with simple string accompaniment in the background. Linda Ronstadt takes the second verse, and her rich, round mezzo soprano tones add depth to the sound. The background remains steady, a slow duple compound strumming support.

When the chorus first comes, the sound bursts into Technicolor. All three singers join together in full-voiced harmony: "Farther along, we'll know all about it . . . we'll understand why." At this point the instrumental accompaniment in the background blooms as well, with a gospel-style piano coming to the fore. The piano takes an instrumental turn, leading to a verse sung by Emmylou Harris, her

knife-edged, crystalline soprano occupying a sonic middle place between the other voices. The song, and the album in general, displays both the distinctive qualities of each singer's voice side by side and the remarkable blend they achieve.

The project had been a long time coming. The idea first hatched following an episode of the short-lived variety show *Dolly!* during the late '70s. The three singers hit it off musically and personally and made initial recordings together in 1978, but all three were so busy with different solo endeavors that the project didn't get off the ground. Their individual accomplishments during the interceding years brought the *Trio* album a deeper patina when it finally did happen. This was due not only to the status of the album's stars, but also to the musicians who played behind them, including multi-instrumentalist virtuoso Mark O'Connor, as well as guitarist and musical consultant on the project John Starling, who also happened to be an ENT (ear, nose, and throat) surgeon.

The album's success was both popular and critical. *New York Times* critic John Rockwell deemed

ABOVE: Dolly with Linda Ronstadt (left) and Emmylou Harris in 1987.

it "a connoisseur's delight." *Trio* won top awards from the Academy of Country Music (Album of the Year) and the Country Music Association (Vocal Event of the Year), along with a Grammy. It remains a milestone achievement. Journalist Sarah Smarsh, who has written extensively about Dolly's significance as a working-class feminist icon, names *Trio* as "one of the greatest collaborative albums of all time." Musicologist Lydia Hamessley frames it as an important precedent to the trio of bluegrass albums Dolly would record around the turn of the century. Her rendition of the traditional Appalachian ballad "Rosewood Casket" alone, the album's tenth track, makes it clear that Dolly never lost sight of her mountain musical heritage regardless of other stylistic explorations.

These roots are in full view during one standout performance by Dolly. Her original song "Wildflowers" describes, in what comes across as metaphor for her own life, growing up as a mountain rose, crowded by other wildflowers and needing room to grow. The rose finally leaves the garden, carried by her trusted friend, the wind.

When Johnny Carson introduced the three singers for their appearance on *The Tonight Show* to promote the album, he noted their collective forty-five Grammy nominations. The three singers performed in custom Western-style outfits—Linda in black, Dolly in red with fringe, and Emmylou in off-white—made for them by Manuel Arturo José Cuevas Martínez, known as Manuel. Manuel had studied the art of tailoring from Nudie Cohn, whose loud, colorfully embroidered creations were seen on everyone from actor Tony Curtis to country music legends like Lefty Frizzell and Webb Pierce and, eventually, rock icons like Gram Parsons.

Linda told Johnny Carson that they wanted *Trio* to sound old-fashioned. In her mind, the concept was that they had been singing continuously from 1907 to 1987. Over the ten years of the project's taking shape, she said, the vision for the final product became clear. The more they sang together, the more they'd realized that the simpler, quieter, more traditional sound was what they were going for. Talking to Stephen Holder of the *New York Times*, Linda put it this way: "Most of the songs predate bluegrass. Unlike bluegrass, the music is quiet, intimate parlor music intended to be appreciated by the people playing it."

The album has remained a landmark collaboration of the late twentieth century. Nearly three decades later, Rhino Records released a three-CD *Trio* box set. It included remastered versions of the group's 1987 and 1999 albums, as well as twenty unreleased songs, some alternative takes, and some new material. Dolly reflected on their years of friendship and musical collaboration, saying, "We're bound together at the song."

Dolly in Bronze

The Sevierville Chamber of Commerce erects a statue for their hometown hero

Early on Sunday, May 3, 1987, Dolly had dedicated the cornerstone for the Dolly Parton Wellness and Rehabilitation Center at the local medical facility in her hometown of Sevierville, Tennessee. Her second ceremony of the day was on the grounds of the Sevier County Courthouse. Dolly joined a small crowd of around five hundred people gathered in front of the Victorian structure built in 1896. The crowd included Dolly's father and Cas Walker, the local grocer who had sponsored Knoxville-based radio and television programs back in the day and given Dolly her first professional experience at the age of ten.

Dolly looked over at Cas, recalled how he predicted she would be a star, and added, "And I couldn't let you down." To the crowd gathered, Dolly said, "It makes me feel like you folks are proud of me, and I've always wanted you to be." When the time came, the cover was removed to reveal a six-and-a-half-foot bronze statue of Dolly seated on a large rock, barefoot and cradling a guitar, dressed simply in pants and a buttoned blouse, with a smile as though she just had a wonderful idea for a song. The day of the unveiling ceremony, Dolly called the statue her "greatest honor, because it came from the people who know me."

Sevierville has a long-standing habit of honoring their hometown hero. The town first celebrated "Dolly Parton Day" on April 25, 1970. The local chamber of commerce named her Citizen of the Year in 1989. But the unveiling of the statue was the

ABOVE: Statue of Dolly in Sevierville, Tennessee, her hometown.

culmination of a project in the works since 1985. A group of local citizens first thought up a statue in Dolly's honor, and presented the challenge to Gatlinburg-based artist, painter, and sculptor Jim Gray. Jim was known for his watercolor and oil paintings of landscapes characteristic of eastern Tennessee, but he embraced the commission. According to Sevierville's local historian, Dolly insisted the funding come solely from private donations and fundraising (including a Dolly Lookalike Beauty Pageant) rather than from public monies.

The idea for her to sit on a rock—the kind found in mountain streams all over the region—came from the artist's son. Step one was creating a small clay mock-up. Step two was locating a rock large enough to hold the completed sculpture. Jim constructed a steel skeleton sufficiently sturdy to support several hundred pounds of clay, and once the clay was in place, the statue was transported to Fredericksburg, Virginia, where it was covered in bronze. All in all, Dolly's likeness took over two thousand hours to complete. The town celebrated the thirtieth anniversary of the statue's unveiling with an exhibit of "artifacts that were part of the statue's creation."

In 2009, Dolly confessed to *Us Weekly* that she once painted her statue's toenails. "She needed a pedicure," she insisted. Dolly also told late-night host Jimmy Kimmel that her dad had visited her statue often after the unveiling ceremony, something she learned from one of her brothers only after her father had died. Dolly's dad would load supplies in the back of his truck and "late at night, he'd go down to the statue and scrub all the pigeon poop off."

ANOTHER STATUE?

A Dolly statue came up again in February 2021, when the *Los Angeles Times* reported Dolly's request to Tennessee lawmakers to remove from consideration a bill regarding a statue in her honor at the state capital building. In 1980, a likeness had been erected of former Confederate general and Ku Klux Klan leader Nathan Bedford Forrest. A movement was afoot to tear it down, which led to questions of who should replace Forrest. In January 2021, State Rep. John Mark Windle had proposed Dolly, for the consistent love she inspired among people from a range of backgrounds, beliefs, and walks of life. Others felt the moment called for honoring a person whose work more directly opposed Forrest's defiance of the nation and repugnant acts of hatred, such as the Black journalist, scholar, and activist Ida B. Wells, or the Nashville lawyer and civil rights leader Z. Alexander Looby. For Dolly's part, she wrote, "Given all that is going on in the world, I don't think putting me on a pedestal is appropriate at this time."

1987–1988

A Missionary, a Beautician, or a Madam

Even Dolly can't quite revive the variety show format with her own The Dolly Show

"[Dolly's stage manager] sidled up to me and said, 'Isn't it amazing the way Kermit can sing like that with somebody's hand up his ass.' Without missing a beat, I came back with, 'Shoot, that ain't nothin'. I did that for seven years on The Porter Wagoner Show.'"*

—DOLLY ON THE DAY KERMIT THE FROG PERFORMED ON *THE DOLLY SHOW*

There are moments on her variety show when Dolly's personality shines through the television like the sparkles on one of her evening gowns. For example, Kermit the Frog once made a guest appearance in an ongoing "date night" skit on *The Dolly Show*. The segment, with guests like Dudley Moore and Bruce Willis, had previously fallen so flat that Dolly acknowledged the awkwardness in the episode's welcoming remarks. Kermit worked much better. When he failed to show up for their date, Dolly found him in a bar, waiting for "another bowl of flies" (insert 1980s laugh track here).

"See, I really thought I'd be your type. I mean, people have always told me I look just like Miss Piggy," she told him. The duo soon performed a duet cover of Sly & the Family Stone's song "Everyday People."

Dolly seems capable of carrying anything. But with *The Dolly Show*, it almost seemed like someone wanted to test her limits. Who decided to open each episode with Dolly in a bathtub, soap bubbles up to her collarbone? Who thought it made sense to cut from that to Dolly's silhouette in a sparkling gown, delivering an opening song to the live audience?

The very first episode set a somewhat bewildering tone. After an extremely awkward "date night" with Dudley Moore, Dolly visited Pee-wee Herman in his playhouse. This led abruptly to a music video skit with wrestler and entertainer Hulk Hogan, in which Dolly played his ringside sweetie, singing a song titled "He's Got a Headlock on My Heart." She also performed a gospel number with Oprah Winfrey, and somewhere in there was a pre-filmed cameo by New York City mayor Ed Koch, who appeared just long enough to deliver an off-color, sexually suggestive remark.

The writers hired for the variety show were past their prime. As Dolly put it in her 1994 memoir, "To them, this was like a new lease on life, a chance to relive their glory days, maybe even buy a new toupee.

To me, it was a disaster." Variety shows had once been a television staple, and *Hee-Haw* had demonstrated that old-school barn dance or vaudeville-style humor could be wed to modern television editing with great success. But this time around, the combination never clicked. Dolly likened the whole enterprise to trying to fit a square peg in a round hold, especially moments like her being asked to sing "Someone to Watch Over Me" on a staircase in a flowing gown. Willie Nelson's 1978 album *Stardust*, Dolly shared, was the only reason she knew those Great American songbook standards, and the song was an odd choice for a performer who, by this time, had amassed a deep and rich catalog of musical material all her own.

The show did have its shining moments. Dolly was once joined by Linda Ronstadt and Emmylou Harris to perform three songs from their acclaimed album, *Trio*, and someone had the sense to just let the cameras roll. Another joy was Dolly gathered around the piano with the Oak Ridge Boys to perform their hit "Elvira." Every week also included a segment—introduced with an excerpt of "My Tennessee Mountain Home"—in which Dolly, seated comfortably with guitar in hand, performed one of her own songs.

In a move that evokes the acme of variety show tradition, Dolly ended each segment by taking questions from the audience, like Carol Burnett had done on her own show. Someone once asked what Dolly would have been were she not a singer. Her reply: "A missionary, a beautician, or a madam."

ABOVE: Dolly poses for a portrait in Los Angeles in 1987.

Nobody Cries Alone
Dolly becomes Truvy in Steel Magnolias

A pivotal scene in the movie *Steel Magnolias* takes place in the beauty salon owned by Dolly's character, Truvy. Shelby, played by Julia Roberts, gazes at her own stunned reflection in the mirror just after her long, auburn-colored hair has been cut short. She bursts into tears. Truvy urges, "Oh, sweetheart, don't. Please don't cry, or I will too. I have a strict policy that nobody cries alone in my presence." Truvy in this moment just might sum up Dolly's "type," if one were to argue that Dolly is a character actor: the gentle-yet-indomitable spirit who radiates positivity in the face of challenges that might drag another person down.

In a story about the particular strength of women amidst the struggles, sorrows, and joys of life, Truvy and her salon are something like an island of calm, community, and connectedness to which other characters can reliably return to renew their strength. Those characters include a legendary ensemble of women on the big screen, including Sally Field, Olympia Dukakis, Shirley MacLaine, Daryl Hannah, and Julia Roberts, who was relatively unknown at the time.

Certain lines seem written for Dolly. For example, at one point Truvy quips, "There's no such thing as natural beauty." But Dolly at the time saw the role as a departure from her three prior movie experiences. In 1989, *Washington Post* writer Rita Kempley quoted her saying, "It's the first time I've played a character who didn't look like me. This is the first time I've been willing to do something where I couldn't have all the big hair and all the big makeup. Oh, it was big hair. But it was not big blond hair."

Whenever *Steel Magnolias* comes up, Dolly remembers working with the other women on the cast as a great blessing. Not that there weren't also challenges. The film's director, Herb Ross, could be difficult and once snapped at Dolly, telling her she couldn't act. She related the exchange to the *St. Petersburg Times* in a 1989 piece on the film's upcoming release. With typical Dolly candor, she reportedly told the director, "Well, hell, I know I can't act! But that's your job. You're the director. You're supposed to help me with my acting. You hired me 'cause you thought I was gonna make you a lot of money. Now earn it."

Whether it's her abilities, Herb Ross's directing, or some combination of the two, Dolly brings sensitivity and depth to her role in *Steel Magnolias*.

ABOVE: Dolly with Olympia Dukakis in *Steel Magnolias* (1989).

In a scene near the end of the film, Truvy's husband Spud, played by the late Sam Shepard, appears fully dressed in his Sunday best, asking to accompany her to the funeral of a friend. This is a surprise to Truvy, coming from a man we've seen up to this point as financially dependent, distracted, and emotionally distant. Her wordless conveyance of quiet gratitude for this moment of grace between herself and her spouse makes this scene so subtly touching.

Robert Harling based *Steel Magnolias* on the real-life story of his sister, who had been a fan of Dolly's and especially loved the song "I Will Always Love You." Some real-life experiences may also have been behind the depth Dolly brought to Truvy's character in the role. She has described the early 1980s as a time of trouble and personal difficulty in her life, in which she wrestled with her relationship with God. Thankfully, Dolly emerged on the other side more in tune with herself, her priorities, and her own inner compass. Dolly would reflect on the phrase "steel magnolia," a woman who "looks soft and pretty on the outside but is as strong as forged metal on the inside." She wrote: "I am proud if people think of me as one. I am also proud that I had a part in making a film that pays tribute to those strong women. *Steel Magnolias* was a fine film with something to say, and I have always thought it should have been a bigger hit."

NO COMPLAINTS FROM DOLLY!

Steel Magnolias includes a Christmas scene, with all the heavy sweaters one might imagine, but the scene was actually shot during a heat wave in Natchitoches, Louisiana. In *She Come By It Natural*, Sarah Smarsh reports Dolly's "heroically easygoing presence" as something her colleagues remembered years later. During filming one day, Shirley MacLaine, Robert Harling, and everyone else noticed Dolly was the only one *not* sweating. As Harling told it, Julia Roberts finally asked Dolly why she never complained. Harling recalled, "Dolly very serenely smiled and said, 'When I was young and had nothing, I wanted to be rich and famous, and now I am. So I'm not going to complain about anything.'"

From the Breadlines

Dolly records White Limozeen *at Treasure Isle Studios*

"I can see that she's the patron saint of Tennessee, and now she's reading books to my daughter on YouTube. Our obsession [with Dolly] is inspired by Nashville's reverence."

—MARC ROSE, ONE OF THE RESTAURANTEURS WHO OPENED WHITE LIMOZEEN, SPEAKING IN 2020 WITH A WRITER FOR THE *NASHVILLE SCENE*

Making the album *White Limozeen* took about five weeks, a pretty typical timeframe according to studio owner Fred Vail, who was there when it happened. It was a piecemeal process. Dolly would be in the studio three or four days, then leave to perform or make a TV appearance. Meanwhile, Vail and producer Ricky Skaggs worked on dubbing other layers for each song. Musicians would come in to record their parts, building the album track by track. These contributing players included studio heavies like Vince Gill on guitar, Lloyd Green on steel guitar, Stuart Duncan on fiddle, Béla Fleck on banjo, as well as Ricky Skaggs, also a consummate bluegrass musician himself.

At the time, Treasure Isle Studios was one of the newer facilities in town. Fred Vail had been in Nashville since the mid-1970s, working in marketing and radio promotion. He had come from California, where his career in music began at a very young age with the Beach Boys during the early 1960s, first as a

concert producer beginning with their first major gig in March 1963, and eventually, at the age of twenty-five in 1969, leading their label, Brother Records. He later moved into promotion, first for Capitol Records and then for RCA. His RCA territory centered on the southeast, including Tennessee, the Carolinas, and Georgia, where his obvious love and enthusiasm for country music led Waylon Jennings to suggest he relocate to Nashville. Vail did, and he eventually left promotions in 1980 to open Treasure Isle, where he built a solid reputation.

Recounting his career during a 2010 interview with the music writer Nancy Cardwell, who was writing a book on Dolly at the time, Vail named a handful of artists whose innate musical gifts had left him stunned. The Beach Boys' Brian Wilson and Ricky Skaggs were on this short list. So was Dolly, whom he described as "a magical singer." Vail said, "I would hear scratch vocals, a reference track that she would be singing with the musicians, and I'd say, 'You don't

ABOVE: Dolly performing, circa 1989.

even have to come back and do a vocal overdub. That's as good as it's going to be.' There are very, very few artists who have that kind of ability."

He also remembered that she never wore a wig when she recorded, an interesting counterpoint to the experience of Jane Fonda and Lily Tomlin during *9 to 5* overnight get-togethers, when they never once saw Dolly without her "regalia." According to Vail, her hair at the time was "kind of dishwater blonde and real short."

The title cut, "White Limozeen," was co-written by Dolly and her old friend Mac Davis, whom she had called out of retirement to collaborate. She told *Interview* in 1989, "I called Mac and said, 'Why don't you put your golf clubs in the closet and get your guitar out?'" He did, and the song they came up with paints a picture with some noteworthy contours: a country girl comes to Los Angeles determined to make it big. Dolly had actually arrived at Mac's house to work on the album's songs in a chauffeured limo and laughed when she stepped out of it, recalling her words to Mac that they should write "like we were *hungry again*." Dolly greeted him, still chuckling over the irony of the moment, and Mac said, "Let's just write that." They wrote two songs that night, the other titled "Wait 'Til I Get You Home," and both made it onto the album.

Fred Vail saw *White Limozeen* as "a fresh start" for Dolly. "She needed to relaunch her country image, for want of a better word." In this she succeeded, with four songs from the album hitting country charts. The two biggest hits were "Why'd You Come in Here Looking Like That," written by Bob Carlisle and Randy Thomas, and "Yellow Roses," written by Dolly. The first is a rowdy, raucous country dance tune with a dash of color thanks to Jo-El Sonnier on accordion.

The other is a standard classic country tearjerker about betrayal at the end of a long love.

Two covers on the album also did well. REO Speedwagon's "Time for Me to Fly," written by Kevin Cronin, sounds like it was begging for a banjo-driven bluegrass treatment all along, with steel guitar guiding the way between verses and chorus. The album's final tune also stands out, a cover of Don Franscisco's majestic contemporary Christian gospel number "He's Alive," a song recounting the events of Easter through the eyes of the disciple Peter. Dolly first heard the song on a long drive from California to Tennessee. She and Carl were crossing the desert, trying to find a radio station in the middle of nowhere, when the song came through the car speakers. They pulled into the next gas station to use the phone (no cellphones in 1989!) to call the station to ask about the artist. Dolly decided the song had to be on the album.

The Christ Church Pentecostal Choir joined Dolly for the climactic finish of "He's Alive" when she performed it at the CMA Awards in 1989, just as they do on the recorded version. Just before she started singing, Dolly said to the crowd, "As Mama would say, I hope you get a blessing out of it." The room full of country music luminaries were on their feet before the song's end.

Homage was paid to the album in a different way in 2020, when the boutique Graduate Hotel in Nashville hired two restaurateurs to open a rooftop bar called White Limozeen. Decked out in all shades of pink, white, and gold, the bar includes indoor as well as outdoor poolside seating, and a menu designed to be eaten casually. Inside, visitors can play Dolly Parton–themed pinball, and outside, view the giant bright pink bust of Dolly Parton made from chicken wire.

Elwanda Takes Manhattan

Dolly hosts Saturday Night Live,
bringing along plenty of her "downhome spirit"

The standout sketch for Season 14, Episode 17 of *Saturday Night Live* (*SNL*) comes near the end of the show. Dolly plays a country girl named Elwanda, pleased to start her job as a cashier in a convenience store only three days after arriving in Manhattan. The sketch pits Dolly's sunshiny spirit against the store's customers: crabby New Yorkers, all full of complaints about waiting in line or being overcharged for merchandise. The locals are played by some of that era's standout *SNL* cast members, including the late Phil Hartman, Jon Lovitz, and Nora Dunn, along with a young Mike Myers and an even younger Ben Stiller.

Elwanda redirects their negative energy by teaching them the "Gator Game." Before long, the customers are counting off 1–2–1–2 to mark themselves as alligators versus crocodiles. To the tune of "Oh! Susanna," Elwanda sings about coming from East Tennessee where "the lakes are full of bass." One customer whips out a harmonica to accompany her. When Elwanda shouts number one, that group stands tall with their mouths agape while the other group crouches low, and vice versa.

The punch line comes at the end of the song. She sings a line about a gift from her father, a pet "so green and full of sass." It "turned out to be a gator and it bit me in the—" Here, Elwanda laughs and points to her backside. Cast member Kevin Nealon as the store owner turns thoughtfully to the camera, and a voiceover describes how "Elwanda's downhome spirit swept Manhattan." The city changed from a "cutthroat metropolis into a sleepy backwoods utopia." Children began playing in the swimming hole at Central Park, he goes on, and a man named "Sweet Ol' Pete" was elected mayor. Though tongue-in-cheek, it is the sketch that features Dolly in her most natural element, a vibrant, positive, unsinkable spirit that people love to love.

During the episode, Dolly also performs two songs with her Mighty Fine Band: "Why'd You Come in Here Lookin' Like That" and "White Limozeen," both off her new album. Otherwise, the episode dwells in the fairly predictable territory of jokes about her breasts and her rural roots. One sketch shows the whole cast gathered around to hear Dolly "tell a mountain story." She begins reflecting on her childhood without a TV, recalling her mother's rich imagination from which she pulled elaborate and entertaining stories. She gives them an example, telling a story about a silver-haired man who lives on a ranch in Nevada with his three sons. After recounting the premise of *Bonanza*, she moves on to other famous TV shows like *I Love Lucy* and *Bewitched*.

During the opening monologue, the camera slowly zooms in on her bust as Dolly talks about the week's preparation for the live show and the hard work of the cast and crew. As she reflects on how "artistic" everything is in New York, a camera operator slowly descends from the ceiling. Dolly declares how crews in Hollywood "would never even try a shot like that." Then the footage cuts to a shot from above of Dolly's cleavage. Of course, Dolly plays along, as though unaware of the middle-school gags unfolding.

A later boob-themed sketch is more developed, so to speak. It features the handful of women in the cast, dressed in exaggerated costumes, as members of the "advanced race of women" that occupy the planet Estrogena. Its leader mocks Dolly—there is no place there for one so "deformed" on Estrogena. The leader banishes her to Earth, "where your undersized breasts will go unnoticed and you may live the rest of your life in anonymity."

ABOVE: Dolly is all smiles at the New York premiere of *Steel Magnolias* in November 1989.

BACK TO HER ROOTS

1991–2000

"It's not a big job being Dolly. It's just my life."

—DOLLY IN CONVERSATION WITH JIM JEROME

FOR *LADIES' HOME JOURNAL*, JULY 1995

OPPOSITE: A portrait of Dolly from the mid-1990s. A version of this photo was used for
the cover of her album *Something Special* in 1995.

Flying High

Dolly releases Eagle When She Flies

"Eagle When She Flies" isn't the first Dolly song to draw inspiration from the famous bird's image. Eagles had also come to mind when, as a younger woman, she'd written through the heartbreak of leaving *The Porter Wagoner Show*. In 1977, Dolly told *Rolling Stone* how much the eagle imagery in "Light of a Clear Blue Morning"—a captured eagle yearning for the sky once it finds freedom—rang true.

Eagle When She Flies makes use of majestic eagles once more, though now from the perspective of a more seasoned, mature Dolly. The title song stands out for its waltz time and even more so for its lyrics. "Eagle When She Flies" displays, as journalist and author Sarah Smarsh describes, "the simultaneous vulnerability and deep power of women." The lyrics point to an unspecified "she," which makes her available for all women to claim. Her soft heart stands alongside her ability to weather whatever trials may come. Her "kaleidoscope" of colors brightens the lives of those around her. At one point, the lyrics list all the things she is: lover, mother, friend, and wife.

Pretty noncontroversial, in terms of roles shared by many women. Yet some radio DJs refused to play the song, apparently objecting to the line in which the sparrow that was the woman becomes the eagle she was meant to be. In 2003, Dolly told *Rolling Stone*'s Jancee Dunn that they wouldn't play it "because they thought it was such a women's-lib song."

There was also the issue of age. Dolly had no qualms about criticizing the radio industry for failing to air new music by established stars. In an era of media conglomeration and subsequently narrowing playlists, the industry was bent toward that which was young, hot, or new. Being dubbed a legend could feel less like an honor, and more like a death knell for one's career and a sentence to the county fair circuit.

That may be why Dolly included a duet with Lorrie Morgan on the girl-fight song "Best Woman Wins," also released on Lorrie's album *Something in Red* at the same time. Another standout song is a sweet duet with Ricky Van Shelton called "Rockin' Years," written by Dolly's brother, Floyd Parton. It is a conversation song about long-lasting love, with both parties conveying mutual commitment to a life together. It would be a great wedding song.

Dolly also collaborated with some of her favorite songwriters on *Eagle When She Flies*. With Carl Perkins she cowrote "Family," which drives home the point that while we get to choose "lovers and friends," the same is not true for family, who call on us to "forgive," "accept," and, at times, recognize ways they "mirror" our own selves. With her old pal Mac Davis, she wrote "Wildest Dreams," a kind of toast and wish-you-well at a parting of ways. Dolly delivers "Dreams Do Come True," a song penned by her Uncle Bill, in a way that weds sensuality with spirituality. *Rolling Stone* writer Jancee Dunn once interviewed the lauded performer and was struck by that "uniquely Dolly blend of sex and scripture."

All in all, *Eagle When She Flies*, coproduced by Steve Buckingham, continues a return started with *White Limozeen* to straight-ahead-sounding country music, after Dolly's ventures into more pop-heavy territory, movie-making, and TV during the 1980s.

ABOVE: Dolly on *The Oprah Winfrey Show* in 1991.

Spreading the Love

Whitney Houston breathes new life into a Dolly classic

Dolly was driving her car when she first heard Whitney Houston's version of her song "I Will Always Love You." She pulled over, stunned. "I thought it was the most unbelievable thing I'd ever heard," she recalled in the 2019 documentary *Here I Am*. "I never even believed my little song could be done like that."

Originally a hit in 1972, "I Will Always Love You" peaked at number one again in 1982 when Dolly re-recorded it for *The Best Little Whorehouse in Texas*. This second achievement made Dolly the first musician to reach the top chart position twice for the same song. On both occasions, Dolly sings her little song as a quiet, introspective, and intimate parting of ways. Her version imbues a sense of melancholy and resignation.

Whitney imagined the song another way: a full, open-throated anthemic farewell and goodbye. She delivered it that way for her movie with Kevin Costner, 1992's *The Bodyguard*, and it remains among the most successful recordings of all time. Whitney's version set new records in terms of international success, spending fourteen weeks at the number one position on *Billboard*'s Hot 100 chart, the longest running number one single ever. Whitney earned a total of eleven *Billboard* awards, topping industry categories from world artist to R&B single. *The Bodyguard* album is the highest-selling movie soundtrack ever and also the top-selling album by a female artist worldwide. Whitney's recording brought at least $10 million in songwriter royalties to Dolly, whose choice to keep the rights, and forego Elvis's offer back in 1974, turned out to be a wise one indeed.

When Dolly performed "I Will Always Love You" in 1993 at a Carnegie Hall performance, after Whitney's hit, she told the audience that her version felt like "trying to follow a road grader with a spoon."

ABOVE: Dolly performs on *The Oprah Winfrey Show* in 1992. OPPOSITE: Whitney Houston in *The Bodyguard* (1992).

Still, she wasn't done with the song. Dolly also recorded it as a duet, with the earnest tenor of Vince Gill, in 1995. That piano-heavy version feels more like a straightforward slow-tempo country ballad, with swelling strings to round out the edges. By 2002, she was doing a bluegrass version "as a playoff" to end her then-current show. As the decades went on, Dolly would credit Whitney's sensational hit with introducing her to a new generation, when "a lot of new, younger people got very involved in my catalogue and started singing my songs all the time."

This level of success must bond a performer and a songwriter, like a chemical reaction neither could have anticipated. Whitney's untimely death in 2012 framed that connection with sadness.

Remembering Whitney during a 2014 interview for *American Songwriter*, Dolly said she'd "always think of it as our song." Writing about the "Dolly moment" in 2021, scholar, columnist, and MacArthur Fellow Tressie McMillan Cottom reflects on the surge in love for Dolly—the reasons she occupies a place of purity outside the divisions characterizing the current age. Reflecting on Dolly's belovedness in a time of personal conflict and political turmoil, Cottom suggests that focusing our collective love on Dolly "is a stand-in for how we can remediate our love for the nation." She adds, "I think we want to be able to feel proud of our country . . . [Parton's] a way to do that without being nationalist." It's like we all just want to keep saying to Dolly, "We will always love you, too."

Aunt Dolly

Dolly becomes "fairy godmother" to Miley Cyrus

The same year Billy Ray Cyrus enjoyed a burst of fame due to his popular hit "Achy Breaky Heart," he also welcomed his daughter Miley. Since Billy Ray and Dolly had become friends while touring together during the early 1990s, he asked if Dolly would be the baby's godmother. "Fairy godmother," Dolly preferred. And so grew a bond between the two families, and particularly between Dolly and Miley.

Their personal connection blossomed into professional ones, beginning with Dolly's occasional appearance on Miley's Disney vehicle, *Hannah Montana*. By 2006, when the program premiered on the Disney Channel, Miley was a musically precocious fourteen-year-old playing an adolescent pop star whose actual identity as "Miley Stewart" was a well-kept secret. Billy Ray played TV father Robbie Stewart to his actual daughter, and "Aunt Dolly" first appeared as the character's godmother in the sixteenth episode of Season 1, "Good Golly, Miss Dolly."

Aunt Dolly arrives with a video camera, which of course leads to an embarrassing mix-up for Miley, in which a taped confession of Miley's true feelings for her crush Jake accidentally lands in Jake's hands. Aunt Dolly appears again during Season 2, in an episode revolving around her long-running feud with "Mamaw Ruthie" (played by Vicki Lawrence) over a high school romance with Elvis (yes, *that* Elvis). During the fourth and final season of *Hannah Montana*, Dolly arrives piloting her personal helicopter, from which she drops a plush ladder for Miley and her best friend to escape the paparazzi. The photographers wait outside the gate of Miley's home, having learned the main character's secret identity. As Aunt Dolly advises Miley how to navigate the relentless attention, a pitfall of life in the spotlight, one wonders how much of the conversation was drawn from real life.

As Miley navigated the tricky road from childhood star to adult performer, Dolly remained a source of inspiration and courage. Miley performed a stripped-down, acoustic version of "Jolene" in 2012 as part of an Internet series of videos labeled "The Backyard Sessions." In 2016, Miley would join Dolly on the reality show *The Voice* to sing "Jolene" with a cappella quintet Pentatonix.

Miley has performed "Jolene" enough that some younger listeners don't even realize its history. Sarah Smarsh writes in *She Come By It Natural*, "A journalist friend of mine once told me that he had been watching the World Cup at a bar in Venezuela with Hugo Chávez when Chávez's daughter told him that she and her friend loved the 'new Miley Cyrus song' about a woman named Jolene. He showed them a video of the Parton original on his phone, and they were dazzled."

In 2020, Dolly and Miley performed the duet "Christmas Is" for Dolly's holiday album A *Holly Dolly Christmas*. The album included songs recorded with Miley's father, Billy Ray; Dolly's brother, Randy Parton; and stars Jimmy Fallon and Michael Bublé.

Dolly remains a champion of her goddaughter. In 2021, she spoke with RuPaul during an interview for *Marie Claire*, noting the spark in Miley's eye and the natural timing she had from an early age. Dolly gave Miley particular props for "being a risk-taker," a quality she herself contains in spades. Dolly said, "We all need to be true to ourselves, and I think that's what she's doing. I think that's the key to everybody's success as a human being and as an entertainer. You have to know what your talents are, what your limits are. But I think you have to be brave enough to try."

ABOVE: Dolly and Miley perform together during the 61st Annual Grammy Awards at Staples Center on February 10, 2019.

Honky Tonk Angels

Dolly teams with country music legends Loretta Lynn and Tammy Wynette for a new album

Dolly had suggested "Hot Flashes" would make a suitable title for the trio album project that included herself (at age forty-seven), Loretta Lynn (fifty-eight), and Tammy Wynette (fifty-one). Loretta suggested "The Good, the Bad, and the Ugly," but never would say who was who. When all was said and done, they called the historic album *Honky Tonk Angels*, an homage to the 1952 Kitty Wells song, "It Wasn't God Who Made Honky Tonk Angels." It was produced once again by Dolly's friend and music-making partner Steve Buckingham. Kitty herself also joined in for a few lines of her signature song, once considered controversial because it dared to insist on male accountability for unfaithfulness in marriage. In many ways, Kitty's recording kicked off the modern era for women in country music, so it was fitting to blend her voice with the powerful trio.

Dolly wrote in her memoir about the song's significance: "Up until that time, it was a lot easier for [married men] to tell themselves that they had been lured into cheating by loose women. Kitty pointed out that they were the ones who had slipped off their wedding bands and gone into the bar in the first place. Right on, Kitty."

Another historic cut off the album finds Dolly, Loretta, and Tammy singing along with a recording of vocals by the late Patsy Cline, on "Lovesick Blues," an Irving Mills vaudeville tune made a country music staple by Hank Williams during the late 1940s. Other classic country and gospel numbers are lifted by the combined forces of these three pioneering singers, songwriters, and stylists, each of whom crafted a distinctive voice over decades of recordings. But the final cut of *Honky Tonk Angels*, a cover of the spoken word classic, "I Dreamed of a Hillbilly Heaven," stands out for its twist on history. Narrated by Dolly, her natural way with a story breathes new life into the material, before Loretta and Tammy join in for the chorus.

"I Dreamed of Hillbilly Heaven" was first recorded in 1954 by Eddie Dean, who co-wrote it with Hal Sothern. It describes a dream of dying and being greeted at heaven's gate by a "doorman" who guides the dreamer around to meet departed country legends. The dreamer asks who else might be joining the heavenly crowd during the upcoming decades and a litany of names is read from a giant "tally book." In this first recording, as in all the covers that followed, the list ends with the singer's own name.

In Eddie Dean's original, the doorman is the famous "cowboy humorist" Will Rogers, prominent during the late 1920s and 1930s. The first figure pointed out is "star lodger" Jimmie Rodgers, the long-acknowledged "father of country music." Hank Williams gets special mention, along with a list of other deceased performers, and then living contemporaries. As future artists covered the song, it became a country music genealogy, with mention of country's central figures amounting to a place of honor and a record of their contemporary currency.

For the version of the song on *Honky Tonk Angels*, Roy Acuff and Tex Ritter greet Dolly the dreamer from onstage rather than at the door, and introduce her to country music greats still singing and performing in the beyond. Conway Twitty, who had recently died, gets a place of honor along with Roger Miller ("he's making everybody laugh"). Patsy Cline, Dottie West, and Maybelle Carter balance out a list that also mentions Marty Robbins, Ernest Tubb, and even Elvis Presley.

When Dolly asks the imaginary Roy and Tex who else might be joining over the next forty or fifty years, the book they hand over names Merle Haggard, Johnny Cash, Willie Nelson, and Randy Travis; Minnie Pearl, Reba McEntire, the Judds, and Tanya Tucker; and younger artists like Vince Gill and Garth Brooks. Dolly's having fun performing this song, and near the end of her litany she pauses, "I said, 'Well where's Porter Wagoner's name?'" A beat for effect. "Oh, there it is." And then, in keeping with tradition, she adds their own three names: Loretta Lynn and Tammy Wynette and Dolly Parton. "That's when I woke up!"

ABOVE: (L to R) Loretta Lynn, Dolly, and Tammy Wynette at the 1993 Country Music Awards.

Always Chasing a Dream

Dolly collaborates with longtime partners and fresh voices for Slow Dancing with the Moon

The album *Slow Dancing with the Moon* contains two extremes. One is captured in the title song, written by Dolly's longtime pal Mac Davis. Friends for decades by then, Mac knew Dolly well and he wrote the song with her in mind. "[Mac] said it's the way he sees me, how I'm always chasing a dream," Dolly told a reporter for *Toronto Star*, "that I'm the same kid he met so many years ago and my spirit has remained the same."

The album's other extreme comes with the song "Romeo," on which Dolly was joined by a number of country stars, including Billy Ray Cyrus, who was hot stuff in country music at the time. There's little of note regarding the song itself, but the music video is a period piece, fun to watch from this distance for its setting (the heyday for clubs featuring country line dancing) and the playful interactions among its cast of characters. At the time, *People* described Billy Ray as "a growling male sex object who is subjected to leering catcalls by Dolly and sidekicks Mary Chapin Carpenter, Kathy Mattea and Tanya Tucker." That about sums it up.

Partnering with Billy Ray on the heels of "Achy Breaky Heart" was a solid way to appeal to a younger audience. The mid-1990s were a tough time to be both ambitious for radio airplay and middle-aged. Music industry resources channeled toward trying to find the next so-called stadium acts. Grown-up country artists in general, and female artists in particular, had difficulty finding slots on the constricting radio playlists that accompanied conglomerated media ownership at the time.

The three younger women joining in the fun on "Romeo" were each experiencing success during what seemed to be a time of expanding opportunity for female country musicians. But this time would prove to be temporary, as country radio airplay for women began a steady nosedive across the first two decades of the twenty-first century. Then as now (as always), Dolly was strategic when it came to finding outlets for her creative energy. In an interview with Jim Jerome for the *Ladies' Home Journal* in 1995, Dolly said, "I'm commercial-minded. If I can't get my own hit, I'm not too proud to hang onto somebody else's coattails."

Slow Dancing with the Moon was produced by Steve Buckingham, with Dolly's Mighty Fine Band backing her up. Out of twelve cuts, eight are her own compositions. Dolly was by then hitting her stride, enjoying the creative and financial freedom her success had brought.

Any potential controversy over the audacious titillations of "Romeo" was deflected by Dolly's donation of proceeds for the single to the American Red Cross. When the *Toronto Star* asked about flak over the song's raciness, Dolly said, "I figure the worse we'll do is feed somebody's kid and rebuild somebody's house, so how hard do you want to be with me?"

The video for "Romeo" ends with Dolly's character leaving the club on the arm of Billy Ray's character. We hear her say, "I am so flattered that you would choose me out of all these young beautiful girls. I tell you, I feel pretty special right now." She turns back to the camera with a knowing wink to us, the viewers. As the two walk away, we hear her add, "But after all, it's only right. I am paying for this video."

ABOVE: Dolly with Billy Ray Cyrus in a 2006 episode of *Hannah Montana*.

Blue Eye Records

Dolly and frequent collaborator Steve Buckingham try their hand at an indie label

The logo for Blue Eye Records is an eye—Dolly's own—gazing out from beneath an arched brow. The eye is blue, though Dolly's are actually hazel. Dolly first wanted to call the label "Blue Indigo Records" because of a dream she had. It turned out someone had copyrighted the name already. "Blue I Records" was the next thought, but that shorthand seemed to cause confusion among people hearing the name, and so Dolly and her longtime musical collaborator and producer Steve Buckingham chose Blue Eye.

Dolly and Steve founded Blue Eye Records in 1994, and it operated for twelve years, followed by Dolly Records in 2007. Founding a label was another milestone in Dolly's journey to creative and financial independence. She already controlled the publishing rights to her enormous song catalog. With her own label, she could record and release music as she saw fit, without navigating the tensions between creative inspiration and the business interests of major label executives.

As Dolly told *Rolling Stone* in 2003, the move gave her creative freedom without "fourteen managers and record executives" trying to have their say. This say would inevitably be shaped by a desire to fit new recordings into the mold left behind by a successful hit. "When the new country came along, any artist over thirty-five was thought to be a has-been," Dolly said. The term "legend" was a euphemism for no-longer-relevant, and Dolly was at a point in her life when she felt "just now seasoned enough to know how to be in this business."

Dolly created recordings on her own terms with her own capital for Blue Eye. The recordings then get leased to other companies who bring them to listeners. This model took some wrangling to figure out. The original arrangement was for Blue Eye Records to be Dolly's own imprint, functioning as a joint business venture with Sony. The first album, *Something Special* (1995), memorably included a duet version of "I Will Always Love You" with Vince Gill.

For the next project, an album of covers titled *Treasures* (1996), Blue Eye partnered with Universal. *Treasures* finds Dolly collaborating with a range of musicians, including the sensational South African mbube group Ladysmith Black

Mambazo, who had first entered the global stage via Paul Simon's *Graceland* album in 1986. She also explores sometimes surprising material, such as Neil Young's "After the Goldrush" and the international hit "Walking on Sunshine" written by Kimberley Charles Rew for the band Katrina and the Waves, of which he was also a member.

Dolly's next album, *Hungry Again* (1998), was an important one for her, from a creative perspective. She describes in the liner notes the creative discipline she brought to bear on the project. Dolly withdrew to the calm of her Tennessee home to give herself over to writing. She reportedly prayed and fasted to tune into her own voice. She later wrote in *Songteller* about how withdrawing from the larger world feeds her musical creativity: "That's when I feel like I am getting into that 'God space,' where I really feel like I'm communicating on a spiritual level. And then the songs start coming, and I go with it. I wrote a lot of songs during that period. Any time I can allow myself the time to do that, my songs are usually better."

Hungry Again was recorded in the Nashville basement of her cousin Richie Owens's home, with musicians who were members of his own bands. The result was an album of originals, received favorably by both critics and audiences. The album was released and distributed by Decca, but a series of poorly timed business moves left the album out to sea. Universal had acquired the Nashville-based label Rising Tide, but after "Universal suddenly sunk Rising Tide," as *No Depression* contributing editor Linda Ray put it, *Hungry Again* was "moved to Decca,

which had its own ideas about the project." In short, the album "climbed onto the country and pop charts without a net, as its label crumbled right out from under it."

Meanwhile, Steve Buckingham made a move unrelated to these shifts in distribution: he accepted a position with Vanguard Records. It was a creative and professional move Dolly encouraged her friend to take. In the end, the move would make possible leaner and more flexible partnerships with the smaller company Sugar Hill Records, acquired during this period by Vanguard. In some sense, working with a smaller company meant less static between Dolly's creative voice—the one coming from her "God space"—and the music being recorded. This would open an entirely new era for Dolly and her music-making.

ABOVE: Dolly with Steve Buckingham at the 2007 Songwriters Hall of Fame Ceremony.

The Imagination Library

*Dolly founds the famed literacy
and education project with her father*

When Dolly began the Imagination Library project with her father in 1995, her goal was to help improve literacy and education success for children in Sevier County, where she grew up. The scope of the project has only expanded. To this day, children who have signed up to participate receive one book every month from birth to kindergarten. The very first book they receive is one of Dolly's own childhood favorites, *The Little Engine That Could.*

There's a lot in that story that speaks to Dolly, her life's work, and particularly to the growth and success of the entire Imagination Library undertaking. Her dad figures prominently in this achievement. Dolly has credited her spirituality and musicality to her mom, but her grit and determination come from Lee Parton, who grew up in a family of fifteen and never had the opportunity to attend school or learn to read.

Yet Lee demonstrated an intuitive grasp of money when it came, for instance, to anticipating the yield for a year's harvest. He repaired anything and everything, and he nurtured his large family despite few financial resources. As Dolly put it for *Parade* twenty years after the Imagination Library's

founding, "My dad couldn't read and write. He was very crippled by that. My daddy was very, very smart, and I thought, 'God, if he'd had an education I wonder what all he might've been?'"

Originally, the idea was to give Sevier County children—maybe those in a neighboring county, if things went well—the chance to enjoy the books Dolly's father never could. But no one could have anticipated the charity's growth. By 2004, the program covered the whole state of Tennessee. It kept growing, and continues to do so. The program currently serves children in communities all over the United States, Canada, the United Kingdom, Australia, and Ireland. The Imagination Library works via partnerships, in which local nonprofits secure funds of $2.10 per month per child registered in their community, while the central organization covers overhead administrative costs. Those costs cover more than two million children every month, and more than 190 million books have been distributed so far.

The Imagination Library is part of the Dollywood Foundation, which in 1988 started with a mission to increase high school graduation rates in the Sevier

County region. Foundation leaders devised the Buddy Program, designed to pair students to support one another in achieving the milestone of graduating high school. Seventh and eighth grade students who participate are paired up, with the promise of $500 upon graduation, provided both they and their designated "buddy" achieve the goal. The first cohort to enroll in the buddy system saw a decrease in local high school dropout rates from thirty percent to just six percent. Dolly also funds college scholarships of $15,000 for Sevier County students, and recently announced a program to pay for further education for employees at her theme parks and resorts.

In 2018, the Library of Congress honored a milestone in Dolly's work with the Imagination Library: Its 100-millionth donated book will be

ABOVE: Dolly reading her book, *Coat of Many Colors*, to children at the Library of Congress in 2018.

housed there forever. Dolly told the Library of Congress interviewer that "of all the things that I have done in my life—and it's been a lot, 'cause I've been around a long time—but this is one of the most precious things, and the proudest I am of any program that I've ever been involved in in my life is working with the little kids."

Dolly returned to the Library of Congress in 2021, when the Imagination Library received the David M. Rubenstein Prize for "an outstanding and measurable contribution to increasing literacy levels." The prize included $150,000 to support the program. By 2021, the program had grown to include two thousand community partners in five different countries.

On July 6, 2022, Dolly was named a Friend of Education, the highest award given by the National Educators Association, for her work championing literacy and learning. Past recipients include Nobel Prize- winner Malala Yousafzai and economist Paul Krugman. At the time of the award, more than 1,600 partner communities participated in the Imagination Library, and the program was being studied for its impact on local literacy within some of these communities.

ABOVE: Dolly with children and parents at the press launch for the Imagination Library and her European Backwoods Barbie Tour at the Savoy Hotel in London on December 4, 2007.

An Impressive Set of Glands

The cloned Dolly the Sheep is named for Dolly the Entertainer

When the Scottish research team at the Roslin Institute in Edinburgh successfully cloned a sheep for the first time, they named it Dolly, in honor of Dolly Parton. The cell from which they had successfully cloned the animal had been taken from a mammary gland of an adult sheep. A member of the team, embryologist Sir Ian Wilmut, commented on the choice of name, "Dolly is derived from a mammary gland cell and we couldn't think of a more impressive pair of glands than Dolly Parton's."

English professor and literature scholar Leigh Edwards, writing about Dolly and gender identity in country music, mused that Wilmut's "comment is one of the more unusual 'boob jokes' in a long line directed at Parton." It goes to show that you can take the boy out of middle school and educate him to be a groundbreaking scientist, but you can't take the middle school boy out of the scientist.

The cloning process had previously only worked using embryonic cells. This time, the cell was taken from the udder of an adult—long dead but whose cells had been frozen. Dolly the sheep was genetically identical to the cloned adult, and unrelated to the surrogate sheep in whom the egg was implanted. At the time of the announcement on February 27, 1997, Dolly the sheep was already seven months old. The news came via a paper in the British journal *Nature*, titled "Viable Offspring Derived from Fetal and Adult Mammalian Cells." Delay of the breakthrough had been due to a pending patent application around the process of nuclear transfer.

The research held promise for understanding age-related diseases. By changing the genetics of a sheep, the animal can produce proteins with therapeutic applications to humans. At the same time, the research sparked ethical debates and fears about potential misuse of cloning technology, including on humans. President Bill Clinton formed a task force to examine the issue from both moral and legal frameworks.

Dolly the sheep's fame sparked a stream of visitors to her pen. In 1999, the local *Edmonton Journal* reported on a Japanese couple who married in nearby Edinburgh and booked the ewe to make an appearance at their reception so they could take photos with her. Unfortunately, she and her scientific handlers turned down a request to appear at Dollywood, due to the logistical and security risks of traveling so far from Scotland.

Dolly gave birth to several healthy lambs during her life, a life cut short by a terminal lung disease. In 2003, scientists at the Roslin Institute made the decision to euthanize her because of the progression of the disease. Her body was preserved and remains on display at the National Museum of Scotland.

Asked how she felt about the naming in 2014, Dolly told an interviewer for Scottish radio, "I never met her but I always said there's no such thing as baaad publicity."

ABOVE: Dolly (the person), circa 1997. INSET: Dolly (the cloned sheep) in 1997.

The Grass Is Blue

Dolly records a bluegrass album

The moment of inspiration came over dinner in an Italian restaurant in Santa Monica. Dolly and her friend, musical collaborator, and business partner Steve Buckingham had run into one another on a plane headed to California and decided to enjoy dinner that night. During the meal, Steve suggested that Dolly do a bluegrass album. He had been working for Welk and Vanguard, which had recently bought the small bluegrass label Sugar Hill Records.

"Yeah, let's do it," Dolly said. "I own myself. I can do whatever I want."

Dolly wrote the title cut for the album that would become *The Grass Is Blue* over a thirty-minute lunch break on the set of the TV movie *Blue Valley Songbird*. She told *No Depression* magazine in 1999 that she "put it down on a tape," sent it to Steve, and said, "Here's our title song." The project moved quickly, from idea to release in about five months, and working with Sugar Hill eased the headaches of partnering with major labels that had dragged down *Hungry Again*. Sugar Hill was large enough to effectively market and distribute the recording, but small enough to keep

the number of decision-makers manageable and the priorities more felicitously aligned.

The Grass Is Blue was also recorded almost entirely live, with only the background vocals layered on after the fact, a decision that signaled a return to Dolly's roots. It was a direction *Hungry Again* anticipated that this album fulfilled. Its opening cut likewise signaled something new. Dolly and an incomparable band of bluegrass instrumentalists take Billy Joel's "Travelin' Prayer" to an entirely new place, and then the final cut is a gospel song called "I Am Ready," written by Dolly's sister, Rachel, and performed entirely a cappella.

Music writer Greil Marcus, reviewing *The Grass Is Blue* in 1999, called it the best album Dolly had made since *My Blue Ridge Mountain Boy* in 1969. His favorite was her cover of the old Appalachian ballad "Silver Dagger," also recorded by Joan Baez in 1960. In the way only Greil Marcus can, he writes: "Parton follows Baez like a girl following her mother through a field, wandering off the path, circling back, then disappearing into the woods. But now it's nightfall, everyone in town is searching and some people are already talking about haunts and ghosts. How it ends: the fiddler, Stuart Duncan, finds her."

The Grass Is Blue won a Grammy, a CMA Award, and also an International Bluegrass Music Association award for Album of the Year. Steve told music scholar Lydia Hamessley how much that last award meant to Dolly. "That's the most surprised I've ever seen her, and the closest to being speechless I've ever seen her," reported Hamessley. "She never expected that, and it meant so much to her that the bluegrass community accepted her for doing this. And believe me, she can do it because that's the roots of her music, mountain music and bluegrass music. And old-time country music."

ABOVE: Dolly performs "The Grass Is Blue" at the 37th Annual CMA Awards.

The House That Holds the Music

Dolly is inducted into the Country Music Hall of Fame

"Please help me welcome, if you will, my friend, Dolly Parton," Kenny Rogers ended his introduction of his old pal and singing partner as she became the seventieth inductee to the Country Music Hall of Fame on September 22, 1999. The announcement came during the televised Country Music Association annual awards. That same year, Dolly was up for Vocal Event of the Year alongside Linda Ronstadt and Emmylou Harris for *Trio II*, the follow-up to their epic recording project from the late 1980s.

A smaller, more formal ceremony had happened earlier at the Hall of Fame itself, an institution described by country music's advocate and ambassador Marty Stuart as "holy ground." Marty was then president of the Country Music Foundation, the institution formed to support the growing industry back in 1961. Its first inductees were country music's first superstar, Jimmie Rodgers; songwriting and publishing pioneer Fred Rose; and honky-tonk icon Hank Williams. Being inducted into the Hall of Fame has continued to be a cherished honor. Marty, who remains an influential musician, described the Hall of Fame as the place "where we all want to end up. Every note of music I play is aimed at this building."

Following Kenny's remarks, Dolly walked onstage to a standing ovation. "I feel like I died and went to hillbilly heaven," she told the audience, referring to one of the songs from *Honky Tonk Angels*, her collaborative album earlier that decade with Tammy Wynette and Loretta Lynn. She then invited singer and multi-instrumentalist Alison Krauss to the stage, along with musicians from her

---

ABOVE: Dolly and Vince Gill performing at the 1999 Country Music Awards.

---

forthcoming album *The Grass Is Blue*, to perform a cover of Blackfoot's "Train, Train" from the new project. After the performance, Kenny presented her with the commemorative plaque to mark the occasion.

In expressing thanks, Dolly began her remarks, "You know, a friend of mine, Mac Davis, once wrote a song called 'Lord, Let Me Die Knowin' My People Were Proud of Me.' And I know that my mama and daddy are up there in Sevierville watching right now." She was talking about the tune "In the Eyes of My People" from Mac's 1972 album *I Believe in Music*, but her meaning came through clearly. She acknowledged her sister Rachel and brother Randy, who were present at the ceremony. She thanked several important people in her life, including Porter Wagoner, Don Warden and his wife Ann, her dear friend Judy Ogle, her Uncle Bill, and several other industry figures important to her early career. She closed by giving "the praise and honor to God for whatever talent and good luck that I've had, so thank you so much." The applause rose from the crowd once more. Dolly also performed a duet with Vince Gill that night, "My Kind of Woman/My Kind of Man," which he'd recorded with Patty Loveless. That recording won an award that night as well. Before singing, Dolly joked, "I'm no Patty Loveless but you're no Porter Wagoner." Dolly had learned about the honor earlier that year via phone call, while she was cooking chicken and dumplings, meatloaf, and a roast. At first, she thought the ringing was from a kitchen timer. Dolly's family was visiting at the time, she told *Parade*. "I was so floored, I screamed at the top of my lungs, and everyone came running, and I started to cry, but I didn't want to screw up my makeup." Dolly jumped up and down with excitement at the news. "I think of myself as still young," she said later. (She was fifty-three at the time.) "I thought if I ever got in the Hall of Fame, I'd be an old woman."

When newspapers and other media began contacting her for a reaction to the news, Dolly said, "What a great honor. I'm really surprised." Then she quipped, "I thought I'd have to be as old as Roy Acuff or as ugly as Willie Nelson to get in the Hall of Fame—just kiddin', boys!"

Alongside Dolly, two late country music performers were inducted into the Hall of Fame in 1999: singer Conway Twitty, who died in 1993, and songwriter and movie singing cowboy Johnny Bond, who'd passed in 1978.

That year also marked the breaking of ground on a new building for the Country Music Hall of Fame. Designed by Ralph Applebaum, the $37 million complex would open in downtown Nashville on May 17, 2001.

"I'm rowdy, I'm playful, I'm passionate, and I'm full of it."

—DOLLY IN AN INTERVIEW CLIP SHOWN DURING HER INDUCTION INTO THE COUNTRY MUSIC HALL OF FAME IN 1999

ABOVE: Reba McEntire (left) and Dolly attend the 2011 Country Music Hall of Fame Medallion Ceremony on May 22, 2011, in Nashville.

A
TWENTY-FIRST-CENTURY
CULTURAL ICON

2001–2013

***

"I think of country radio like a great lover. You were great to me,
you bought me a lot of nice things, and then you dumped my ass for younger women."

—DOLLY IN HER 2012 BOOK *DREAM MORE*

OPPOSITE: Dolly outside her offices in Nashville, Tennessee, in 2001.

The God Zone

Dolly is inducted into the Songwriters Hall of Fame

"It starts with a song, and I hope it'll end with a song."

—DOLLY IN CONVERSATION WITH EMILY LORDI FOR THE *NEW YORK TIMES* IN DECEMBER 2020

Songwriting is the creative act Dolly loves most of all, the gift she values above her many other gifts, since the beginning of her journey. So, being inducted into the Songwriters Hall of Fame in 2001 was a particularly notable moment of recognition in a long line of acknowledgments. The same year she was inducted, fellow honorees included Billy Joel, Willie Nelson, Elvis Costello, Dionne Warwick, and Paul Williams. Immediately following the ceremony, Dolly was interviewed at the event. She said, "Writing is my first love . . . It's my doctor, it's my therapist, it's like everything, but it also gives a voice to a lot of folks that really don't know how to express it. I feel like that it's a God-given gift, and it's a very personal thing to me, so this means more to me than all the other awards I've won."

Dolly's songwriting inspiration springs from multiple reservoirs. Her childhood memories constitute one rich source of feelings and images. "The days of Mama and Daddy and my grandmas and grandpas, and church days," she once said. "All I ever have to do is close my eyes and just kind of go inside." Early musical experiences at home and in church have remained with her so that even modern songs find her "pulling stuff from those days before I ever left home." Dolly also draws on her own emotions, which dwell close to the surface, and on her sense of empathy as a deep-feeling person. She sees herself as "a very sensitive person. I hurt deep. But I have to hurt deep and I have to feel all those feelings in order to write. And I cannot harden my heart against things. I've been through it all, seen it all, been it all, felt it and been able to write about it."

Among the ingredients in Dolly's secret sauce are strong dashes of discipline and routine. She typically rises early to write, often by three o'clock in the morning, which is her time of greatest inspiration. She calls it her "wee-hour wisdom." Talking with journalist and theater critic J. Wynn Rousuck in 2006, Dolly said, "I kind of get in my God zone, I call it—my God space, or just my creative place. It's like a little field of energy that I get in." Her longtime friend and musical collaborator Steve Buckingham recalled her sharing that she likes the early morning talks with God "because she feels there aren't as many people up at that time of

the morning to talk to him, so she feels she has a freer line."

While inspiration tends to visit early in the morning, Dolly continues to craft all the way up to the final mix of a song, tweaking a line here and there, adjusting a melodic turn once she hears it fleshed out with instruments or harmonies. That level of involvement is only available to an artist who has carved space to be in control and command of her creative output. It's a process she began when she took ownership of her song catalog and has continued through the creation of a series of her own record labels. Creative control is a central component of Dolly's ability to continue being a productive artist over so long a career. She summed it up best for *Music Week*'s George Garner in 2020:

"Well, it's always good to be in control of as much as you can be—in control of the things that you are . . . It's great when you become your own boss, and you can call the shots."

The Songwriters Hall of Fame was founded in 1969 by the composer Johnny Mercer, with a mission to recognize the craft's great contributors. To be considered for the award, a writer must have a commercial release at least two decades prior to being honored. Six years after being inducted, Dolly was recognized by the institution a second time as the recipient of its highest honor, the Johnny Mercer Award. Only songwriters already in the Hall of Fame are eligible, and they must be judged to have "established a history of outstanding creative works." Dolly has certainly done that.

ABOVE: (L to R) Honorees Paul Williams, Dolly, and Willie Nelson during the 2001 Songwriters Hall of Fame induction.

Blue Mountain Music

Dolly records Little Sparrow, *the second of her three bluegrass albums*

"I had to get rich so I could sing like I was poor, which is what I've done."

—DOLLY, TALKING TO *PEOPLE* IN 2001

ittle Sparrow, the album that followed *The Grass Is Blue*, served as a kind of musical bridge between bluegrass and other styles. Dolly coined the phrase "blue mountain music" to characterize what she hears as a meeting between bluegrass and old-school mountain music in her sound. She sometimes reached outside either genre and interpreted songs through that blue mountain lens, to great success. Specifically, she earned a Grammy for Best Female Country Vocal Performance for her cover of Collective Soul's "Shine," which appeared on *Little Sparrow*.

The title song off the album is based on the old ballad "Come Ye Fair and Tender Maidens," the kind of song Dolly used to hear her mother sing. As musicologist Lydia Hamessley notes in *Unlikely Angel*, her book about Dolly's songwriting, this was not the first time Dolly made a new song from something old. "Sandy's Song" adapts "Greensleeves." "Shine On," from the 1990s album *Hungry Again*, is set to the tune of "Amazing Grace." "Silver Dagger" reworks a traditional ballad associated with Joan Baez and Bob Dylan during the 1960s, but the song itself has roots at least back to the early nineteenth century.

Part of the momentum behind *Little Sparrow* was the overwhelmingly positive reception with which *The Grass Is Blue* was embraced. This had come as a surprise to Dolly, and a very happy one, according to producer Steve Buckingham. *Little Sparrow* also includes a few cover songs, which, as Steve said, were meant to "take the focus off, as Dolly calls it, the cartoon [of her persona] and put the focus back on her artistry: that voice, that singer, that musical talent, that songwriting talent, and the way she could interpret other people's song" through that "blue mountain" lens.

OPPOSITE: Dolly promotes *Little Sparrow* in Los Angeles in 2001.

A Living Legend Takes an Iconic Stage
"I like them hoo-hoot songs, too . . ."

By the time Dolly taped an episode of the long-running PBS television music showcase *Austin City Limits (ACL)*, both she and the series had achieved the status of cultural icons. *ACL* was by then in its twenty-sixth season and had far outgrown its original Austin-based foundations in 1970s "cosmic cowboy" culture. What began as a stage emphasizing mainstream country evolved into singer-songwriter and roots music, and finally emerged by century's end as an eclectic showcase unbounded by one musical genre. It remains so today.

Musicians famously love *Austin City Limits* for how the television production stays out of the way of live performance. The results are relatively simple, but rare on the small screen, where the typical start-and-stop production method kills musical spontaneity. The approach and exquisite quality mean that *ACL* performances by legends no longer with us—like Fats Domino or Waylon Jennings, Ray Charles or Nanci Griffith—remain lasting testimonies to their artistry. It likewise means that a performance by a living legend like Dolly Parton offers a precious glimpse into top-shelf music-making.

ACL had tried and tried to book Dolly. Executive producer and the show's longtime guiding light Terry Lickona talked about it as far back as 1990, telling the *Chicago Tribune*, "She's always busy doing something else." Ten years later, Terry's persistence paid off.

The taping coincided with Dolly's release of *Little Sparrow*, the second of three albums that marked a return to her Appalachian roots, and onstage at *ACL*, we witness Dolly's full musical power. She opens with a two-cover medley: the blues rock hit "Train, Train," made famous by Blackfoot during the late '70s, and "Mule Skinner Blues," the Jimmie Rodgers classic that had earned her solo acclaim early in her career. The transition between the two tunes pivots on a long-held note: "goodbye" in the first becomes "good morning, captain" in the next. When she finally releases that high lonesome pivot note, Dolly fans her face lightly with her hands in mock exhaustion. "Glad I got big lungs," she adds. She ends this set opener with a big smile and says to the audience, "I don't know what you get when you cross a mule and a train. Do you?"

Throughout the concert, Dolly plays rhythm guitar, closely surrounded by a half circle of musicians, including two harmony singers and a

ABOVE: Dolly performs at the Hammersmith Apollo in London in 2002.

full bluegrass backing band—fiddle, mandolin, guitar, banjo, dobro, and bass. At the center, Dolly wears a cream-colored satin top under a brown leather jumper, with a slitted skirt and fringes that brush just above her knees. Orange sunburst and flower designs cover the ensemble, embroidery and sequins associated with country music since tailors Nudie Cohn and Manuel Cuevas made them so popular back in the day. Dolly turns to face her band members when they solo, passing a chance to demonstrate their instrumental chops, one to another. There is an intimacy to the atmosphere, with the musicians onstage but also with the crowd, who occasionally erupt with applause for a particularly virtuosic solo.

Dolly then sings "Mountain Angel." Although this was a new song for *Little Sparrow*, it fit the Appalachian ballad tradition of tragic storytelling. This particular tale describes a young woman giving her heart to a stranger, only to have it crushed when he abandons her, pregnant with a child who dies at birth. The woman spends her remaining life wandering the hills before death finally takes her too, alone and stretched across her baby's grave. High, wailing "hoo-hoots" imbue the tune with a haunting beauty. They signify the woman's spirit still echoing through the mountains. When the song ends, Dolly prompts her audience to try these out. "Hoo-hoot" swells from the audience in one voice, and she signals them to try them once again. A beat, and then she laughs: "Lord, that'd scare the hell out of me if I was back home."

At the time of the taping, *ACL* performances still occurred in KLRU's studio 6A, which held fewer than four hundred people. Viewing the episode, one gets the sense Dolly connects with every person in the room, and that the same would be true for audiences larger or smaller. Associate producer Leslie Nichols, in an interview for an *Austin City Limits* oral history project in 2007, recalled this particular episode's rehearsal. She and another colleague had pulled their chairs close to the stage to watch, so Dolly was only about six feet away. She sang "Mountain Angel," looking directly at them, and the two colleagues sat crying their eyes out from start to finish. When the song ended, Dolly paused and said, "That was plumb pitiful, wasn't it?"

In the singular way of *ACL*, this episode captures Dolly in action as singer, instrumentalist, band member, and charismatic performer. Dolly likewise enjoyed the moment and, as Terry recalled during a 2009 panel celebrating *ACL*'s induction into the Rock and Roll Hall of Fame, Dolly told him *ACL* was the most fun she had ever had doing television.

LETTING IT ALL COME OUT

After each *Austin City Limits* performance, executive producer Terry Lickona interviews the artist backstage. On this occasion, Dolly expressed her memorable experience on *ACL*:

I love songwriting better than anything else. In fact, I've been writing songs since I was a little bitty kid. My mama used to keep stuff that, before I could write, she'd keep things, she'd write 'em down that I had made up because she was just fascinated that I could rhyme everything so good. Plus I listened to everything. I'm very touched by everything I hear. And most of the songs that I sing, if I haven't suffered that or lived that story, somebody I love has lived that or suffered that . . . I'm glad I can write because it's my therapy. I'd probably be a total lunatic. I'm just a little crazy now but I'd probably be nuts if I couldn't write. What I love to do is to be able to really just let it all come and then let it all come out.

SET LIST FOR THE *ACL* EPISODE (SEASON 26, EPISODE 18, 2001):

"Train Train" (*The Grass Is Blue*, 1999)

"Mule Skinner Blues" (*The Best of Dolly Parton*, 1970)

"Little Sparrow" (*Little Sparrow*, 2001)

"Shine" by Collective Soul (*Little Sparrow*, 2001)

"Mountain Angel" (*Little Sparrow*, 2001)

"Marry Me" (*Little Sparrow*, 2001)

"A Tender Lie" (*Little Sparrow*, 2001)

"I Don't Believe You've Met My Baby" (*Little Sparrow*, 2001)

"Coat of Many Colors" (*Coat of Many Colors*, 1971)

"I Will Always Love You" (*Jolene*, 1984; *The Best Little Whorehouse in Texas* soundtrack, 1982; and with Vince Gill on *Something Special*, 1995)

Appalachian DNA

Dolly continues to make music her own way on Halos & Horns

"The difference in bluegrass and country, for those of you who don't know: it's like in bluegrass, you work twice as hard and get half the money, but you have twice the fun."

—DOLLY IN A SPEECH TO THE NATIONAL PRESS CLUB IN 2000

By the time Dolly recorded the third of her trio of bluegrass-flavored albums, she had established that her bluegrass impulse was not a passing fancy. On the contrary, it was more like a return to where she came from—what she liked to call her "Appalachian DNA." The first album, *The Grass Is Blue*, had been named Album of the Year by the International Bluegrass Music Association (IBMA) in 2000, an award that delighted and surprised Dolly. The award also closed a loop for a musician grounded in mountain music, who had ventured far and wide musically and come back full circle. As Dolly said, "It's not like I came in the back door with this music. I've been doing it on my front porch for years."

Halos & Horns maintained the same spirit as the previous two solo records, but bypassed their personnel of studio heavy-hitters. Instead, the album featured less well-known musicians, a number of whom performed regularly at Dollywood. Dolly produced the project herself and wrote twelve of its fourteen songs. The title cut was one such original,

a country waltz about the nature of human beings hovering somewhere between sinners and saints. Asked about it by a reporter in 2002, Dolly said, "I think that all people who were brought up in a fundamental church like I was are left with some sort of guilt when they stray a little bit. But I don't agree with it. What I say is I'm too good to be bad and too bad to be good—I'm sort of caught somewhere in the middle."

"Sugar Hill" is a sweet, guitar-strum-heavy reflection from a mature point of view on early memories of an enduring love. "These Old Bones" conveys the story of a soothsaying mountain woman, simultaneously feared and sought after by her neighboring mountain folk. Both songs would inspire episodes of her *Heartstrings* series on Netflix years later.

Two more songs from the album, "Not for Me" and "Dagger Through the Heart," portray shades of sorrow and heartbreak, while "What a Heartache" and "Shattered Image" each appeared before on previous

ABOVE: Dolly performs in the United Kingdom in 2002.

recordings. The first was on the soundtrack for the 1984 movie *Rhinestone* with Dolly and Sylvester Stallone, then appeared again on *Eagle When She Flies* (1991). The second debuted in 1976 on *All I Can Do*. Another song, "John Daniel," is a character song with a religious bent, painting a picture of a mysterious newcomer. "I'm Gone" is a departure song with a freight-train rhythm that Dolly harnesses to ebullient effect. Two songs were written in response to the tragedy of 9/11, "Hello God," which music writer Bill Friskics-Warren described as "an update of Mr. Dylan's 'With God on Our Side,'" and "Raven Dove."

While original material makes up most of *Halos & Horns*, the two cover songs on the album make clear Dolly's instinct for choosing songs from other genres that work well in a "blue mountain" setting. She reinterpreted Bread's 1971 easy listening hit "If," and then made a striking treatment of Led Zeppelin's "Stairway to Heaven."

Dolly had recorded rock songs before. Some, like REO Speedwagon's "Time for Me to Fly" and Billy Joel's "Travelin' Prayer," had been suggested by Dolly's husband Carl. But Carl had not thought "Stairway to Heaven" was a good idea, perhaps because he was a hard-core fan of the original. "He's been a 'Led Head' from day one and also loves bluegrass and big-band music," Dolly told *People*, noting that the song and the band were among Carl's favorites. Dolly, too, had come to love the tune over the years. "It was kind of like 'our song' because at romantic times or sweet times, we'd just be riding around in the car and if that would come on, Lord, he'd just knock us out of the car turning it up full blast."

In the end, the cover was a success. The *New York Times* review praised how it "transforms the song's vaguely spiritual musings into an admonition against placing one's faith in earthly treasures."

DEFIANTLY HERSELF

Rolling Stone writer Jancee Dunn summed up her impressions of Dolly on the back end of her three bluegrass albums that marked a new artistic era and the new century for Dolly: "The mountains are around her and within her, and what sustained her at age seven sustains her at fifty-seven—her family, her time with the Lord and the music. She may have adapted to the seismic shifts of the industry, but throughout she has stayed defiantly herself."

Shock and Awe

Dolly takes stock with Larry King and Oprah Winfrey

Larry King evidently sent a tape of him singing the Broadway tune "Hello, Dolly" to convince Dolly to come on his show. It worked. Her appearance was her first with Larry in nine years, but she would return multiple times in the coming years. During their conversation, Dolly volleyed Larry's abrupt, sometimes rapid-fire style of questions with her typical grace and good humor, regardless of whether their aim was personal ("Is the love life ok?") or business-minded ("How is Dollywood doing?").

Their conversation took place the night before she was to headline a musical July Fourth celebration at the Capitol Building in Washington, DC. Larry asked about rumors of plans to bring back the trio of stars for a follow-up movie to *9 to 5*, to which Dolly joked they needed to hurry, or the movie would be set in a nursing home. Dolly had recently performed in Atlanta to help Jane Fonda raise funds for her charity, the Georgia Campaign for Adolescent Power and Potential (GCAPP), whose focus at the time was on supporting and uplifting pregnant adolescents.

Larry brought up some recent news, including the 2003 tribute album *Just Because I'm a Woman* on Sugar Hill Records, where fourteen artists interpreted songs from Dolly's catalog, from Shania Twain covering "Coat of Many Colors" to Norah Jones doing "The Grass Is Blue." They talked about an upcoming album titled *For God and Country* that included patriotic songs, gospel standards, spirituals, and a few new songs of her own, with a tour planned that would put Dolly on the road for the first time in several years. Larry wanted to canvas her history with Porter Wagoner, whom Dolly had recently helped induct into the Country Music Hall of Fame in 2002, an occasion that included some touching moments of their performing together. Several years later, she would wipe tears from his eyes as she sang "I Will Always Love You" on the occasion of his fiftieth anniversary of being on the Opry, both aware he was dying of lung cancer at the time.

Dolly is a coveted guest on television talk shows for the sparkle and spontaneity she brings to the conversation. No matter the question, Dolly's answers seem thorough and thoughtful, prepared in a way that makes clear she gets asked about the same topics over and over again. At the same time, she conveys an openness to the unexpected, moments when she can insert levity and humor. As Larry put it during a 2009 interview, "One thing you can always count on, Dolly is never dull."

When Dolly spoke with Oprah Winfrey that same year, she was joined by Shania Twain and Melissa Etheridge, both contributors on the tribute album. Their conversation brought out generational dynamics highlighted by the album, but also shared experiences as they spoke about how it feels to perform in a club versus in a stadium of 150,000 people or more. Oprah had interviewed Dolly before and their rapport dates back at least to 1987, the same year Oprah actually sang a duet on Dolly's TV variety show. Dolly appeared as an Oprah guest that year, talking mostly about her weight loss. She returned in 1992 when the film *Straight Talk* was being released.

During the 2003 visit, Oprah turned the conversation toward plastic surgery. Dolly was unguarded on the subject. Gesturing toward Shania, seated next to her, Dolly joked, "I was already into plastic surgery when they were still sleeping on plastic sheets." In Oprah's probing style of interview, she wanted to dig deeper into the topic of her breast enhancements. Dolly took the questioning in stride. Looking down at her chest, she replied, "I call these my weapons of mass distraction—Shock and Awe."

In conversation with both Oprah and Larry, the topic turned to Dolly's work ethic. "I count my blessings more than I count my money," she told Larry, an attitude she credits to her upbringing. And while she has acknowledged having plenty of it, money is not what motivates her. She told him. "I really love the work, I love the creative end of it, I love seeing and making and helping things happen, and it really is a great thing. I know that I'm very fortunate but I don't take a bit of that for granted." The conversation with Oprah turned toward Dolly's experience with depression during the 1980s. In retrospect, she told Oprah, it was "one of the best things that ever happened to me, because it made me take inventory. I'd never slowed up. I've been working since I was ten years old."

> "I'm really a working girl. This is really a way of life for me and I just pray every day that I'll be guided in my life, and in my career. When I did get to see my dreams come true, I always joked and said, 'I have dreamed myself into a corner'—meaning that I have seen my dreams come true and now I have to be responsible for them. I feel blessed; what a wonderful problem to have, so to speak. I just [make sure I] know what's coming next, brace myself for it, and take care of business."
>
> **—DOLLY ON HOW SHE DOESN'T THINK OF HERSELF AS A STAR, DURING A DECEMBER 2020 INTERVIEW FOR MUSIC WEEK**

PHOTOGRAPHER/©ABC/GETTY IMAGES.

ABOVE: Oprah Winfrey visits *The Dolly Show* in 1987.

Helping Eagles Fly

Dolly receives an award from the
US Fish and Wildlife Service

The week around July 4, 2003, was especially busy for Dolly, and what she described on *Larry King Live* as an "all-American weekend." She was in Washington, DC, for her Independence Day performance at the Capitol, but she was also there to help open a new bald eagle refuge exhibit at the National Zoo.

During the opening ceremony on July 2, Dolly also received a Partnership Award from the US Fish and Wildlife Service. Dignitaries including National Zoo director Lucy Spelman and Secretary of the Interior Gale Norton were on hand, as well as Deputy Secretary Steve Griles, who presented the award.

The opening also featured a gift from Dollywood: a bonded pair of eagles, female Sam and male Tioga, from the raptor sanctuary housed at Dolly's famous theme park. Due to permanent wing injuries, the birds were "non-releasable," meaning they were unable to survive in the wild.

Both Sam and Tioga were rescue birds, found injured in the wild and rehabilitated through the work of the American Eagle Foundation (AEF), which was founded in 1985 and based at Dollywood since 1991. AEF founder and CEO Al Cecere began his conservation efforts in 1983, after seeing an image of two dozen bald eagles slain by poachers in the Dakotas. He began as a volunteer, but eventually left his work in the entertainment industry to create a nongovernment organization leading the recovery of these magnificent birds.

ABOVE: Dolly stands next to America the bald eagle in 2003.

Dolly's award acknowledged her contributions toward bald eagle conservation via partnership with the AEF. Over the thirteen years of AEF's existence, Dollywood had contributed several million dollars to the nonprofit to keep its education program and rehabilitation efforts going. Education programs include four "Wings of America" shows per day at the park, to introduce Dollywood visitors to various birds of prey, eagles included. Rehabilitation facilities include the Eagle Mountain Sanctuary, a 1.5 million cubic feet aviary that houses the world's largest group of non-releasable bald eagles.

The opening of the National Zoo's eagle exhibit was one of a year of events celebrating the National Wildlife Refuge System's one-hundredth anniversary. The system began in 1903 at the behest of Theodore Roosevelt, whose goal in creating it was to protect natural resources. The US Fish and Wildlife Service oversees 542 wildlife refuge areas, over 94 million acres available for hiking, fishing, and hunting, with at least one per state. In addition, the service oversees national fish hatcheries, fishing resource offices, and field stations that support local ecology.

Several years before the award, bald eagles were removed from the endangered species list, a testament to the success of wildlife rehabilitation efforts. Bald eagles were chosen to symbolize the United States of America partly because they are a species only found in North America. Indigenous communities had embraced the bald eagle as a symbol of their own long before it became America's national bird. During the ceremony, Dolly expressed pride over the partnership and her opportunity to "play a special role in dedicating the new eagle exhibit celebrating America's wildlife refuge system."

Dolly continued to be involved in efforts to raise awareness and appreciation for bald eagles both as national symbol and as important predators in the food chain. In April 2008, she participated in releasing a fourteen-week-old eaglet into the wild from the shore of Tennessee's Douglas Lake. The bird had fallen from its nest on Sanibel Island in Florida and been nurtured back to health by AEF. Before it took flight, Dolly named it Liberty.

Given the eagle's deep symbolism around US national culture, AEF founder and CEO Al Cecere proposed Dollywood with its emphasis on heritage as a natural partner for the preservation-focused nonprofit. If Dolly is the human star of the partnership, its feathered star is a bald eagle named Challenger (named in memory of the space shuttle disaster), who was non-releasable due to "human imprint" and became the first eagle ever trained to "free-fly" at large events, both indoors and out. One of his most famous early appearances was during the 1996 Olympics in Atlanta. After 9/11, Challenger began to appear regularly at football games, baseball games, and other major events, often during a performance of the national anthem. He also appeared on television regularly, including *Dateline NBC*, the *David Letterman Show*, and *Good Morning America*. While Dolly has said she never plans to retire, Challenger, after hundreds of demonstrations for audiences across the US, left the public eye in 2019 at the age of thirty.

It Becomes Something of a Habit

Dolly is honored in Washington, DC

"I've often said that I feel like I'm as old as yesterday, but as new as tomorrow."

—DOLLY DURING A 2018 INTERVIEW AT THE LIBRARY OF CONGRESS

At the start of the twenty-first century, Dolly found herself being called again and again to Washington, DC, to receive recognition from the nation's most prestigious institutions for celebrating and nurturing American culture. In 2004, she accepted the Living Legend Award from the chair of the Library of Congress. Dolly thanked everyone who played a part in "allowing all this to happen to a little Smoky Mountain girl. And thank you for allowing me to see my dreams come true and making me believe that I mean something to somebody."

The yearly ceremony celebrates people who make vast contributions to American culture, honoring artists and entertainers, filmmakers and activists, writers and sports figures, physicians and public servants. Dolly was chosen for the honor by curators and specialists at the Library of Congress. The award put her in company with other notable Americans, including fellow musicians Tony Bennett, Dave Brubeck, Johnny Cash, and Ray Charles. As part of the ceremony, Dolly taped a performance for broadcast in May on the Great American Country cable television channel.

The following year, Dolly was named one of ten National Medal of Arts recipients, an award given by the National Endowment for the Arts (NEA) and noted by journalist Sarah Smarsh as the pinnacle of national recognition "for contribution to creative fields." The NEA, founded in 1965, has several awards, including the Jazz Masters Fellowship, the National Heritage Fellowship, and the National Medal of Arts, which is "the highest award given to artists and arts patrons by the US government and presented by the President." The other nine honorees for 2005 were actor Robert Duvall, musician Wynton Marsalis, author Louis Auchincloss, orchestra director James DePreist, jazz saxophonist Paquito D'Rivera, film animator Ollie Johnston, choreographer Tina Ramirez, and arts advocate Leonard Garment. The Pennsylvania Academy of the Fine Arts was given an institutional award.

The National Medal of Arts is given in conjunction with the National Humanities Medal, both determined via nominations by advisory councils for the NEA

ABOVE: Dolly performs during the final night of her 2005 tour in Myrtle Beach, South Carolina.

and National Endowment for the Humanities (NEH), respectively. The day before the NEA honors, National Medals of Freedom are presented; Muhammad Ali was among the fourteen recipients in 2005. The ceremonies take place in the Oval Office, given by the President, with a formal dinner in the evening.

Dolly was unable to make it that year due to her schedule around a new album and work on *9 to 5: The Musical*. She became the first person to receive a Presidential Medal of Arts outside Washington, DC, when NEA chair Dana Gioia traveled to Chattanooga, Tennessee, in September 2008. The delayed bestowment took place at a meeting for the National Assembly of State Arts Agencies.

But Washington was not done with Dolly. The Woodrow Wilson International Center for Scholars of the Smithsonian Institution honored her in 2007 for "outstanding commitment to integrating politics, scholarship, and policy for the public good." In 2011, "Coat of Many Colors" was added to the National Recording Registry created by Congress to recognize the nation's most important sound recordings. By that time, the song had expanded in its significance from being a deeply personal anecdote to a song that, in Dolly's words, "addresses difference in people." "It's about acceptance," she said.

THE HIGHEST CIVILIAN HONOR

Not every time Dolly is offered an award does she accept. She was twice offered the Presidential Medal of Freedom between 2016 and 2020. She told the *Today Show* that the first time, "I couldn't accept it because my husband was ill." The second time, "I wouldn't travel because of the COVID." In an appearance on *The Late Show with Stephen Colbert*, former president Barack Obama said not awarding Dolly the honor while he was in office was a mistake. He had assumed she already had this nation's highest civilian honor.

"Travelin' Thru"

Dolly writes a song for "the little movie that could"

Duncan Tucker's short film *The Mountain King* had gained notice in festivals around the turn of the twenty-first century. But his new movie, *Transamerica*, was to be his first feature-length film, written and directed by him and completed on a shoestring budget.

Duncan needed the perfect song for the film's end credits. Dolly struck him as just the person to write it.

Her first response was that she didn't have the time. Dolly was on tour for *Those Were the Days*, an album of bluegrass-style interpretations of John Lennon's "Imagine," Joni Mitchell's "Both Sides Now," and other iconic tunes of the 1960s and '70s.

"Would you at least try?" Duncan asked.

She would at least do that.

Duncan shared all that he had hoped the song would convey, and sent her the film's rough cut. Dolly took it all in and, sure enough, one morning the song took shape. Duncan had told her "he wanted the song to be about redemption and about people's feelings." He told her "it should be a song you could sing in churches and you could sing in dancehalls." Once Dolly got the idea for it to have the feel of a gospel tune, she wrote it in a day. It worked. Dolly drew from a personal relationship with one of her longtime employees, whom she had never known was transgender. "And when I found out," Dolly said, "I discussed that whole thing with them, knowing how good they were and what they went through. It gave me a personal insight and inspiration to get in the song."

Dolly was in Detroit when she finished the song and called Duncan. By coincidence, he too was in town for some promotional screenings and so he dropped by the bus to hear it. The song was a perfect fit. She made him a demo recording right there. As Duncan effused to *CMT*, "She sings the hell out of it. She kept the arrangement really simple, so her voice can come out front and center, which is what I wanted. I think Dolly has such soul and such guts in her voice."

It was fortuitous that the song's arrangement was simple, because time was short. The completed film needed to be in California in approximately one week. Dolly was headed to Kentucky, so she invited Duncan to join her as she stopped off in Nashville to record it in a day. The end result, "Travelin' Thru," was nominated for both a Golden Globe and an Academy Award. Dolly performed the song at the Oscars, but it was ultimately beaten out by "Hard Out Here for a Pimp" from *Hustle and Flow*.

"Travelin' Thru" conveys a journey, a person searching to find home and human connection. Its themes speak to the human urge to seek love and

a sense of belonging. The song evokes Christian imagery in overt ways, referencing the crucifixion and resurrection as symbols for the universal experiences of suffering and renewal. It likewise evokes recurring gospel imagery of the "weary pilgrim" and folk music traditions with deep roots, including the song "Wayfaring Stranger." "Travelin' Thru" would be equally at home at a show-business awards show and in a Sunday-morning service.

These universal references take on specific dimensions related to *Transamerica*'s story of Bree, a transgender woman anticipating her upcoming gender-confirming surgery. She is detoured by an unexpected phone call from the seventeen-year-old son she never knew about. Bree, in a remarkable performance by Felicity Huffman, travels across the country to bail the errant youth out of jail, introducing herself only as a "church lady," and the two embark on a road trip back to California. Their secrets and struggles gradually come to light, including their relationship as parent and child, highlighting the movie's themes of shared humanity. The end result is, as Dolly described it to *New York Daily News* in 2005, "a beautiful movie."

Writer and English professor Emily Lordi suggests that Dolly's decision to write the song fit country music's tradition of giving voice to outsiders. Expressing perspectives from the mainstream society's periphery—people who might be described as wayfaring strangers—has long typified country music. Only beginning with Nixon and doubled down on by Reagan in the 1980s did country music become coopted by conservative political ideologues.

Dolly has been a target of hate mail and threats for her support of the LGBTQ+ community. When asked about such backlash, Dolly has responded, "I'm not God, I'm not the judge. I love people and I don't judge anybody, because I was judged—and still am—for the way I look. I might look cheap but I'd like to think I'm a quality person."

For Dolly it ultimately comes down to love and to living a life defined by love. It seems directly connected to her spirituality. She said, "Some people are blind or ignorant, and you can't be that prejudiced and hateful and go through this world and still be happy. One thing about this movie is that I think art can change minds. This is a very real, sincere treatment of people living in the wrong bodies. It's still just as odd, even for an accepting person like me, but I don't pass judgment. It's all right to be who you are."

> "I'm old enough and cranky enough now that if someone tried to tell me what to do, I'd tell them where to put it."
>
> **—DOLLY, IN A WIDELY QUOTED DOLLYISM AROUND THE TIME SHE WAS TURNING SIXTY (OR "SEXTY," AS SHE PUT IT TO A REPORTER)**

The Universal Experience of Loss

Dolly duets with Brad Paisley

lthough she spent decades recording critically acclaimed albums and stretching her musical talents into other creative fields, Dolly's duet with Brad Paisley was her first trip to the top of *Billboard*'s Hot 100 Country chart in almost a decade and a half. (Her most recent number one on the list had been "Rockin' Years" in 1991.) Their duet, "When I Get Where I'm Going," appeared on Brad's fourth album, *Time Well Wasted*. The song was written by George Teren and Rivers Rutherford, a personal expression of grief experienced by Rivers after the death of his grandfather. Brad was touched by the song due to the loss of his beloved aunt to cancer, and Dolly's own recent experience of losing a close friend also drew her to the song.

Brad's aunt had been a big fan of Dolly's, and Dolly's voice would bring an added dimension to the record. "Her voice is angelic and that takes it to a more spiritual realm instantly," Brad said of Dolly's voice, ". . . and my aunt loved her and thought she was great."

"When I Get Where I'm Going" was released as a single, and was nominated for Single of the Year, Vocal Event of the Year (which it won), and Video of the Year at the Country Music Association Awards. The

song is an expression of faith, picturing the afterlife as a simultaneous embrace of love and release from fear. In a quiet ballad with wistful strings, Brad paints an image of release following death with whimsical images like riding a raindrop and more down-to-earth longings like reunion with departed loved ones. Dolly joins him on the chorus with harmonies that complement Brad's soothing baritone. The song's bridge speaks of the pain, confusion, and toil of life, but returns to hope when speaking of an afterlife of light and "amazing grace." The song ends with prominent unresolved piano chords that signal a journey yet unfinished.

The video features Brad playing his guitar and singing in a Northern California forest. These musical scenes are interspersed with cuts to people holding images of presumably departed loved ones. Near the end, Dolly holds a photo of her Grandpa Jake at the piano. We also see Brad in old film reel footage with his grandfather, as well as him holding a photograph of his aunt. This moving montage includes other people, some well known and others not, all holding images of loved ones. The Olympic ice skater Scott Hamilton, for instance, holds a picture of his mother,

and John Carter Cash holds a photo of Johnny and June Carter Cash.

Writing a review for *the New York Times*, Bill Friskics-Warren summed up the song as "a statement of faith featuring a goose-bump-inducing vocal from Parton that's free of the cheap piousness that's alarmingly prevalent in country music today." Brad's three albums before had established him as a singer and songwriter with a sense of humor, as well as an appreciation for country music history. He typically included outtakes and cornball humor segments on his albums that harkened back to the "radio barn dance" variety shows epitomized by the *Grand Ole Opry*. These radio broadcasts were precursors to early country music television programs like the *Porter Wagoner Show* that first introduced Dolly to a national audience.

Brad is also a capable guitar picker, so his albums consistently feature at least one instrumental song and, like Dolly's, at least one gospel song. In the case of "When I Get Where I'm Going," his voice melded with Dolly's to set the song and the larger project apart. So moved was Dolly by the song, she wrote a letter to its writers to thank them for creating "one of the greatest songs that I have ever heard." She wrote, "I just lost a dear friend, and they played it at his funeral. It was his favorite song ever. But all of my living friends love it, too . . . I truly am as proud to have been a part of that [song] as anything I've ever done in my whole life."

ABOVE: Dolly and Brad Paisley during rehearsals for the 2001 Grammys.

Only a Dream

Dolly receives Kennedy Center Honors

"What's that saying? A peacock that sits on its feathers is just another turkey?
Well, I don't want to be another turkey."

—DOLLY, INTERVIEWED IN THE *KNOXVILLE NEWS SENTINEL*, SEPTEMBER 16, 2006

When Reba McEntire introduced Dolly as one of five recipients of the twenty-ninth annual Kennedy Center Honors, she kicked things off with a story. In 1977, Reba was backstage at the *Grand Ole Opry*, getting set to make her debut. She planned on singing two songs for this momentous occasion. Shortly before her entrance, a stage manager came and told her she would need to cut one song. "Dolly Parton has just walked in the back door," Reba recalled him saying, "and Dolly's gonna sing."

Reba recalled a resplendent Dolly in a black chiffon pantsuit adorned with sparkling butterflies, her hair "all airy and shiny, looked like cotton candy." Reba expressed gratitude for Dolly's influence, one that shaped not only her musical journey but also that of "every girl in country music for the last thirty years."

Reese Witherspoon took the stage next, talking about memories of wanting to be Dolly when she was growing up, and noting how Dolly never forgot where she came from. Carrie Underwood sang "Islands in the Stream," and halfway through was joined onstage by Kenny Rogers. Dolly smiled to see her old friend,

and began to mouth the words along with the song. Alison Krauss, Suzanne Cox, and Cheryl White performed "Jolene" as a harmony trio, and Alison remained onstage to sing harmony behind Shania Twain, who took on "Coat of Many Colors." Shania sat with guitar in hand, strumming while a pedal steel player laced her notes with color and texture. Vince Gill closed the set with the only song that could on so momentous an occasion: "I Will Always Love You."

Dolly sat beside her friend, fellow musician, and producer Steve Buckingham, who had also accompanied her to other ceremonious occasions in recent years, including inductions into the Country Music Hall of Fame in 1999 and the Songwriters Hall of Fame in 2001, and the Library of Congress Living Legend Award ceremony in 2004. They sat in the same row as then-President George W. Bush and First Lady Laura Bush, along with fellow honorees Smokey Robinson, Andrew Lloyd Webber, Zubin Mehta, and Steven Spielberg. At the end of the presentation, all the evening's performers returned to the stage to join the audience in a standing ovation. Dolly rose from her seat as well, applauded for the friends and fellow musicians who had honored her from the stage, and held up her award in appreciation.

The gala and show at the Kennedy Center are only part of the hoopla surrounding Kennedy Center Honors. Before the publicly aired event on December 26, there was a formal ceremony at the State Department, followed by a White House reception. Arts reporter Jacqueline Trescott spoke with Dolly for the *Washington Post* in between the awards announcement and the actual ceremony. Dolly told her, "You never know what you are going to do with your life. As you get older, you hope people remember you. You always welcome the awards. It makes you feel like your life is worthwhile. And for the elite to select you—I didn't have much of an education, only a dream."

She added a moment of reflection on the breadth of her fan base, one that has only continued to expand since this momentous occasion: "I am amazed. I see the old fans, with the blue hairs. And then I see the blue hairs with the spikes and piercing. They know I love them all."

ABOVE: Dolly with President George W. Bush and First Lady Laura Bush (center) and fellow Kennedy Center honorees (L to R) Smokey Robinson, Andrew Lloyd Webber, Steven Spielberg, and Zubin Mehta.

Dixie Fixin's

Dolly shares recipes from her life

"If I had to choose between a slice of chocolate cake with a foot-thick layer of frosting or a heaping bowl of potato salad, I'd dig into that salad without thinking twice."

—DOLLY EXPLAINING HER PREFERENCE FOR STARCHY FOODS, WHICH SHE ATTRIBUTES TO THE RARITY OF SUGAR IN THE HOUSE WHEN SHE WAS GROWING UP, IN *DOLLY'S DIXIE FIXIN'S*

On more than one occasion, Dolly has quipped, "I have always said my weakness is food, sex, and music . . . but not necessarily in that order." So it seemed only natural for her to publish a cookbook, which she titled *Dolly's Dixie Fixin's*. The cookbook collected recipes that open windows into different parts of Dolly's life as they share some of her favorite foods.

Dolly once told *Chicago Tribune* writer Bonnie Churchill, "Next to singing, cooking is one of my most fun things to do." It was a skill she learned early on in life. Dolly and older sister Willadeene often did the cooking in a household where they were the two oldest girls and their mother was often sick or tending to eight younger siblings. Dolly explained, "My mama, grandma, and auntie taught me, and by the time I was nine I was really good at cooking soul food. With our large family, it was a necessity to cook big and often."

In *Dolly's Dixie Fixin's*, Dolly shared that she still tended to cook in large batches, even when it was just her and Carl, or herself away from home. That way, she had quick meals to grab when her schedule was tight. Around the time she was putting the cookbook together, for example, she was also recording the album *Those Were the Days*, and she described in the book making soup for the crew. Cheese and Bacon Soup and Bodacious Bean Soup, recipes included in the book, were among these communal meals. She wrote, "I like to think it made a difference in the experience making that album—at least my fiddle player thought so!"

Dolly prefers to travel by bus with her band when she can, and they try to stop for picnics at mealtimes rather than at truck stops. Dolly told *Playboy* in 1978, "We have water fights, cake fights, food fights . . . like brats. It's like a family. When the day comes when I can't enjoy it or there's no fun doin' it, there's lots of things that I can find joy in, and I would." When unable to make food, Dolly and her crew know the stops along their travel routes to find comforting food on the road. One chapter in *Dolly's Dixie Fixin's* covers favorites from some of these diners and restaurants. As Dolly put it, "when you go from one place to

another by bus as much as I do, you've got to have your food treasures!"

Some recipes reveal the extent of the poverty her family experienced during her childhood. The very first recipe in the book is for "cornmeal mush," which is exactly what it sounds like: cornmeal and water with a little salt, thickened and served with syrup. A variation at the bottom of the page is good for leftovers, where slices of the firmed-up mush can be buttered, dipped in flour, and fried in a skillet. Another recipe includes the "left-handed gravy" her father would make, so named for no other reason than

that he was left-handed and everyone noticed the rare occasions he prepared food in the kitchen.

The chapter on holiday gatherings includes an anecdote about a New Year's Eve tradition in her family. Every year, her mother made a pot of black-eyed peas and her father would drop a silver dollar into the pot. The person who got the silver dollar was destined to have a good year. "After he passed away, I got Daddy's silver dollar," Dolly wrote. "I drop it into my black-eyed peas to this day. Evidently it's working, because I feel like the luckiest girl in the world."

ABOVE: Dolly performing at a pre-Oscars party in 2006.

Jack-of-All-Trades

Dolly hires Danny Nozell,
a manager for a new era of her career

Dolly had been without a manager for around a decade and was doing fine when she first hired Danny Nozell as a consultant in 2004. The next year, his role expanded to tour consultant, and gradually he was performing other duties. Danny told *Music Week* writer George Garner in 2020, that "from stage manager to tour manager to tour accountant and security; I was doing it all!"

Along the way, Danny felt a growing intuition. He saw a stellar performer who still actively wrote and recorded excellent music, who controlled both her own publishing catalog and her own recordings, and who maintained an incredible work ethic. Yet she had no website, and her tours were booking midsized venues and selling around two thousand seats per show. He saw a vital entertainer with potential beyond the "living legend" status that, despite its nice ring, often relegates aging stars to relative obscurity beyond awards show tributes.

Dolly's recent trio of bluegrass albums had earned critical accolades and new audiences, as well as reconfirming her rootedness in musical traditions associated with the Appalachian Mountains she

called home. Danny saw potential to reach newer and younger fans both in the US and abroad, particularly in Europe. He believed in Dolly's expansive gifts as a songwriter and performer across typical boundaries of genre and audiences. This belief, coupled with his knack for modern marketing strategies and timing, bore fruit. When Dolly hired Danny as her manager in 2006, it signaled a new phase of her career characterized by sold-out concerts in huge venues and a widespread awareness of Dolly as a cultural icon of international proportions.

His approach was based on careful research and analysis of her past touring schedules and album sales, after which Danny took on the role of promoter so that each date could be booked individually rather than as a package. Promotional efforts were similarly curated for each location. The result, as Danny shared with *Music Week*, was that "in 2006 I sold out the first ever complete tour for Dolly Parton with hard ticket dates." Since then, Dolly and Danny have continued to work together closely. Danny got her back into international touring by ordering custom buses that are "like a condo on wheels." Danny helps her

navigate the multidimensional aspects of her business ventures, which range from personal appearances to branding deals. When you spot Dolly moving in public, entering a concert hall, approaching the stage to receive an award, or boarding an airplane, it is most often Danny's arm she holds until she lands at her next spot.

Dolly has a knack for surrounding herself with highly effective people, and those people tend to respond with admiration and gratitude. Danny told *Music Week*, "Dolly gave me an opportunity that no one else would give me—Dolly Parton didn't need me even back then. When I came in, she needed me for nothing. She didn't need me financially. She didn't need to be a star. She was already a star."

ABOVE: *Dolly with her manager, Danny Nozell.*

Both a Star and an Idol

Dolly pops up on Dancing with the Stars *and* American Idol

In 2007, Dolly appeared on *Dancing with the Stars*, the popular US version of Britain's *Strictly Come Dancing*. She performed a version of "9 to 5" for the pro-dance segment, during which professional dancers Mark Ballas, Cheryl Burke, Derek Hough, and Julianne Hough performed without their amateur partners. Dolly wore a blousy buttoned shirt, opened wide over a red tank top with a plunging neckline. Black suspender straps attached to a shorts-length jumper with a black, laced-up, cinched closure around the corset region. Patterned black stockings covered her legs from shorts to heels. The band was outfitted in leather, and the song's arrangement added repetitions like "workin', workin', workin'" that fed the choreography.

On April 2, 2008, Dolly was the featured artist for *American Idol* during its seventh season. She performed a song from her 2008 album *Backwoods Barbie*, "Jesus & Gravity," written by Craig Wiseman. For this show, Dolly wore a white jumpsuit with gold trim and sparkles around a jacket with vest-like points along its bottom. Both her sleeves and a sort of train trailing behind her were made of sheer, chiffon material. After her performance, she thanked the Mighty Fine Band and the choir backing her up, and teased judge Simon Cowell about his visiting Dollywood.

In addition to performing, Dolly was on hand to coach *American Idol* contestants in a show dedicated solely to Dolly's songs. Dolly was gracious. She complimented David Cook's voice as he performed "Little Sparrow." Carly Smithson had the "kind of voice" the song "Here You Come Again" was written for, and her slow-tempo version offered a chance for her to show it. Dolly thought David Archuleta, who sang "Smoky Mountain Memories," had the "voice to become a great singer." Dolly also said she could see herself writing songs for Michael Johns, who sang a husky rock-ballad version of "It's All Wrong, but It's All Right."

In short, Dolly was everywhere those two years, promoting the first mainstream country album she had released in a decade. As she told the audience at the end of her *Dancing with the Stars* performance of the song "Better Get to Livin'," "And you better do it too. Get out there and do it." She was taking her own advice.

ABOVE: Dolly with *Dancing with the Stars* professional dancers Mark Ballas, Jr. (left) and Derek Hough.

Dolly Goes Broadway

The legend takes on a new challenge
with 9 to 5: The Musical

The show *9 to 5: The Musical* premiered in Los Angeles in September 2008, then opened on Broadway in April the next year. This was an era of what came to be dubbed "moviecals," musicals based on movies like *Shrek*, *Dirty Rotten Scoundrels*, or *Legally Blonde*. By the time of its opening, the project had been in the works for more than four years. It began as an idea for producer Robert Greenblatt, who told NPR that he began thinking of the "theme song, which is so identified with the movie. And I thought, if we could take that feeling and translate it to other moments in the show and other characters, then it might turn into a musical."

He brought in Patricia Resnick, who had written the original screenplay, to write the musical's book. The two of them then approached Dolly about writing the score. She was eager to take it on, even though she had never written a musical before. She assured them there would be no hard feelings if the end results didn't work. They could still use the theme song if they didn't like the new songs. In short, she was willing to "give it a whirl." Dolly retreated to her lakeside cabin and ended up writing somewhere around two dozen songs in about

two weeks. The first song she wrote was "Backwoods Barbie," which also became the title song for a 2008 album, a manifestation of the kind of flexibility an artist has when she controls her own creations.

Dolly described writing for Broadway as being freeing, in the sense of development. A normal country song aims at radio airplay and therefore conforms to certain constraints. The song must generally be under three minutes and have a typical structure (verses, chorus, and bridge). For Broadway, songs can be more expansive. "I had the luxury of just writing until I told the story of what I thought these characters would say," Dolly said, including the character of Doralee, the role Dolly played in the film. Writing from multiple perspectives of different characters all within the context of a coherent show was a challenge Dolly relished. "I was shocked myself that I drew from this well I didn't even know I had dug, you know," she told NPR. "I could have just as well dug a grave for myself, I think, as a well. And I write all sorts of songs, anyway."

On Broadway, Doralee was played by Megan Hilty, joining an original cast under the direction of Tony Award winner Joe Mantello. Stephanie J. Block played

Judy, Jane Fonda's role in the film, and Allison Janney played Violet, Lily Tomlin's part. Dabney Coleman's role as Mr. Hart was translated to Broadway by Marc Kudisch. Each of these characters required different types of songs, which Dolly delivered.

Ever the savvy businesswoman, Dolly had part ownership in the show. In 2009, her score was nominated for a Tony Award, bringing Dolly to reflect, "That's a long way to come from Locust Ridge, Tennessee, in Sevier County to Broadway." The song "Get Out and Stay Out," performed by Judy in the musical, won an audience favorite award on Broadway.com. But even before these official recognitions, Patricia Resnick knew the songs were going to work. When she first received Dolly's CD of potential songs, Patricia popped it into the car stereo. "My kids in two minutes were immediately singing half of them," she told NPR, "so I knew we were in good shape."

Bringing Dolly onto the project turned out felicitous in more than one way. During previews, one performance had to be halted for forty-five minutes due to a technical malfunction. Dolly was in the audience that night and took to the stage to sing "I Will Always Love You" and other songs until the problems were resolved and the show could go on. Asked if she might ever return to Broadway, her response was enthusiastic. She would love to do further projects, but they would be "born and raised out of my own gut and my own soul and my own head."

ABOVE: The opening night of *9 to 5: The Musical* in Los Angeles in 2008, featuring members of both the orignial film's and show's casts.

"Just think: I'm Doctor Dolly!"

*Dolly receives an honorary doctorate
from University of Tennessee*

Dolly walked onto the stage at the Thompson-Boling Arena in Knoxville, Tennessee, to accept her honorary doctorate from the University of Tennessee, belting out the tune "Rocky Top," written by Felice and Boudleaux Bryant and first recorded by the Osborne Brothers. Dolly had recorded the song in 2004 for her live album *Live and Well*, but long before then—since 1972, in fact, when it was first played during a football halftime show—it has been an adopted theme song for the University of Tennessee. It became the state of Tennessee's official song in 1982.

Technically speaking, Dolly already had an honorary doctorate, bestowed in 1990 by Carson-Newman University in Jefferson City, Tennessee. But it had been nearly two decades since that honor, and Dolly reflected early in her speech at the University of Tennessee that she was a bit nervous. She knew that on an occasion like this, people expected to hear sound life advice, something she made it a habit not to give.

"Information, yes, but advice, no," she said, adding that "what has worked for me might not work for you." She gave an example: "Well, take for instance what has worked for me: wigs, tight clothes, push-up bras, high

heel shoes—five-inch high heel shoes." Some of her advice, she joked, might lead the young men of the Class of 2009 "on a little different career path than you might have planned. And you girls better be careful, too."

She recalled her first case of nerves, when she sang onstage for the first time before an audience not made up of siblings or animals hanging around the front porch. The studio audience at the *Cas Walker Farm and Home Hour* had loved it, however, and wanted more. Unfortunately, Dolly realized that she only knew one song. So she simply sang it again. "Don't you worry, though," she added to the Knoxville crowd of college graduates and their families, "because I'm not going to repeat this speech. I don't care how much you like it."

Dolly structured her speech along the four parts of the mission statement for her Imagination Library: dream more, learn more, care more, and be more. She encouraged the graduates to dream, recounting high moments in her own life when she had ignored the discouragements of others to stay true to her vision. She added that she still had dreams to pursue and didn't anticipate slowing down. "I would certainly rather wear out than to rust out," she said, adding, "I just hope that I drop dead right onstage one of these days, doing exactly what I want to do."

She encouraged them to learn as much as they could. Dolly had never cared for school, but shared her gradual realization "that the more you learn about everything, the easier it is to do it." She said they should care in ways that come through in "how you prepare and how you keep your commitments." She added that caring for people meant "you won't judge them and then you will learn to appreciate the uniqueness in every single soul." Finally, she encouraged them to be more, reflecting that "people will remember us for who we were" more than for any achievements.

As Dolly wrapped up to go change into her cap and gown, which she would wear for the ceremonial part of the occasion, she said that she was off to "try to get my little hat on if I can do all that and then come back out here and get my honor." After the ceremony, "Dr. Dolly" joked, "When people say something about 'double D,' they will be thinking of something entirely different."

ABOVE: Dolly receives her honorary doctorate from the University of Tennessee in 2009.

Lessons Through Rhyme

Dolly writes her first children's book,

I Am a Rainbow

In 2009, Dolly turned her gift for rhyming to a new pursuit: She wrote a book about emotions for children. Rhyming had come easily to Dolly since she was little, and her knack for it surprised and impressed her mother enough that she saved the words for "Little Tiny Tasseltop," the song Dolly wrote as a young girl. The gift remained with Dolly, continuing to find new outlets via the seemingly unquenchable drive to create that characterizes her life.

Dolly's *I Am a Rainbow* ascribed colors to emotional states in straightforward ways. Illustrator Heather Sheffield depicted a diverse cast of boys and girls in scenes that sparked strong feelings. A boy frightened to swim showed his cowardly emotions in yellow; someone jealous of another's birthday present turned green. Happy children were rosy, and a girl with cotton candy was tickled pink. The arc of the book was that emotions were not always in our control; however, "how you act IS a different deal."

Dolly intended the book to open talk about feelings between parents, children, and educators, helping children identify and navigate their own emotions and behaviors. She told Larry King in 2009 that "it is about all the different moods of children. And it's very simple and very sweet and kind of done in rhyme and it's just talking about, you know, the colors and the moods of children." Dolly even wrote a song to go with the book, and sang it when she read her book as part of her

ABOVE: Dolly signs copies of *I Am a Rainbow* at the Country Music Hall of Fame in Nashville in 2009.

Goodnight With Dolly series of online storybooks early during the era of COVID-19 quarantine.

Dolly had talked about wanting to write a children's book for a long time. Work with the Imagination Library naturally pulled her in the direction of writing for children. Above all, it sounded fun. As Dolly remarked to *Time* magazine, "What a great way to go into your second childhood. Children have always responded to me because I have that cartoon-character look. I'm overexaggerated and my voice is small and my name is Dolly and I'm kind of like a Mother Goose character. So I think that it's going to be a fun thing."

Dolly has also been the subject of an illustrated children's book. Simply called *Dolly Parton*, the book was written by Maria Isabel Sanchez Vegara and illustrated by Daria Solak and covered the highlights of Dolly's career up to that point. It was published in 2019 by Frances Lincoln Children's Books as part of their Little People, Big Dreams series, which also includes books on Frida Kahlo, Marie Curie, Maya Angelou, Amelia Earhart, and Rosa Parks. You know you're a cultural icon when you're the subject of a children's book aimed at the youngest audiences.

In a handful of pages, the little book conveys the story of a woman possessed of tremendous talent, driven both to perform and to help others, open to wonderful ideas, and in possession of the resources to carry them out. At one point, the text mentions Dolly's love of wigs and makeup, and a butterfly—her signature symbol—lands on a container on a dressing table. "Maybe some people thought it was too much, but children loved her look and she did, too," it reads. "After 50 years onstage, little Dolly has become the most respected country performer of all time."

DOLLY THINKS YOU CAN

Within a decade of her children's book, Dolly recorded a children's album called *I Believe In You* in 2017. Its title song referred to her favorite children's book, *The Little Engine That Could*, first published in 1930 by Watty Piper. *The Little Engine That Could* is the first book that children enrolled in her Imagination Library program receive. To write *I Believe In You*, Dolly holed up in one of the treehouses or playhouses she kept on her properties for all the children in her life, to take herself back to her own childhood and sense of childlike wonder.

Food Fight

*Dolly returns to the big screen, joining
Queen Latifah in* Joyful Noise

The image of Queen Latifah holding Dolly Parton in a headlock really sticks with a person. It happens at the end of the "food fight" sequence in the 2012 film *Joyful Noise*. Queen Latifah's character, Vi Rose Hart, threatens to tear the wig off the head of Dolly's character, G. G. Sparrow. The characters are positioned as rivals at the start of the story, about a small-town church choir with aspirations to compete at the national level gospel competition. The choir director and G.G.'s spouse, played by Kris Kristofferson, passes away during rehearsal, and G.G. is passed over for the vacant role in favor of the traditionalist Vi Rose. Tensions build, not only about the choir but also regarding the budding romance between G.G.'s grandson and Vi Rose's daughter. That leads to the food fight at a local diner, with Dolly pitching hard dinner rolls at Queen Latifah, who uses a metal serving tray as a shield.

This food fight scene, along with the film's overall verve, are among reasons why the media

critic Rebecca Nicholson wrote a *Guardian* piece titled, "Hear me out: why *Joyful Noise* isn't a bad movie," in June 2021. The piece was part of a series devoted to defending "maligned films," and she enumerated what made this one worth the watch, despite glaring imperfections and some odd, quirky choices by director Todd Graff.

For Dolly's part, she agreed to do *Joyful Noise* because she liked the theme of people facing hard times and pushing through with resilience and faith. Dolly wrote twelve songs for the project, three of which appear in the movie. By this time in her career, Dolly occupied a distinct space in American culture where her public persona and the characters she played on screen were blurry and fluid. Thus, some of the words Vi Rose aims at G.G. in the restaurant scene feel pulled right from snarky comments aimed at Dolly. Vi Rose mocks G.G.'s apparent plastic surgery and her need to be loved by everyone. You can easily imagine Dolly hurling G.G.'s response at any of her real-life critics: "Who gives a rat's ass if I've had a few little nips and tucks. God didn't make plastic surgeons so they could starve."

In 2012, Dolly did an interview with *Huffington Post* entertainment editor Caroline Frost, anticipating the film's UK release. She said that the three days of filming that scene left her feeling a bit sore. "Everybody always likes to talk about my plastic surgery, but the writer was being a little sensitive about that," Dolly explained. "I told him, 'Go for it, I don't care what you say about me, as long as you give me some back.'" Frost writes, "On screen, as in life, Dolly isn't down for long."

ABOVE: Dolly and Queen Latifah in *Joyful Noise* (2012).

STILL ROCKIN'

2014 AND ONWARD

"There's so much darkness in the world.
I just hope that I can be a force for good and a light for others."
—DOLLY, IN *SONGTELLER*

OPPOSITE: Dolly performs during the 37th Annual Rock and Roll Hall of Fame Induction Ceremony in 2022.

She Loves Crazy
Dolly releases Blue Smoke
and plans a global tour to promote it

When Dolly launched a tour around the album *Blue Smoke*, it was on a larger scale than past tours, including dates (as well as custom buses) in Australia and Europe. Her manager, Danny Nozell, brought in a booking agent named Neil Warnock, whom he knew from previous work with the heavy metal band Slipknot.

Neil was now with the Agency Group, and he joined to help make plans for sell-out crowds in arena-sized venues like the O2 in London, which holds twenty thousand people. Neil flew to Nashville for a strategy meeting and was surprised to learn it was being held in Dolly's kitchen, where Dolly made him a cup of tea. There at her table, Warnock presented his vision for the tour. Recounting the moment to a *Music Week* reporter, he explained, "She basically said, 'Are you crazy?' I said, 'Yeah, are you?' Thankfully, she said yes, absolutely, she loves crazy, so we were off."

Blue Smoke opens with the title cut, an upbeat "heartbreak train" song with choo-choo rhythm, steel guitar evoking a train's whistle, and references to the "clickety-clack" of a train called *Blue Smoke*. The rest of the album mixes tempos and moods, originals and

covers and old ballads, duets and solos. Dolly described it as an album with "mountain music flavor." In a similar arrangement to the 2011 album *Better Day*, the songs were recorded on her own label, Dolly Records, and licensed to Sony for distribution.

"Unlikely Angel" is a slow-tempo song about finding love at a time when love seems impossible. It had originally been composed for the 1990s television movie of the same name, starring Roddy McDowell and Dolly as angels. The song had never appeared on an album until this one.

Dolly's cover of Bob Dylan's 1963 "Don't Think Twice, It's All Right" makes it seem destined for a "country-bluegrassy" treatment, to quote Dolly's description, all along. A standout cover on the album is her take on Bon Jovi's 1988 rock anthem "Lay Your Hands on Me," which keeps the song's rock feel but adds new lyrics to transform it into a gospel song. Dolly loved the song the first time she heard it and thought its title chorus fit the spirit of Pentecostal-style worship she grew up enjoying. Jon Bon Jovi and guitarist Richie Sambora gave her their thumbs up to reenvision the song and appreciated the transformation enough that

Sambora has more than once joined Dolly onstage to sing it.

Dolly and Kenny Rogers perform "You Can't Make Old Friends," a duet that seems written for their longtime camaraderie. Willie Nelson joins her for "From Here to the Moon and Back," a song Dolly once told a reporter was inspired by Carl. Dolly had performed the song with Kris Kristofferson during the 2012 movie *Joyful Noise*. The murder/love ballad "Banks of the Ohio" and a song called "If I Had Wings" draw on what Dolly called her "old world mountain voice" in the album's liner notes.

Two songs with single-word titles stand out on the release. Dolly wrote "Home" with producer Kent Wells, and she wrote the album's final song, "Try," for the Imagination Library. In the coffee table book based on her lyrics, *Songteller*, Dolly wrote that she thinks of "Try" as "my song."

Blue Smoke was first released in Australia to coincide with the early portions of the tour there. After a few dates in Arizona and other western US states, Dolly traveled to Australia. While there, she helped launch the Australian wing of the Imagination Library, which basically operates the same way as its US precedent. Australia became the fourth country and third continent to include communities joining the literacy program. Dolly returned home for more US dates, beginning in Oklahoma and then the Midwest, before a longer stint in Europe, including a sold-out show at the O2 and the climax of the European leg of the tour at the historical Glastonbury Festival.

ABOVE: Posters for Dolly's Blue Smoke World Tour.

Glastonbury Festival

Headliner Dolly wows the crowd at Worthy Farm

Several months after her festival appearance, Dolly confessed to freelance writer Deborah Evans Price that she had felt uncharacteristic nerves while waiting to take the stage at the Glastonbury Festival, the UK's biggest music celebration, in late June. "I thought it was more for a rock crowd, and I just hoped that I would fit in. I was standing backstage all nervous and thinking, 'Oh, I hope they like me. I hope that everybody's right that this is a good thing to do.' And then I heard them say my name, 'Dolly! Dolly! Dolly!' and I thought, 'I guess they do know who I am.'"

When Dolly walked onto the Pyramid stage, the event's main stage, those nerves fell away. She wore a sparkling white pantsuit, which she had joked with British reporters would go well with the mud that typifies the event. She told a *Sun* reporter, "I grew up in mud. I was on the farm and had to trudge through the mud to feed the animals, so I'm OK with that." The rain that had drenched crowds the day before had cleared away by her Sunday afternoon slot, a time typically reserved for "legends." Dolly found herself at ease in front of the largest crowd ever to gather at Glastonbury in its then nearly fifty-year history. Memorable moments that afternoon included a sing-along to "9 to 5," and Dolly's production of a small rhinestone-

studded, custom-made saxophone to play "Yakety Sax," the tune made famous as the theme song for the classic British TV program *The Benny Hill Show*. Dolly was also joined onstage by Richie Sambora, guitarist for Bon Jovi, and they performed "Lay Your Hands on Me," a song Dolly introduced as "just a conversation with the Lord."

The Glastonbury Festival of Contemporary Performing Arts began in 1970 with around 1,500 attendees paying an admission fee of £1 each. Visitors to the 900-acre site of Worthy Farm also received free milk. The event was started by Michael Eavis who, now with his daughter Emily, has kept it going and growing ever since. The festival today receives television coverage on three different BBC stations. In 2014, tickets cost £210 and organizers anticipated up to 200,000 fans. The first 120,000 of those tickets sold out in a record one hour and twenty-seven minutes.

The same year Dolly performed, the band Arcade Fire closed out the first night, Metallica headlined on Saturday, Jack White and Elbow were scheduled for the main stage, and Robert Plant also performed. Other Sunday performers included British acts Ellie Goulding, Massive Attack, and Kasabian. According to the *Birmingham Mail*, Dolly's performance "attracted the biggest crowd of the festival."

This performance marked the end of the tour, her first on the scale her manager Danny Nozell had envisioned and worked toward since taking on the job in 2006. An international publicist, Steve Cuest, recalled traveling to the US to meet with Dolly and her team in anticipation of the tour. "We did some interviews and Dolly had laid out two tables: one with delicious Southern food and one with scones and cream, PG Tips and what have you, to welcome the Brits. I knew then that this was the start of a great relationship."

Journalist Sarah Smarsh, in her book *She Come By It Natural*, frames this specific performance as a "tipping point" in terms of Dolly's rise to icon-level fame: "When she finally took the leap in 2014 as a Glastonbury headliner, not even Parton understood what was about to happen: An estimated 180,000 people gathered to see her—the biggest crowd in festival history, surpassing numbers for a Rolling Stones performance. Another 2.6 million watched live on the BBC, the network's largest-ever audience for its festival coverage."

Once the festival ended and cleanup began, crews discovered an abandoned dog, a white lurcher, in one of the five thousand tents left behind on the grounds. They nicknamed it Dolly and took it to a local animal shelter. Dolly offered to adopt the dog and take it back to Tennessee if no one came forward to claim it. Dolly the dog was reunited with its owner a few days later.

ABOVE: Dolly performs on the Pyramid stage at the 2014 Glastonbury Festival.

Dream More

Dolly places a song in a time capsule at the DreamMore Resort at Dollywood, to be opened in 2045

In 2015, the opening of Dolly's DreamMore Resort at Dollywood was marked with the creation of a time capsule containing a song Dolly wrote but did not share. "I have written a song that nobody's going to hear until I'm ninety-nine years old," she told Kelly Clarkson on her talk show seven years later, in 2022. "And I might be there, I might not be." In *Songteller*, Dolly likened the burial of the song to burying one of her kids, or putting the song on ice. The capsule will be unearthed in 2045, the resort's thirtieth anniversary.

The song is buried in a vessel built of chestnut wood by Dolly's Uncle Bill, the same uncle so instrumental in getting Dolly started in the music business. Bill spent the last decades before his passing in conservation efforts for the American chestnut, a tree important to the region, both for wildlife and for people. The impressive tree, native to the eastern United States, was nearly wiped out by blight in the early 1900s due to the import of chestnut trees from the Asian continent. The imported trees carried a fungus to which the native trees were vulnerable, and billions of trees were lost as a result. Efforts in conservation and scientific communities to develop a resistant variety are ongoing. Uncle Bill and his wife Sandy were deeply involved in supporting those efforts.

When the digging crew arrives in 2045 and unlatches the box, they will find three versions of the song: sheet music, cassette tape, and CD. A CD player and a cassette player are also buried, in case those are as hard to come by at that point as an eight-track player is today. It bothers Dolly to think that the song might not survive its burial, if any of the materials should disintegrate, but only time will tell. Dolly also told Kelly that the fact that no one will hear the song for that long is driving her crazy. "I wanna go dig that up so bad," she said. "And it's a really good song!"

In summer 2022, the American Chestnut Foundation presented the Chestnut Champion Award along with a small seedling to Dolly on behalf of her late Uncle Bill. The award is a large, framed image of chestnut tree trunks, surrounded by a handmade wooden frame, made of chestnut, using ebony guitar pins and a guitar string for hanging in honor of Uncle Bill's life as a musician. As for the seedling, it will be interesting to see how big it has gotten by 2045.

ABOVE: A fountain at Dollywood's DreamMore resort.

Smoky Mountains Rise

Dolly hosts a telethon to raise money
for her beloved home

On December 13, 2016, Dolly hosted a three-hour event called Smoky Mountains Rise: A Benefit for the My People Fund. The Fund was established to support relief efforts for more than 1,300 families who had lost their homes due to the devastating Sevier County wildfires earlier that year. The wildfires caused fourteen deaths and destroyed more than 2,400 buildings, resulting in over $500 million in damage. Timing played a factor in the extent of the destruction, as the flames were fed by winds sometimes gusting up to ninety miles per hour.

Dolly began the telethon seated on a stool, a mountain dulcimer across her lap. In blue jeans and a white blouse with a light blue sequined vest on top, she strummed chords on the dulcimer to accompany a slow intro. The bass kicked in, along with gentle shaking percussion and light banjo picking for the mid-tempo, intimate performance of "My Mountains, My Home," a song she had performed in 2009 at the seventy-fifth anniversary of the Great Smoky Mountain National Park.

The next hour, she performed "Smoky Mountain Memories," this time standing. Quiet

piano accompanied the song, which she began by playing the wistful melody on a vertical wooden flute, an instrument like a recorder. More than twenty country music performers showed up to sing, too, including Chris Stapleton, Don McLean, Chris Young, Alison Krauss, and the duo Big and Rich. Kenny Rogers performed "Islands in the Stream" with Dolly in a casual performance also marked by good humor. "Is this getting higher," Dolly asked, "or are we just getting older?" Cyndi Lauper performed "Time After Time" with a dulcimer and Reba McEntire sang "O Come All Ye Faithful."

The telethon included live and pre-taped performances, as well as large donations from celebrities and small donations from people across the United States. Donations came in from performers on hand but also those afar, including Paul Simon and Kenny Chesney. The Academy of Country Music and the Country Music Association contributed, as did Taylor Swift and Dierks Bentley, who each donated $100,000.

Before the telethon began, Dolly appeared on television to announce it. "Those of us who

are lucky enough to call the mountains of East Tennessee home, we think of ourselves as mountain tough," she said. "You know, but sometimes we need to admit that we need a little help. And we're also smart enough to know who our true friends are when we run into trouble." Half a million dollars came in before the telethon began. The day after the telethon, the *Tennessean* reported that nearly $9 million had been raised, and donations were still coming in. *Billboard* magazine would later report more than $13 million raised.

The original goal of the My People Fund was to provide $1,000 per month for six months to each family. Nine hundred families signed up, and each received an additional $5,000 at the end of six months. Journalist Sarah Smarsh characterized the program as remarkably "low on red tape." Its

only requirement was proof of address. In 2022, *Billboard* reported that "the fund also donated around $8.9 million to those in need. The initiative still helps residents pay for rent and utilities, plus food and mental health resources."

Country music legend Loretta Lynn had been among the friends who assisted with fundraising efforts in 2016. When floods destroyed areas of Loretta's home territory in Middle Tennessee in October 2021, Dolly returned the kindness, helping raise $700,000 in relief funds for residents who had lost their homes and livelihoods. Dolly said in a statement, "This was just one small way I could help Loretta's people for all they did to help my people. I hope that this money can be put to good use to help the people of Middle Tennessee with what they need during their recovery."

ABOVE: Dolly performs during the 2016 Medallion Ceremony at the Country Music Hall of Fame.

Golden

Dolly celebrates her fiftieth wedding anniversary with Carl and marks the occasion with an album of love songs

"Sometimes we'll stay over at a Days Inn where we can just pull up and sneak me in. We don't care, as long as the bed's clean and there's a bathroom. That's how we live."

—DOLLY TALKING ABOUT HER MARRIAGE IN PARADE IN 2015

On May 30, 2016, Dolly and her husband Carl Dean renewed their wedding vows to celebrate their golden anniversary. The ceremony took place in a small chapel on their property, with a modest gathering of close family and friends and a photographer on hand to capture the special event. Dolly wore a beautiful gown and, as she told Deborah Price Evans *for Rolling Stone*, she "dressed that husband of mine up. He looked like a handsome dude out of Hollywood."

The occasion also inspired an album of love songs titled *Pure & Simple*, produced by Dolly and released on her own Dolly Records label in partnership with Sony Music Nashville. The album explored different facets of love, including one about new love titled "I'm Sixteen," a cheating song titled "Can't Be That Wrong," and one about friends with benefits titled "Outside Your Door."

Three songs were specifically about her relationship with Carl. Two of them, "Say Forever You'll Be Mine" and "Tomorrow Is Forever," she

wrote early in her career and first recorded during the 1970s. The third, "Forever Love," was new, and specifically for the renewal of their vows. As she told Price, "I purposely tried to write a wedding song and I thought it would be a good wedding song for anybody's wedding." The song opens with strings, and then the lyrics describe the singular feeling of true love, depicting the beloved as both the author and the "poetry, story, and song" of their shared life. Guitar arpeggios bring in a light, soaring chorus melody, with tender words about the joy, laughter, and "storybook feelings" of this "forever love."

Over the years Dolly and Carl have made it a habit to revisit some of the significant sites related to their lasting romance. The Wishy Washy Laundromat where they first met no longer stands, but as Dolly told Canadian reporter Richard Ouzounian in 2006, "It's long gone now, but they built a little city park where it used to be, and sometimes Carl and me would pull in with our RV and sit in the park and eat some fast food, and I think that my life has been so sweet."

They also return regularly, if stealthily, to the small Georgia town of Ringgold, where they married with only Dolly's mother, the pastor Don Duvall, and his wife in attendance. They had chosen the town because "we knew that was where you could get your license and get married the same day." They married on a Monday and headed straight back to Nashville for work the next day. Dolly once told a Chattanooga television news station that she and Carl return every few years to Ringgold, find an out-of-the-way spot, and enjoy a picnic. "They never know we're there," she added.

Asked her secret for a long marriage, Dolly said it was the same that's "true of all relationships—no matter what they are—you have to respect each other. We make each other laugh." She often describes herself and Carl as opposites, which is part of "what makes it fun." They also clearly enjoy one another's company, and life's simple pleasures. "I love hanging out with my husband, riding around in our little RV," she said. "Even when I get off the road after traveling thousands of miles, I'll say, 'Get the camper; let's go somewhere.' He'll say, 'Are you kidding? Ain't you tired of riding?' 'No, I'm a gypsy. I want to do that.' My life is fairly simple when I'm out of the limelight."

ABOVE: Dolly accepts the Tex Ritter Award at the 51st Academy of Country Music Awards on April 3, 2016, in Las Vegas.

Rainbowland

Dolly creates and collaborates with a younger generation

Dolly had told Larry King in 2016 that she was working on a song with her goddaughter Miley Cyrus. The next year, that collaboration became part of Miley's album *Younger Now*. Some saw the album as a departure from Miley's extended post-adolescence, a hard break from her Disney Channel image that had included a series of "wild child" displays seemingly intent on shock. Dolly defended her goddaughter during that phase of her life to the *London Evening Standard* in 2013, saying, "It's not easy being young. It's hard to know what to do. You've almost got to sacrifice your damn soul just to get anything done."

Dolly and Miley had sung together before, including memorable performances of "Jolene" that circulated on the Internet, but this was the first time they created a song together from scratch. Since both kept busy schedules, they wrote over the phone and sent tapes back and forth, layering harmonies and adding ideas for lyrics. The end result, "Rainbowland," is joyful, and sends a message the world needs, Dolly told *Rolling Stone*: "If we could just do a little better, try a little harder, try to get along a little better, we could live in Rainbowland. If nothing else, if we tried a little harder at least we'd be a little more colorful than it is right now, a little brighter, a little shinier out there."

One *New York Times* write-up dubbed the song a "pro-gay anthem." By 2022, when writer Amie Windsor posted a piece for the *Sonoma County Gazette* in honor of Pride month titled "Dear Readers: Love is Love," she, too, referenced the song, including a call for action in the name of love: "It's the time when we need to truly focus on the fact that we are living in a rainbowland (Thank you, Miley Cyrus)."

"Rainbowland" was not Dolly's sole 2017 collaboration with a younger artist. She also sang with Kesha, for the other artist's new album *Rainbow*. Like the reaction to Miley's release, Kesha's album was framed critically as an artistic turn toward her Nashville roots. Dolly joined Kesha on a rendition of "Old Flames Can't Hold a Candle to You," a song first recorded with success in 1978 by Joe Sun. Dolly herself had included a successful version on her 1980 album *Dolly, Dolly, Dolly*. The 2017 recording brought an added layer of meaning, since "Old Flames Can't Hold a Candle to You" had been written by Kesha's mother, songwriter Pebe Sebert. Dolly told *Rolling Stone* that the song had always been among her favorites, and recalled how she jumped at Kesha's invitation to recut the song with her. "I said, 'Why did you choose to do that song? That's an unusual choice for you.' She said, 'Well, because my mother wrote it.'"

WE ARE WHO WE ARE

In September 2016, Larry King asked Dolly her position on LGBTQ+ rights. Dolly did not equivocate in her answer. "I do not believe that we should criticize and judge other people. I think we should be accepting and loving," she said. "We are all God's children. We are who we are and we should be allowed to be who we are."

Larry asked about reactions she gets from certain faith-based communities who disagree with her point of view. Dolly drew on her own deep-rooted formation in the central Christian dictate to love one's neighbor. "If you're the fine Christian that you think you are, why are you judging people?" she said. "That's God's job." Dolly took the lessons she learned from scripture about not judging others to heart, adding, "I've got too much to do on my own to try to do God's work too."

ABOVE: Dolly and Miley perform at the 2019 Grammys.

Another Girl in the Movies

New songs and new interpretations for Dumplin'

In May 2018, *Billboard* announced an upcoming speaking engagement at a Nashville music business conference featuring Dolly and producer Linda Perry. The topic was their recent collaboration to make a song together. Dolly had agreed to work with Linda to write a song for the soundtrack for the upcoming movie *Dumplin'*. The two hit it off so well in the Nashville studio where they holed up together that they ended up with not one but six new tunes.

Based on Julie Murphy's 2015 novel by the same name, *Dumplin'* follows teenager Willowdean "Will" Dickson as she fights for the acceptance of her former beauty pageant mother and her small Texas town. Dolly's music plays an integral role in Will's journey beyond self-doubt to embrace her own value. Her recently departed Aunt Lucy instilled in her this deep love for Dolly, a woman that both Will and Lucy saw as confident and unshakable. So it made sense to bring the legend herself onto the project. With her music so central to the plot, the movie couldn't be made without Dolly's thumbs up. Thankfully, when the filmmakers approached Dolly's team, they learned she was already familiar

with the story. Dolly had a copy of *Dumplin'* on her shelf, had read it, and thought the story was cute.

As Linda put it in the documentary *Dolly & Friends*, which covered the process of writing and recording those songs, "I think we both just come from not sitting down and thinking about writing. We just are sitting and feeling our way through it." Linda and Dolly went back and forth with director Anne Fletcher and actor/producer Jennifer Aniston, and every time the filmmakers heard a new song, their response was yes, they could fit it into the film. Dolly told *The Hollywood Reporter* that the end result came from "two very strong women that love to write and love to create things."

Linda is arguably best known as founder and lead singer for the band 4 Non Blondes. Since the band's run between 1989 and 1994, she has built a career as a songwriter, with hits for pop singers Christina Aguilera and Pink, and as a sound producer. For the *Dumplin'* soundtrack, she and Dolly both created new material and reimagined old songs. For instance, Linda envisioned a fresh take on a perennial Dolly hit. "I called my string guy and, I'm like, I need you to do an arrangement—like 'Eleanor Rigby'—but to 'Jolene,'" she explained. The

result appeared on the movie soundtrack, a slow, floating, and ethereal take on the original.

Their whole artistic partnership worked, despite their strikingly different backgrounds. The way Linda described it, "We are bringing both of our worlds into this project . . . There's that friction of her style versus my style—instead of battling, we're coming together." For Dolly's part,

"I welcomed her input. It kind of put me in a new place. And she welcomed mine, 'cause it put her in another place."

The place they created together made room enough for some monumental studio pairings. Dolly recorded duets with Sia ("Here I Am") and Elle King ("Holdin' on to You"), and Mavis Staples joined her on the new song "Why," about love and

---

ABOVE: Dolly performs onstage with Linda Perry at a luncheon for *Dumplin'.*

---

acceptance, which Dolly said she wrote "with her in mind." In the documentary, Mavis reflected that "the message in the song is just what I've been singing for years. And so it's just right on time for me, and right on time for today." The project's most straight-ahead country song—"If We Don't"—includes Alison Krauss on fiddle and Rhonda Vincent on mandolin, their voices a beautiful triple blend with Dolly's. Other memorable pairings include Dolly covers featuring Miranda Lambert ("Dumb Blonde") and Macy Gray ("Two Doors Down").

Of the original songs, "Girl in the Movies" received the most critical attention, with both Golden Globe and Grammy nominations. It was also one of Dolly's favorites. Its quiet, contemplative opening, dominated by the sound of her guitar, evokes the popcorn smells, sweet candy tastes, and fuzzy, velvety feel of movie theater cushions, drawing the listeners in through their senses. It's the stuff of her most enduring songs. "With Dolly, you get story," Linda said, describing Dolly's "old school" approach to songwriting. And the unfolding story, as Dolly describes it, is "about a girl that spends her life looking at other people." But then the girl decides to change that, and the song builds that sense of determination in its empowering, anthemic chorus about *being* "the girl in the movie." The song parallels the film's emotional arc for Will, as she moves from grief and anger into acceptance, confidence, and her very own happy ending. That journey is made all the more satisfying by Dolly's contributions.

UP FOR THREE

Dolly's wicked sense of humor was on display during a guest appearance on *The Tonight Show Starring Jimmy Fallon* on December 1, 2018, in anticipation of the release of *Dumplin'*. She joked that her husband Carl was more excited that she was doing a movie with Jennifer Aniston than about her own songwriting for its soundtrack. "See, I think he kind of fantasizes, like, a threesome with us," she laughed. In response, Jimmy did a little comedic shudder and yelled at the camera, "Carl, go to bed!" As the audience laughter quieted, Dolly added, "I mean, he can't even get it out to pee, much less get it up for three." Jimmy fell sideways from his chair, hitting the floor, and Dolly added, "He's going to kill me for saying that."

Votes for Women

Dolly sings "A Woman's Right," in case anyone wasn't following

In 2018, Dolly contributed to WNYC Studios' collaborative recording project *27: The Most Perfect Album*. An eclectic mix of artists was tasked with writing songs, one for each of the twenty-seven amendments to the Constitution. Artists ranged from They Might Be Giants to Kash Doll, Aisha Burns to Huey Supreme. For the Nineteenth Amendment—the one giving women the legal right to vote—they enlisted Dolly.

Dolly's song, which was accompanied by a beautifully animated video, is a short history lesson about the Nineteenth Amendment delivered in the simultaneously entertaining, uplifting, and empowering way that only Dolly can do. Both video and song begin with sounds of women's voices chanting "We Want the Vote," evoking decades of action related to the suffrage movement leading up to the amendment's historic passage.

A male voice presents the facts: the Nineteenth Amendment's ratification on August 18, 1920, and its function to recognize women's right to vote. Then Dolly begins talking, noting 1840 as the beginning of women's fight to vote and

the foundation of the National Woman Suffrage Association (NWSA), led by Susan B. Anthony, and the American Woman Suffrage Association, led by Lucy Stone. (The two organizations merged in 1890.) "But"—Dolly pauses for effect—"women have been fighting for their rights since the very beginning of time."

The *Washington Post* quoted Dolly in a statement at the time of the song's release as saying, "Being lucky enough to be a successful woman in business, I wanted to exercise my right to write about the Nineteenth Amendment to praise and uplift women."

A few years before, Dolly had appeared on *Larry King Live*, where Larry read her a viewer question: Did Dolly consider herself a feminist? "I'm very feminine and I'm all for women," Dolly replied, walking the same line she usually walked when faced with the question. As she told Jad Abumrad in the first episode of the podcast deep dive into her cultural significance *Dolly Parton's America*, "Everybody goes to extremes sometimes. I do not like extreme things. I do believe in making a point and making it well. I don't believe in crucifying a whole group just because a few people have made mistakes. To me when you say just the word feminist is like 'I hate all men.'"

She elaborated during the conversation with Larry King. "I just try to raise the women up and do what I can. I'm very proud to be a woman. I'm very proud of all the accomplishments that women do." She added that her work around *9 to 5* was a point of pride, as that early mainstream call for pay equality led to changes in the modern day. As Sarah Smarsh points out in *She Come By It Natural*, Dolly's power as a feminist comes through in what she does and who she is. Someone demanding that she follow one specific script or incorporate particular vocabulary is liable to miss the point laid out by the facts of her life—not to mention her rocking tune about it.

ABOVE: Dolly at the grand opening of Dollywood's 2018 season.

Truly Kind

Dolly is named MusiCares' Person of the Year

Dolly stepped up to the microphone at the end of a tribute concert and fundraiser for MusiCares wearing a beige body suit decorated with black sparkling designs from top to bottom, a shimmering black fringe skirt around her waist. "It's a long, long way from the hills of East Tennessee to the Hollywood Hills, but it has been a wonderful journey," she told the crowd. MusiCares, the charity arm of the Recording Academy, which began recognizing artists for their craft and their philanthropic contributions in 1991, was founded in 1989 to offer a range of support services and emergency assistance to professional musicians and their families in times of need. They convened on the night of February 8, 2019, to honor Dolly as their Person of the Year.

The celebration included a concert, which began with Miley Cyrus and Shawn Mendes performing "Islands in the Stream," with Mark Ronson on guitar. Midway through the song, right before she began a solo verse, Miley said, "I love you, Dolly." It was a sentiment repeated by artists all night long. Members of Little Big Town served as hosts, joking with one another about who loved Dolly the most. Band member Philip Sweet

said he did, since he once dressed up like Dolly for Halloween, to which Kimberly Schlapman countered that she had named her baby for Dolly. She won.

Memorable performances included Willie Nelson and Brandi Carlile performing the song Dolly and Willie had successfully recorded during the 1980s, "Everything Is Beautiful (In Its Own Way)." Katy Perry appeared all in lavender—from her boots to the cape with her name on the back— alongside Kacey Musgraves in shimmering silver to sing "Here You Come Again" as a duet. Leon Bridges was likewise memorably dressed in a muted green suit decorated with embroidered cacti, horseshoes, and a red barn; his name was also on the back of his jacket. Bridges sang "Not Enough" with Mavis Staples, backed by Jon Batiste and a huge gospel choir.

Norah Jones and the Brooklyn-based country duo Puss N Boots performed "The Grass Is Blue" and Chris Stapleton gave an electric guitar-driven rendition of "9 to 5" made complete by a punching horn section. The song "Do I Ever Cross Your Mind" became a trio with Jennifer Nettles, Margo Price, and Cam, backed by mandolin picking and a plaintive fiddle. Lauren Daigle performed "The Seeker," moving it from an introspective beginning to a subtle groove carried forward by percussion on the box cajon. Yolanda Adams brought the crowd to their feet with a Whitney-inspired performance of "I Will Always Love You." Emmylou Harris and Linda Ronstadt introduced a short video tribute to Dolly, reflecting on their decades of friendship and music-making together.

At the end of the night, Miley introduced the closing performance of the concert: Dolly singing "Coat of Many Colors" with musician and producer Linda Perry on guitar. In summing up all that she loves about Dolly, Miley described a life spent "teaching us all what it means to be truly kind, to be individual, to never give up, and to never judge a book by its cover, or its huge boobs and big hair."

The Recording Academy had already honored Dolly with a Lifetime Achievement Award in 2011. Dolly joked during the 2019 ceremony that she hoped to be around long enough to next receive a Betty White longevity award. The event reportedly raised $6.7 million for MusiCares. Before the public concert, there was a silent auction, dinner, and a live auction, and according to a clip from *Entertainment Tonight*, Miley bid over $100,000 for the prize of spending the day with Dolly and getting one of her outfits.

ABOVE: Dolly accepts the MusiCares Person of the Year award in 2019.

Tugging on Heartstrings

Dolly teams with Netflix to bring her stories to life in an emotional series

In June 2018, Dolly announced that her own Dixie Pixie Productions was partnering with Warner Bros. Television to create a limited-run series to stream on Netflix. The resulting project was an eight-part series titled *Dolly Parton's Heartstrings*, executive produced by Dolly. Each episode is based on one of her most iconic songs. Dolly introduces the episode, which then unfolds as an hour-or-so-long self-contained narrative.

"All of my life I've been writing songs and telling stories, but I always thought they should make movies out of my stories. So, we sent to Netflix and they fell for it"—Dolly laughed here—"and they said, well, let's do it." Dolly had worked already with Warner Bros. to create movies for NBC with great success. *Dolly Parton's Coat of Many Colors* had drawn over 13 million viewers in 2015, followed by *Christmas of Many Colors: Circle of Love* (over 11 million viewers) the next year. Dolly also served as an executive producer on *Christmas of Many Colors*.

Heartstrings allowed Dolly to stretch her acting muscle once more. She performed as herself at a wedding reception in the episode "Two Doors Down," and played Babe, the owner of a local juke joint, in "Jolene," the first in the series. Babe is a riff on Dolly's public persona: a gentle mentor in a motherly relationship with the titular Jolene, but also tough and savvy. Dolly could call on some of her earlier acting work to bring Babe to life, summoning up a sad but wise woman running a successful business establishment whose moral grounding some would question. (In this case, it's a honky tonk, but not unlike a certain little "chicken ranch" in Texas.)

The series is also an example of Dolly's remarkable business acumen—and timing. Her instinct for the viability of limited-run streaming series and for choosing business partners fits a career-long pattern of savoir faire. In particular, Dolly noted how much she appreciated how Netflix was "willing to spend the money for marketing and promoting their things. They're also willing to give you creative control and that's very important to artists and to people that really have a real feel for what they want the things to be."

ABOVE: Dolly (center) and the cast and crew of *Dolly Parton's Heartstrings* at the show's premiere in Dollywood in 2019.

Have Faith

Dolly cuts an EDM mix that gets everyone shakin'

"I always know inside myself what's right and what's wrong to do, and this felt really right."

—DOLLY TALKING ABOUT THE GALANTIS COLLABORATION WITH *ROLLING STONE* IN 2019

The song "Faith," a track by the duo Galantis, carved out new territory for Dolly when the single reached the top position on the Swedish charts and number twenty-eight on *Billboard*'s US Hot Dance/Electronic Songs in 2020.

Galantis is a Swedish duo comprised of Linus Eklöw and Christian Karlsson. The Dutch singer and producer Dennis Princewell Stehr, better known as Mr. Probz, also sang on the track. John Hiatt's 1987 song "Have a Little Faith in Me" was the starting point for "Faith," building from the original's first line and general melodic contours. Along the creative process, Galantis had a vision of collaborating with Dolly on the song, since they were big fans, but they thought it unlikely she would agree. They sent it to her as a long shot.

For Dolly, it was love at first hearing. "It's all about uplifting mankind and believing in a higher power," she told *Rolling Stone*. "All the things we need in this dark, ol' dreary world right now." While Dolly songs like "Baby I'm Burnin'" and "Jolene" have been remixed as dance versions, this was the first time Dolly fully collaborated on a project with an electronic dance music (EDM) group. She later said that she was open to doing other dance music in the future if this cut proved successful.

For their part, the two Swedes found Dolly a hoot to work with. After the project, they spoke to *bangshowbiz.com* about how funny she was in the studio, and how game she was for most anything. For example, when they asked if she would play the part of the bus driver in the song's music video, she agreed—with the caveat that she design her own clothes.

"Faith" was released as a single and also appeared on Galantis' album *Church*. The album also included collaborations with artists like OneRepublic, John Newman, and Passion Pit. The duo's outlook on the whole undertaking seemed in line with Dolly's own: "Church doesn't necessarily refer to a building or specific religion, but instead to people banded together in similar belief for a better humanity."

ABOVE: Dolly speaks at the 2019 CMA Awards.

The Collaboration

Dolly makes a surprise appearance
at Newport Folk Festival

For the 2019 Newport Folk Festival, singer-songwriter Brandi Carlile was given the programming reins for the Saturday night headliner by the festival's executive producer, Jay Sweet. She spent the year leading up to the weekend of music compiling the roster for a performance simply titled "♀♀♀♀: The Collaboration." When showtime finally arrived, Courtney Marie Andrews, Lake Street Dive, Candi Carpenter, and Molly Tuttle kicked things off with Joni Mitchell's "Big Yellow Taxi." Yola and the First Ladies of Bluegrass performed "Sisters Are Doin' It for Themselves," the song originally made famous by Annie Lennox and Aretha Franklin. Amy Ray sang with Lucy Dacus on the Indigo Girls' tune "Go." Sheryl Crow sang "If It Makes You Happy" with Maren Morris, and then "Strong Enough" with Yola and Maggie Rogers.

The 1990s anthem "What's Up" was performed by the song's writer Linda Perry, Jade Bird, and the supergroup known as The Highwomen, made up of Maren Morris, Amanda Shires, Natalie Hemby, and Brandi herself. Brandi and Judy Collins sang another Joni Mitchell folk classic, "Both Sides

Now." Then The Highwomen were joined by Sheryl and Yola for the song "Highwomen."

This particular set was gilding for a Newport Folk Festival that had featured more women than at any time during its sixty-year history. The performer list included Kacey Musgraves and another collaborative dynamo, Our Native Daughters, made up of four Black banjo players, vocalists, and songwriters Amythyst Kiah, Allison Russell, Leyla McCalla, and Rhiannon Giddens.

Attendees and performers alike exploded in delight when Dolly walked out onstage that Saturday. Jay Sweet told author Marissa R. Moss for her book *Her Country*, "Everyone had this look as if they had met fucking Snow White." Dolly and The Highwomen sang "Eagle When She Flies," "Just Because I'm a Woman," and "Jolene," and Dolly duetted with Brandi Carlile on "I Will Always Love You." The show closed with "9 to 5," a performance *Rolling Stone* writer Suzy Exposito described as "a little sobering," asking, "how many more years will it take until we achieve a wider-scale semblance of

gender parity in music, much less any industry in the United States?"

In her 2022 book *Her Country: How the Women of Country Music Became the Success They Were Never Supposed to Be*, author Marissa R. Moss describes how they pulled off Dolly's surprise appearance. She arrived in secret, exiting a plane she herself funded, draped with a long, hooded black cape. She remained out of sight until showtime.

Her Country also details how three modern musical pioneers—Kacey Musgraves, Maren Morris, and Mickey Guyton—have found ways around a systemic, structural set of barriers, rooted in gender and racial biases so deep they were not even recognized as such. These performers subvert the accepted notions of "how things are," finding new ways to share their music, connect with their audiences, and tell their truths through supposedly career-ending songs. This generation of country music women carries forth the clarity of vision Dolly brought to her own career.

ABOVE: (L to R) Amanda Shires, Maren Morris, Dolly, Brandi Carlile, and Natalie Hemby perform during the 2019 Newport Folk Festival.

Don't Be Chicken Squat

Dolly donates $1 million to vaccine research

In the forty-nine-second video clip, Dolly sits on a soft bench in front of a backdrop with the logo for Vanderbilt Health. Directly behind her sits a desk with an open laptop on it. She sings to the tune of "Jolene": "Vaccine, vaccine, vaccine, vaccine, I'm beggin' of you, please don't hesitate." She repeats the melody for the next line and ends "cause once you're dead, then that's a bit too late." Dolly smiles at her own turn of phrase, but then turns serious, encouraging people to take the vaccine. She ends with a Dolly-style admonition: "Don't be such a chicken squat, get out there and get your shot."

Early in the COVID-19 pandemic, in a gift announced in April 2020, Dolly donated $1 million to Vanderbilt University for coronavirus research, partially funding the biotechnology firm Moderna's vaccine. By November, the *New England Journal of Medicine* published findings that Moderna test trials demonstrated a ninety-five percent effectiveness rate. The list of funding sources for that paper included the Dolly Parton COVID-19 Research Fund.

The donation came about because of a conversation between Dolly and Vanderbilt doctor Naji Abumrad. The two first met in 2013 when Dolly was taken to the hospital after a car accident. She was treated by Dr. Abumrad, and the two formed a lasting friendship. According to a story on NPR, Naji and Dolly had a conversation near the beginning of the crisis, in February or March 2020, in which Naji shared with her that Vanderbilt researchers were making progress in the race to find a vaccine for the devastating virus. Dolly posted an encouraging comment on social media: "When I donated the money to the COVID fund I just wanted it to do good and evidently, it is! Let's just hope we can find a cure real soon."

In 2020, Dolly also released a single called "When Life Is Good Again." The song is a pop-style epic power ballad, complete with heavy drum beat and a backup choir, and the lyrics list a number of simple pleasures made impossible by COVID, as the singer promises to live a better life once the pandemic is over. Dolly's voice of reassurance that "everything's going to be all right" was more than welcome, as Melinda Newman, a journalist writing for *Billboard*, named her "comforter-in-chief."

While the donation garnered a great deal of notice as a sign of hope in dark times, it was not Dolly's first donation to medical research at Vanderbilt, nor was it her last. In October 2017, Dolly donated $1 million to the Children's Hospital's Pediatric Cancer Program in honor of her niece Hannah, who had been treated there successfully for leukemia when she was a young child during the early 1990s. The gift was also dedicated to Hannah's parents and to Dr. Abumrad. The hospital opened a butterfly garden named for Hannah Dennison the following year. Dolly released her first children's album, *I Believe In You*, in 2017, which included the song "Chemo Hero," written in honor of her niece.

In June 2022, Dolly donated another $1 million to Vanderbilt's Division of Pediatric Infectious Diseases, for research on childhood infectious diseases caused by bacteria and viruses. Dolly was quoted in a press release from Vanderbilt saying that she loves all children: "No child should ever have to suffer, and I'm willing to do my part to try and keep as many of them as I can as healthy and safe as possible."

The Southern culture writer Rick Bragg, in a paean to Dolly in *Southern Living* in May 2022, wrote about growing up loving Dolly. He first saw her on a small black-and-white Philco TV, where to him she seemed to appear in color. And then he found out about Dolly the philanthropist: "I discovered that there was a whole other human story here, one of great heart and generosity, of a woman who hated ignorance and gave out books to fight it, who used her celebrity to do some good in this sorry ole world."

ABOVE: A sign in New Orleans meant to evoke the lyrics of Dolly's song "Jolene" in 2021.

Comforter-in-Chief

The "book lady" reads bedtime stories to a country rocked by crisis

Less than a month after the full pandemic lockdowns began, and phrases like "social distancing" and "these uncertain times" entered common parlance, Dolly began a ten-week web series titled "Goodnight with Dolly." Every Thursday evening at 7 pm EST beginning April 2, 2020, children (and their parents) could look forward to seeing the "book lady" propped up in bed in her PJs, her glasses resting near the end of her nose, ready to share a children's book.

The first book Dolly read was her favorite, *The Little Engine That Could* by Watty Piper. The Imagination Library website posted the video, which cut between Dolly reading to images from the book itself. Beneath the video, parents could find links to activity sheets, reading tips, and suggestions for related books. There was also a note on the "Goodnight with Dolly" page that said the series was a gift from Dolly to all families, and a reminder: "Free of charge but not free from obligation as the message will be to pass on the love and keep hope alive because we are all Together, You and I."

The "Goodnight" episodes also included links to music on the streaming platform SoundCloud, either a full song or an excerpt. Many of the songs were from Dolly's 2017 children's album *I Believe In You*. The title song was inspired by the Watty Piper classic, including its "woo woo woo" chorus of train sounds. In another installment, a different song from the album, "I'm Here," was linked beneath Dolly's reading of *Llama Llama, Red Pajama. Max & the Tag-Along Moon* was matched with the song "From Here to the Moon and Back," off the *Joyful Noise* soundtrack. The only book with no music link was Loren Long's *There's a Hole in the Log on the Bottom of the Lake*, which is itself a song and includes music in the back of the book.

During what *Time* dubbed "the golden era of livestreaming," Dolly was not the only celebrity helping assuage anxieties during rough times. DJ and rapper D-Nice threw dance parties from his kitchen via Instagram Live. Talk shows carried on via split screen, with late-night hosts holed up at home, from Seth Meyers in his attic to Stephen Colbert speaking memorably from his bathtub but more often from his living room, with his wife acting as his crew. In addition to entertainment, the COVID-19 quarantines were a time when computers became something of a lifeline. Business meetings and school classrooms limped along via virtual platforms, loved ones kept in touch over video calls and virtual game nights, and story times helped entertain children stuck at home for weeks and months on end.

Other well-known figures also read children's books online. Michelle Obama, Kate Winslet, and Tom Hardy, for example, all posted book readings for children during the early months of lockdown. Few, however, already had in place a program and a platform to expand the effort in multiple directions at once, both creative and educational. Dolly's Imagination Library was already in full swing, with a web presence that "Goodnight with Dolly" could fold into seamlessly.

"Goodnight with Dolly" began when the pandemic forced postponement of the release of *The Library That Dolly Built*, a documentary about the Imagination Library that got pushed from April to December 2020. Members of the documentary's production team found themselves with the time and energy to apply to the online storytelling series. "Goodnight with Dolly" enjoyed over 13 million views worldwide, and earned one Gold and three Silver Telly Awards, which honor work in video and television production across any platform.

ABOVE: A mural painted on the wall outside The 5 Spot, a music venue in East Nashville, created by Nashville-based artist Kim Radford.

The Dolly Lama

Dolly is an angel in

Christmas on the Square—*and in life*

There's a scene in the Emmy-winning Netflix musical *Christmas on the Square* when Dolly reveals herself as an angel to the story's protagonist Regina Fuller, played by actor Christine Baranski. Dolly had appeared at the start of the film as a particularly bedazzling street beggar who holds a sign asking for "change." Regina has returned to the hometown her father founded, hardened by her big city life as a successful businesswoman. She is determined to sell the entire town to a developer to make way for a giant mall, which requires evicting all residents from their homes and businesses. To make matters worse, she's announced her intentions on Christmas.

Christmas on the Square is a classic holiday tale of transformation, very much in the tradition of Charles Dickens. Thus, the "change" Dolly was hoping for turns out to be a change of heart and not pocket change. In the scene when Dolly's character first appears in her heavenly glory, she floats, seated on a cushion-sized cloud, robed in sparkling white with her wings peeking up from behind. She

dispenses good-natured advice and wisdom, which seems a natural fit for Dolly.

The rest of the story unfolds around Regina's central conflict, carried along by fourteen songs, all composed by Dolly. We meet the local pastor and his wife, who have just completed fertility treatments in hopes of bringing a child into the world. They sing love songs. Regina's long-ago friend laments the impending loss of her made-from-scratch business and of the town she led as its first female mayor, and sings a "set you straight" number to her former pal. Regina's high school sweetheart and first love Carl sings about the priceless value of memories in his secondhand store. A widowed father and his young daughter with an "old soul" come to play a central role in Regina's moral dilemma.

The whole town sings and dances beautifully, in full-production numbers choreographed by Debbie Allen, also the movie's director and executive producer, best known for her work on *Fame* (1980). Debbie commented after working with her that Dolly's "comprehension of music is encyclopedic." In the Christmas Eve climax, Dolly appears decked out in full angelic splendor, her wings now fully extended.

Dolly has come into an almost angel-like status in popular culture, as a presence somehow able to avoid the worst of the divisiveness and conflict that characterize the modern age. She exists as an idea quite apart from the living, breathing person who built a decades-long entertainment career. The word "brand" has become shorthand for any entity whose identity emerges at an intersection of different signifiers. Nicknames like "Dolly Lama," books of Dollyisms, T-shirts displaying phrases like "What Would Dolly Do?" and "Y'all Need Dolly," votive-style "saint" candles with Dolly's likeness: these all carry layers of meaning that are fairly framed as the "brand" that is Dolly. Perhaps the most remarkable aspect of Dolly's existence on the level of brand is that it most signifies acceptance, kindness, hard work, and integrity. It seems the world really does need Dolly, and the positive qualities for which she stands.

ABOVE: Dolly in *Christmas on the Square* (2020).

Dolly Parton, Thriller Author
Dolly co-authors Run, Rose, Run
with James Patterson

In *Run, Rose, Run*, a young woman named AnnieLee Keyes heads to Nashville in pursuit of a dream to become a country music star. But she is also pursued by a troubled past that trails her ever more relentlessly. AnnieLee's musical journey is buoyed by a fortuitous relationship with Ruthanna Ryder, an aging country legend who has withdrawn from public performances following her own life's painful events.

Knowing the identity of its co-author, it is nearly impossible not to project bits of Dolly onto both of *Run, Rose, Run*'s lead characters. AnnieLee is the young, gifted songwriter with guts, determination, and a clear vision of her goals and the compromises she is willing to make—and not— to reach those goals. Ruthanna is the experienced older musician with hard-won insight into the country music business accumulated over a long career. Like Dolly, the fictional Ruthanna enjoys creative and financial freedom, doing as she pleases and helping who she pleases along the way. Some of Ruthanna's advice and warnings to AnnieLee ring particularly true, like her descriptions of the

decline of women's voices on country music radio since 2000: "When you were little, just learning how to sing along with the radio, women musicians sang about a third of the songs played on country stations. Now they're barely above ten percent."

To accompany the novel, Dolly wrote and recorded an album of twelve songs, also titled *Run, Rose, Run*, and released it on her own Butterfly Records, in partnership with Ingrooves/UMG. The songs shift perspectives between different characters, and some are even woven into the plot itself.

Creating this album was not unlike the challenge Dolly took on in writing the score for *9 to 5: The Musical*, or *Christmas in the Square* for that matter, conveying multiple viewpoints within the course of a larger creative undertaking. It likewise falls in line with the way Dolly's songs have inspired retellings via different media, with songs like "Coat of Many Colors" inspiring movies, TV episodes, and more than one illustrated children's book.

When James Patterson contacted Dolly in February 2020 with the idea of cowriting a book

about a country music singer, they had at least
two things in common. Both have been longtime
literacy advocates, and both tell stories people want
to enjoy. James knew Nashville from his days as a
student at Vanderbilt and of course Dolly knew the
city well. At her suggestion, they met to chat. A few
hours later, they decided to make the deal. COVID
forced their collaboration to take place largely at
a distance, but between faxing and video calls, the
project kept moving forward.

Once the novel and album were released
on March 7, 2022, James and Dolly did press
interviews to promote the work. On one occasion
in Nashville, reported in an unsigned piece for
the *Daily Mail*, Dolly seemed to be having fun with

this contemporary creative duo. James had put on
a Western-style jacket with designs to match those
on her black pants. Dolly winked and said, "I got
him dressed up almost like one of my early duet
partners."

While storytelling and collaboration both come
naturally to Dolly, the nature of this particular
project was a first for her, for James Patterson,
and possibly a first for anyone. Spotify pitched
the simultaneous release of novel and album to
promote an "immersive listening experience." To
read lyrics on the page by a character in a story, and
then hear those songs realized by Dolly Parton, adds
depth to both experiences.

ABOVE: Dolly and James Patterson discuss their book collaboration *Run, Rose, Run* at SXSW in 2022.

When Faith is "Riding the Fence"

Dolly sings a song of hope with an old friend during a difficult era

Dolly's longtime hairstylist Cheryl Riddle brought her a recording of a new song by a friend of hers. The friend happened to be the legendary country music performer and songwriter Bill Anderson, and Cheryl thought he and Dolly would make a great duet. Dolly must have thought so, too, because she recorded herself doing the song and sent it back to Bill. "She just made the song and the record just come alive," Bill said in a June 2022 interview for the podcast *The Music Universe*. "It took on a whole new life, as everything does when Dolly Parton touches it."

The song was titled "Some Day It'll All Make Sense." Written by Bill, Bobby Tomberlin, and Ryan Larkins, it was a song that resonated deeply with listeners hearing it two years into the COVID-19 pandemic. This new recording became the driving force behind a larger project, collecting sixteen of Bill's most beloved songs from a career spanning seven decades. By 2022, Bill Anderson—nicknamed "Whispering Bill" for his soft style—was the longest-running living member

of the *Grand Ole Opry.* The Country Music Hall of Fame had seen fit to honor his career and his legacy with an exhibit titled for a line in his first hit song, "City Lights," recorded in 1958 by Ray Price: "Bill Anderson: *As Far As I Can See.*" Bill's MCA collection shared the title of the exhibit and accompanied a digital release of seven previous albums by Bill, all from the 1960s, his heyday as a performer.

Shortly after the recording, Dolly and Bill released a bluegrass version of "Someday It'll All Make Sense," which featured Sierra Hull on mandolin and her spouse Justin Moses on fiddle and dobro. This version of the song was nominated for a 2023 Grammy for Best American Roots Performance. Dolly was also nominated for a collaboration with Reba McEntire in the category of Best Country Duo/Group Performance. Shortly before the ceremony, where their song was beaten out by Aaron Neville and the Dirty Dozen Brass Band's "Stompin' Ground," Bill spoke about his work with Dolly to Nashville writer Gayle Thompson. "She's amazing. I've been so blessed. I

ABOVE: Dolly and Bill Anderson perform during the *Grand Ole Opry* 85th Birthday Bash in 2010.

mean, I pinch myself sometimes that this has really all happened. If we do win a Grammy on Sunday, that'll be the cherry on top of the sundae. And if we don't, it's still been a fun ride."

Dolly and Bill got together to shoot a video for the song during a three-hour session directed by Trey Fanjoy, whose reputation is built on videos for artists like Taylor Swift and Reba McEntire, Steven Tyler and Paul McCartney, and others. The video for "Someday It'll All Make Sense" is stylized, shot in black and white, with opening credits that summon up images of classic movies.

According to country music writer Gayle Thompson, interviewing Bill for her blog *Everything Nash*, three hours was all the time Dolly had in a day whose schedule also included filming videos for England's Queen Elizabeth for her Platinum Jubilee and NASCAR. Bill noted that, when realizing they had finished the shoot ahead of schedule, Dolly announced she had fifteen minutes for anyone wanting photos or autographs. The lessons Dolly learned once upon a time with Porter, about demonstrating appreciation for her fans, have remained with her.

Bill's album includes one more duet with Dolly, but this one is a historic artifact. In 1964, Dolly and Bill recorded a demo of a song, "If It Is All The Same To You," that he would go on to successfully record with Jan Howard. It appeared on Bill's 1969 album of the same title. As Bill remembered it, Dolly was newly arrived to Nashville, and he had never heard of her. He just "needed a girl singer" to make seven or eight demos at Bradley's Barn studio in 1964, and "Dolly Parton showed up, thank goodness, and did a great job on this song." Someone found the demo on an old tape, cleaned it up, and added it to Bill's retrospective release, making them the final cuts, back-to-back, on *As Far As I Can See*. Bill said with a laugh, "To hear Bill and Dolly from 1964 and then Bill and Dolly from 2022, you can hear us age. You can hear our arteries hardening over the years."

During the late 1960s, Dolly was beginning a long series of successful duets with Porter Wagoner, while Bill began a series of duets with Jan Howard. During the video shoot, they talked about this history, wondering to one another what Porter and Jan might be thinking and saying, looking down on their 2022 project. The answer: "God, I had no idea their careers would last this long."

At a time when Dolly was creating remarkable collaborations with a young generation of artists across a variety of styles, this particular project demonstrated her love of collaborating with old friends as well. "Working with my ol' buddy Bill Anderson was the most meaningful fun I've had in years," she reportedly said of the project. For Bill's part, he mused on two songs "connecting the dots across more than fifty years. How cool is that?"

Doing Good

Dolly is awarded the Carnegie Medal of Philanthropy

"If I can just do my small part in this world, then that's all that I'd ask in this world."

—AN EXCERPT FROM DOLLY'S SPEECH ACCEPTING THE CARNEGIE MEDAL OF PHILANTHROPY IN OCTOBER 2022

"I was afraid I was going to have to take my hair off to get this on," Dolly joked as she held up the medal around her neck for all in Gotham Hall in New York City to see. Then she expressed the pride she felt to "be amongst these great people doing all these great things to try to help the world, as they say." Among others, Dolly was referring to the three other honorees for the Carnegie Medal of Philanthropy, an award sometimes called the "Nobel Prize for Philanthropy." It has been given every two years since 2001 (with the exception of 2021, skipped due to the ongoing COVID-19 pandemic) and so far, sixty-five philanthropists have received the commendation.

Dolly would later acknowledge, "I get paid more attention than maybe some others that are doing more than me." Though her fellow honorees may have been less internationally recognizable, they shared her conviction to alleviate suffering and uplift people in need. The industrialist Manu Chandaria ran a foundation in Kenya supporting health care, education, and environmental initiatives, as well as working to end poverty. The Dallas entrepreneur

Lyda Hill focused on cancer and mental health research and support for women in STEM fields, as well as boosting efforts of local nonprofits. Like Dolly, Lyda donated toward vaccine research early in the pandemic.

Investors Lynn and Stacy Schusterman were the first mother-daughter duo to receive Carnegie recognition for their work around education, voting rights, gender equity, and criminal justice in Oklahoma, and their support of "Jewish communities and a secure, inclusive Israel." Daughter Stacy accepted the award on behalf of the Schusterman Family Philanthropies, founded in 1987. In her remarks, she called for greater collaboration among philanthropic efforts and for work toward manifesting the lofty ideas upon which the US was founded. "When we say, 'All men are created equal,'" she said, "it is clear 'men' does not yet mean all Americans, including women, gender expansive people, and all ethnicities, races, and religions."

Dolly's honor was focused on her contributions to improving literacy, although her philanthropic efforts range wider, from destigmatizing people suffering from HIV/AIDS in Los Angeles to partnering with PETA to end the practice of chaining pets outside. If one goal of the Carnegie Foundation is, as its website states, to "inspire a culture of giving," Dolly certainly embraces that. In 2022, the Dollywood Parks and Resorts also began its Care More Initiative, providing a day off for employees to "volunteer at a nonprofit of their choice."

Any hope that the spirit of philanthropy is contagious was buoyed by the announcement the month after Dolly's Carnegie honor that Amazon CEO Jeff Bezos and his partner Lauren Sanchez would bestow upon Dolly the second annual Courage and Civility Award. The award came with a $100 million gift to apply toward any charitable cause Dolly chose. The previous year, CNN commentator

and activist Van Jones and World Central Kitchen chef José Andrés had received the inaugural award. In 2010, José mobilized a tremendous, ongoing effort to provide meals to people in the wake of disasters both natural and humanitarian. He was given the Carnegie Foundation's Catalyst Award the same year Dolly received her medal.

Midway through her remarks, Dolly led the attendees in a sing-along. Setting the beat with her acrylic nails in the way she used them to distinctive effect in the rhythmic opening of "9 to 5," she taught them a ditty she had written for the Imagination Library: "Books, books, I love books, the way they feel and smell and look . . ." Later, Dolly gestured again to her medal and quipped, "I'll probably sleep in this tonight."

ABOVE: Dolly performs at the first annual Kiss Breast Cancer Goodbye Benefit Concert, held at the Country Music Hall of Fame's CMA Theater in October 2021.

Dolly Rocks

The country legend is inducted into the Rock and Roll Hall of Fame

"I have no regrets. I will never apologize for trying. And when I'm old and rocking away in my rocking chair, I'd rather regret a few things I did, than to regret a whole bunch of things I didn't do."

—DOLLY IN A RECORDED INTERVIEW SEGMENT SHOWN DURING THE ROCK AND ROLL HALL OF FAME INDUCTION CEREMONY

"I'm a rock star now!" Dolly exclaimed, after Pink officially inducted her into the Rock and Roll Hall of Fame. The tribute that followed included a motley crew of musicians. Brandi Carlile and Pink performed "Coat of Many Colors," backed by members of the Zac Brown Band. Sheryl Crow and Zac Brown sang "9 to 5" as a duet.

Then out came Dolly in a form-fitting black latex jumpsuit. From the bottom of the capri-length pants, swathes of sheer black fabric extended down to her high heels. A sequined overlay fell across her shoulders like an epaulet, and thin silver cords dangled around the shoulders, arms, and hips. The outfit's plunging neckline was intersected by the strap of Dolly's electric guitar slung across the front of her body.

Dolly put her hands on her hips. "I figured if I'm going to be in the Rock and Roll Hall of Fame, I'm going to have to earn it." With that, she struck a loud chord on the electric guitar. "And you thought I couldn't rock!"

The song that followed was one Dolly had written for the occasion. The lyrics described her coming of age during the early era of rock and roll and her plans to rock "till the cows come home." Not every country music legend could take the stage at age seventy-six and perform a newly penned song so perfectly pitched for the occasion. Maybe no one but Dolly could pull off the balance between not taking herself too seriously while also demonstrating the serious depth of her songwriting chops.

The final performance of the tribute was a group rendition of "Jolene," where other 2022 inductees joined in. Eurythmics vocalist Annie Lennox shared the first verse with presenter Pink. Duran Duran lead singer Simon Le Bon and rock legend Pat Benatar joined together on the second.

ABOVE: Dolly speaks during her induction into the Rock and Roll Hall of Fame in 2022.

Finally, Rob Halford of the heavy metal band Judas Priest sang with Dolly on the chorus. Sheryl Crow and Brandi Carlile were also on hand to sing the final verse.

Before the songs began, Pink had recounted Dolly's musical achievements: writing the most-selling song by a female artist ever, recording twenty-five songs that reached the top position on the *Billboard* country music charts, forty-two top-ten country albums, and 110 charted singles over more than four decades. Pink appropriately led and closed her introduction with Dolly's songwriting, describing Dolly's body of work as "a narrative of painful, beautiful, poetic, melodic commentary on what it's like to be human, and on what it's like to be a woman in America." After a big round of applause, Pink added, "She can make you feel like God is listening and that help is right around the corner." Dolly "is the only author of her story," Pink said, "and what an incredible story that you have written, Dolly Parton."

A recorded tribute segment included Dolly's goddaughter Miley Cyrus reflecting on Dolly's kindness. "The way she'll treat her biggest fan, the way she'd treat her worst enemy, is all the same," she says. "I have had such a great role model as a musician but also just as a person. She's just the kindest of all."

DOLLY PLANS TO CONTINUE ROCKING

Not long after her induction into the Rock and Roll Hall of Fame, Dolly announced she was working on a rock album. She envisioned bringing in classic rockers, including Nancy and Ann Wilson from the band Heart, as well as recent stars like Ed Sheeran, whose voice she thought would blend well with hers. She also wanted to redo "Stairway to Heaven," this time without the bluegrass flavor, and hoped to reunite Led Zeppelin band members who hadn't played together for a decade and a half. She told music writer Holly Gleason that she aimed to "do it more true to the regular record. I'm trying to see if Robert Plant might sing on it. Maybe Jimmy Page might do the pick-up part on it. I'm looking forward to dragging in some of the great classic people, girls and boys, to sing on some of the songs."

May It Be More Merry and Bright

Dolly and Miley Cyrus host the
NBC party ringing in the New Year

Dolly and Miley kicked off the second annual celebration of *Miley's New Year's Eve Party* with a duet performance of Joan Jett's '80s anthem "I Love Rock and Roll." Viewers had already learned that Dolly was to undergo a "Miley-fied makeover" for the occasion, and there she appeared, decked out in a black bodysuit with sheer leopard-print trim and cut-outs that started at the hips and ran down the outside of both legs. Dolly took the high harmony on the outro chorus and Miley asked the crowd as the song ended how they liked "Rock and Roll Hall of Fame Dolly."

The remainder of the two-hour celebration featured a mix of artists performing on one of two stages at an outdoor venue in Miami, interspersed with shots of the partying crowd, short pre-recorded comedy sketches involving *Saturday Night Live* (*SNL*) cast members and writers, and live interactions with comedians and crowd members. The comedy trio of Ben Marshall, John Higgins, and Martin Herlihy, better known as Please Don't Destroy, led a couple of sketches,

including one where they pitch bad sketch ideas to Dolly until she appears to run away via a series of flips, leaps, and other acts of physical derring-do. One standout sketch had Miley and Dolly coaching their "understudies," played by *SNL* cast members Chloe Fineman and Sarah Sherman, respectively. Chloe made her voice husky and added "y'all" to the end of every sentence; Sarah put on a blond wig and an identical outfit to Dolly's. "I feel like something's missing," Dolly said, sending Sarah back for certain . . . *additions*. Sarah-as-Dolly returned and spun around to model her improved chest, knocking to the floor the champagne bottle, glasses, and other objects sitting on a waist-high table. Dolly joked, "I do it all the time."

A performance highlight was Miley leading the crowd in a mass sing-along of her *Hannah Montana*–era hit, "Party in the USA." Dolly, now dressed in a shimmering white floor-length gown, then joined Miley for a duet on the distinctively post-*Hannah* song "Wrecking Ball." The line, "I will always want you" in "Wrecking Ball" marked an easy pivot into Dolly's iconic "I Will Always

Love You." Godmother and goddaughter led the crowd, who sang along as Dolly waved her arm to conduct. In a final duet performance, Dolly appeared in hot pink and black, coordinated with Miley's outfit, to sing the Patsy Cline classic "Walkin' After Midnight," followed by another crowd sing-along on—what else?—"Jolene."

Near the end of the show, a final comedy sketch showed Dolly and Miley sitting down to talk about plans and resolutions for the new year. Dolly pointed to work she was doing for the upcoming movie based on the novel she co-wrote with James Patterson, *Run, Rose, Run*. She was also working on a rock-and-roll album and beginning to build a new hotel at Dollywood. Miley said that was a lot to pack into one year; Dolly quipped that she was only talking about January.

Miley planned to read more. In response, Dolly brought out the book she was (supposedly) currently reading: a giant tome labeled *Roman History*. It was taking her a while, she said, because it was all in Latin. Amazed, Miley asked Dolly if she had any downtime planned for 2023. Dolly reached down beside her seat to pull up an eighteen-inch carved figure of a man from the waist up, mounted on a black base. "Of course," she said offhandedly, "and that's when I do my sculpting."

"Nice bust," Miley said.

To which Dolly replied, "If I had a nickel . . ."

ABOVE: Miley and Aunt Dolly at the 2019 MusiCares Person of the Year event honoring Dolly.

BORN TO TELL SONGS

Sources related to Dolly's childhood range from her own published memoirs to numerous interviews appearing in newspapers, magazines, television, radio, and the internet. For discussion of her childhood fascination with butterflies, see *My Life and Other Unfinished Business*; Hirschberg, 2021 interview for *W*; Smarsh, 2020, *She Come By It Natural*; Daly, 2016. On "Little Tiny Tasseltop," see Price, 1990. Dolly discusses her iconic look in the 2009 special *Live in London*, also mentioned in Smarsh (123); on wanting to be "trash," see *Here I Am*, 2019. On Dolly's Uncle Bill see the website https://dollyparton.com, which includes her tribute after his passing. Dolly recalls speaking to Cas Walker for the first time in numerous sources, including *Songteller*. On Dolly's early appearances on radio and TV, including the "Nickels and Dimes" anecdote, see *My Life and Other Unfinished Business*; also see Jones, *Vanity Fair*, 2015. On Dolly's first *Grand Ole Opry* appearance, see Grobel, 1978; "Oh Mister Cash" and "She's gonna be in real trouble" appear in *My Life and Other Unfinished Business* (116); "I promise" quote comes from Snyder, 1978; on Uncle Bill "dogging" Chet Atkins, see Hirshey 1979; for the Leinbaugh's anecdote, see *Dolly's Dixie Fixin's*. Sources for Dolly's Mercury Records session include John Rumble's entry on "Shelby Singleton" in the Oxford Music Online database. Several quotes and information about this period of Dolly's life come from *My Life and Other Unfinished Business*, including fundraising for the high school trip to NYC and what items she carried with her to Nashville (139); Carl's first and last attendance at an awards ceremony (159), the wig anecdote (146), and the story about "Just Because I'm a Woman" (222-23). Sarah Smarsh's quote about the "sexual double standard" is found in *She Come By It Natural*.

BIG DREAMS WITH BIG WINGS

For quote on wrecking her first car, see Price, 2014; Dolly's reflections on Porter, and on her writing process for "Down from Dover" come from Abumrad, 2019; the story about Porter offering to absorb any lost royalties is told in Campbell, 1975, among other places; for quotes related to "Down from Dover" being banned from radio and ahead of its time, see DeMain, 2004 (33–34); also quoted in Hamessley 2020 (152). Dolly also reflects on writing "Down from Dover" during interviews for the 2019 documentary *Here I Am*. The "simply complicated" quote comes from a *New York Post* piece by Jan Hodenfield dated August 6, 1975, and is quoted in Hamessley, 2020 (54), among other places. For list of tearjerker songs, including "Coat of Many Colors," see Sutton, *It's a Southern Thing*, 2020. For quotes about the little girl named Jolene, see Vitale, NPR, 2008; also see Morris, 2013. For quote about writing "I Will Always Love You," see DeMain, 2004 (36); Dolly's reflections on songwriting as it relates to turning down Elvis and on having never met him come from DeMain, 2001.

TIDE'S GONNA TURN

For Dolly's comment on touring frustrations, see Grobel, 1978; on Sandy's vision for her career, see Snyder, 1978; for Sandy's quote about plans for Dolly's career, see Hance, 1976; Dolly's quote about her "big plans" comes from Nash, 1977. For quote about bringing in Gary Klein to produce, see Snyder, "Dolly's Gamble," 1978; on unprecedented success of "Here You Come Again," see Otis, 1978; the quote about simplicity and quotes about writing "Two Doors Down" come from Grobel, *Newsday*, 1979. Quotes about Dolly's wardrobe malfunction come from Schwed. The 2004 *PopMatters* review *of Just Because I'm a Woman* is found at https://www. popmatters.com/various-justbecauseimawoman-2496132480.html. Dolly's quote regarding the *Playboy* cover is found in Schmidt, 2017 (80). On Carol and Dolly's press conference, see Litsch, 1979.

FIND YOUR PLACE AND SHINE

Perspective on *Best Little Whorehouse* (including "blood on the project" quote) comes from *My Life and Other Unfinished Business*; on requirements for future projects, see Thomas, 1981. Dolly's quote about Dr. Thomas is from Vandergriff, 2009. On "Islands" being originally intended for Diana Ross, see Newman, *Billboard*, 2021; Kenny's quote about bringing Dolly in for a duet is from Dukes, 2022; Dolly talked about their long friendship for a TV interview with WBIR in October 2017. Barry's quote comes from Eells, 2014. Dolly's view on never wanting to retire and the wig quote are from Warhol, 1984 (in Schmidt [235; 231]). Dolly posted about the second Walk of Fame star on Twitter (@DollyParton) on June 25, 2018; general understanding of the process for choosing honorees comes from *Jet* magazine and the Walk of Fame website. On Dollywood as a smart business decision, see Smarsh (117); on the Dollywood Foundation philanthropy, see Jaehne, 1990; on the tensions between tourism and conservation, see Bellows, 2009; and Schmidt, 2017; on the Back Porch Theater, see Nash, 2002. On Dollywood as a place for fans to play, see Gross, *New York Times*, 2003. Cottom, 2021, explores Dolly's significance in the context of social movements sparked by 2020 police killings. For coined term "Dollyverse," see Abumrad, 2019. On tensions between success and longing for home, see Watson, 2016, and Drew, 2021. Dolly discusses the symbolism of the sand dollar in *My Life and Other Unfinished Business* (290); Gail Berman's story is found in Barnes, 2016. On Dolly's childhood application of medicine for makeup, see *St. Louis Post Dispatch*, 1987; Gloria Steinem quote comes from Kai Green, "50 quotes"; on Dolly's attitude toward feminism, see *Dolly Parton's America*; on Dolly's awareness of how she looks, see Jefferson, 1979; for Dolly's attitude about turning 40, see McHenry, 1986; on "surprise" related to the *Ms.* award, see Steinem, 1987. Dolly stated that she, Emmylou Harris, and Linda Rondstadt were "bound" during a conference call with music writers, including Konc, 2016. Information about the Sevierville statue is found in McMahan, 2016; *Us Weekly*, 2009; and Smarsh, 2020, who also shared the Jimmy Kimmel story. On Dolly's words to Herb Ross, see Lipper, 1989; quote about the strength of women comes from *My Life and Other Unfinished Business*; the sweater anecdote is found in Smarsh, 2020 (130). Sources about creating *White Limozeen* and Fred Vail's work with the Beach Boys include Cardwell, 2011, and *USA Today*; for story about songwriting with Mac Davis and the anecdote about first hearing "He's Alive," see Stadiem, 1989.

BACK TO HER ROOTS

On eagle imagery in "Light of a Clear Blue Morning," see Flippo, 1977; Smarsh's description of "Eagle When She Flies" is on p. 87; on DJs refusing to play it, see Dunn, 2003. On the record-setting success of Whitney Houston's cover, see Ellison, 1995; on Dolly's 1993 Carnegie Hall performance, see Pareles, 1993; on Whitney's version bringing younger audiences, see Garner, 2020; on bluegrass version for early 2000s shows, see Jeremy Rush, *Goldmine*, 2002. On Miley being a risk-taker, see Charles (202); Vera, 2020; and, for quote, Smarsh (147). For quote from Steve Buckingham about *Honky Tonk Angels*, see Cardwell, 2011. On *Slow Dancing*, see *People*, 1993, and an uncredited piece for the *Toronto Star* in 1993. On naming Blue Eye Records, see Caldwell, 2011 (127); also Ray, 1999, and *Songteller*, which is also a source of insight on Dolly's favorite kid's book and her parents' influence. On being the "book lady," including quoted comments from a 2013 *PBS Newshour*, see Smarsh, 2016. The Scottish radio quote comes from Smith, 2021; on the wedding in Edinburgh, the British art exhibit, and the invitation to Dollywood, see Weiss, 1999. Details about the restaurant meeting and recording *The Grass Is Blue* come from Cardwell (128); on Steve Buckingham's perspective and Dolly's surprise, see Hamessley, 2020 (83); also see Marcus, 1999. The Marty Stuart and Dolly quotes are found in Strauss, June 1999; Dolly's words during the performance come from Strauss, September 1999; on her reaction to the news, see Brady, 1999, and Churchill, 1999, also where the Acuff/Nelson quip appears.

A TWENTY-FIRST-CENTURY CULTURAL ICON

On Dolly's songwriting inspiration, see Dunn, 2003; the quote about deep feelings comes from *Dolly & Friends: The Making of a Soundtrack*, 2018; on Buckingham's insights, Dolly's "wee-hour wisdom," and her ongoing songcrafting, see Rousuck, 2006; on creative control, see Garner, 2020. In addition to sources mentioned in the entry, perspective on Dolly's covers comes from Tirella, 2001. On band personnel for *Halos*, see Dunn, 2003; review commentary for "Hello God" and "Stairway to Heaven" comes from Friskics-Warren, 2002; for "sinners and saints" quote, see Heathcote, 2002; on Carl's love for Led Zeppelin, see *People*, 2022; Carl's outlook on "Stairway," his rock song suggestions, and the upcoming re-recording appear in Gleason, 2022. For information about Challenger, see McKenzie 2011; on the 2003 ceremony and the partnership, visit the AEF website. The *Today Show* quote is found in Kabota, 2021; the National Medal of Arts is discussed in Smarsh (166) and https://www.arts.gov/about/what-is-the-nea; on the 2008 medal presentation, see blog entry for the Wyoming Arts Council dated September 12, 2008, https://wyoarts.state.wy.us/parton-presented-national-medal-of-the-arts-at-annual-nasaa-conference. On Duncan asking Dolly to write "Travelin' Thru" and her personal inspiration, see Lowman, 2006, and Shelburne, 2006; on the film's shoestring budget, see Stricker, 2006; on hate mail, her gay following, and her perspective, see Cooper, *The Tennessean*, 2006. Quotes about the duet with Brad Paisley come from Dolly's website at https://dollyparton.com/life-and-career/music/when-i-get-where-im-going-duet-brad-paisley/476. On Dolly's award ceremony attendance with Steve Buckingham, see Rousuck, 2006. One place to find the "food, sex, music" quote is *Songteller* (223); on learning to cook with Willadeene, see Churchill, 1999; see Parton 2006 for soup quote (47), on road food (30), and for quote about the silver dollar quote (94); also, Dolly talks about writing songs while cooking in King, 2003. On pre-Nozell era ticket sales and his quotes, see Garner, 2000; also see Lordi, 2020, and Woods, 2021. A major source for perspectives on the Broadway musical is Lunden, 2008. The "Dr. Dolly" quote is found in White, 2009. Dolly expanded themes of her UT graduation speech for her 2012 book *Dream More*. For Dolly's perspective on making *Joyful Noise*, see Ahmed, 2012.

STILL ROCKIN'

On Warnock's kitchen conversation, see Roberts, 2014; Dolly's quotes about the album are from Lewis, 2014, and *Songteller* (371). Dolly described her backstage Glastonbury nerves in Price, 2014; details about the performance come from Merrill, 2014; for Steve Guest quote, see Roberts, 2014; also Smarsh (146). Sources on the time capsule include *Songteller* (372) and Smith, 2022. On the 2021 donation five years after Dolly's telethon, see https://www.billboard.com/music/music-news/dolly-parton-good-deeds-timeline-9487782; also see Smarsh (150). On Carl's dressing up and Dolly's composing "Forever Love,"

see Price, 2016; on Ringgold, see *People*, October 2022, and Sexton, 2012; on her secret to a long marriage and driving around in their RV, see Price, 2014; on she and Carl being opposites, see *Radar*, 2015. Insight and information on "Rainbowland" come from https://999thepoint.com/dolly-parton-miley-cyrus, including Dolly, 2013; Bilbo, 2018; and Gold, 2017. The *Washington Post* piece on "More Perfect" is dated September 17, 2018. On Dolly's perspective about working with Netflix, see Jacobsen and Beachum, 2020; also see Roberts, 2019. On the Galantis collaboration, see Spanos, 2019. Dolly's tweet about the vaccine donation is found in Clouse, 2020; also see NPR's *All Things Considered*, 2020, and Bragg, 2022. "Goodnight With Dolly" sources include Berman, 2020; https://donate.imaginationlibrary.com/goodnight-with-dolly; and Vasquez Russell, 2021. For Debbie Allen quote, see Lordi, 2020. Information about Spotify comes from Smyth, 2022; the Nashville press interview appears in *The Daily Mail*, 2022. On the Bezos award, see Brasch, 2022; for Schusterman quote, Care More initiative, and Dolly's quote about recognition, see Gamboa, 2022. For rock album plans, see Gleason, 2022.

SOURCES

BOOKS AND BOOK CHAPTERS

Cardwell, Nancy. *The Words and Music of Dolly Parton: Getting to Know Country's "Iron Butterfly."* Praeger Singer-Songwriter Collection. Santa Barbara, CA: Praeger, 2011.

Connors, Charlotte. *How Dolly Parton Saved My Life.* New York: Broadway Books, 2008.

DeMain, Bill. *Behind the Muse: Pop and Rock's Greatest Songwriters Talk About Their Work and Inspiration.* Cranberry Township, PA: Tiny Ripple Books, 2001.

DeMain, Bill. *In Their Own Words: Songwriters Talk About the Creative Process.* Westport, CT: Praeger, 2004.

Edwards, Leigh H. *Dolly Parton, Gender, and Country Music.* Bloomington, IN: Indiana University Press, 2018.

Ellison, Curtis W. *Country Music Culture: From Hard Times to Heaven.* Jackson, MS: University Press of Mississippi, 1995.

Emery, Ralph, with Patsi Bale Cox. *50 Years Down a Country Road.* New York: William Morrow, 2000.

Hamessley, Lydia R. *Unlikely Angel: The Songs of Dolly Parton.* Women Composers. Urbana , IL: University of Illinois Press, 2020.

Havighurst, Craig. *Air Castle of the South: WSM and the Making of Music City.* Music in American Life. Urbana , IL: University of Illinois Press, 2007.

King, Larry L. *The Whorehouse Papers.* New York: Viking Press, 1982.

Marcus, Greil. *Real Life Rock: The Complete Top Ten Columns, 1986-2014.* New Haven , CT: Yale University Press, 2015.

Mellard, Jason. *Progressive Country: How the 1970s Transformed the Texan in Popular Culture.* Austin, TX: University of Texas Press, 2013.

Morris, Mitchell. *The Persistence of Sentiment: Display and Feeling in Popular Music of the 1970s.* Berkeley, CA: University of California Press, 2013.

Moss, Marissa R. *Her Country: How the Women of Country Music Became the Success They Were Never Supposed to Be.* New York: Henry Holt and Company, 2022.

Nash, Alanna. *Behind Closed Doors: Talking With the Legends of Country Music.* New York: Knopf, 1998.

Parton, Dolly. *Dolly's Dixie Fixin's: Love, Laughter, and Lots of Good Food from My Tennessee Mountain Kitchen.* New York: Viking Studio, 2006.

Parton, Dolly. *Dream More: Celebrate the Dreamer in You.* New York: Penguin, 2012.

Parton, Dolly. *My Life and Other Unfinished Business.* London: HarperCollins, 1994.

Parton, Dolly, with Robert K. Oermann. *Dolly Parton, Songteller: My Life in Lyrics.* San Francisco: Chronicle Books, 2020.

Parton, Dorothy Jo Owens, with Javetta Saunders and R. Jerry Horner. *Dolly's Hero Shares Mighty Mountain Voices.* Self-published. Dorothy Parton, 2007.

Sánchez Vegara, Ma Isabel, and Daria Solak. *Dolly Parton. Little People: Big Dreams.* Mankato, MN: Frances Lincoln Children's Books, an imprint of The Quarto Group, 2019.

Schmidt, Randy L. *Dolly on Dolly : Interviews and Encounters with Dolly Parton.* Chicago: Chicago Review Press, 2017.

Smarsh, Sarah. *She Come By It Natural: Dolly Parton and the Women Who Lived Her Songs.* New York: Scribner (Simon & Schuster), 2020.

Watson, Jada. "Region and Identity in Dolly Parton's Songwriting," in *The Cambridge Companion to the Singer-Songwriter*, edited by Katherine Williams and Justin A. Williams, 120-30. Cambridge: Cambridge University Press, 2016.

West, Andrew. *The Art of Songwriting.* London: Methuen Drama, 2016.

ONLINE RESOURCES

Abumrad, Jad, host, and Shima Oliaee, producer. "Sad-Ass Songs" [Episode 1]. *Dolly Parton's America* (podcast). October 15, 2019. Accessed June 26, 2022. https://www.wnycstudios.org/podcasts/dolly-partons-america/episodes/2.

Ahmed, Beenish. "In Tough Times, Dolly Parton Makes a 'Joyful Noise.'" *NPR* (website), January 18, 2012; https://www.npr.org/2012/01/18/145397009/dolly-parton-makes-a-joyful-noise-on-big-screen.

American Eagle Foundation website, unsigned blog posts dated July 2, 2003, and April 10, 2008; https://www.eagles.org/music-legend-dolly-parton-names-releases-rescued-eagle.

Aniftos, Rania. "A Timeline of Dolly Parton's Good Deeds." *Billboard* (website), August 3, 2022; https://www.billboard.com/music/music-news/dolly-parton-good-deeds-timeline-9487782.

bangshowbiz.com. "Galantis: Dolly Parton is like a stand-up comedian." *BANG Showbiz (UK)*, February 10, 2020. *NewsBank: America's News Magazines.* https://infoweb-newsbank-com.eu1.proxy.openathens.net/apps/news/document-view?p=AMNP&docref=news/17904D6CD88B2848.

Bilbo, Thomas, 2018. Comment on Miley Cyrus. "Rainbowland." *YouTube*, September 28, 2017.

BradPaisley. "Brad Paisley - When I Get Where I'm Going (Featuring Dolly Parton)." *YouTube*, October 3, 2009; https://youtu.be/yYHT-TF4KO4.

Carter, Jimmy. "Dolly Parton Debuts on *The Porter Wagoner Show* September 1967," May 8, 2022; https://www.youtube.com/watch?v=202J3LeYdEY.

CBS Mornings. "Dolly Parton Sings a Song She Wrote as a 5-Year-Old," May 5, 2016. https://www.youtube.com/watch?v=0HCoMd_wmDg.

Chang, Juju, and Victoria Thompson. "Dolly Parton on Gay Rumors, Losing a Drag Queen Look-Alike Contest and New Memoir." *ABC News* (website), November 26, 2012; https://abcnews.go.com/Entertainment/dolly-parton-gay-rumors-losing-drag-queen-alike/story?id=17812138.

Christian, Margena A. "How Do You Really Get A Star On The Hollywood Walk Of Fame?" *Jet* 111, no. 15 (April 16, 2007): 25–30. https://search.ebscohost.com/login.aspx?direct=true&AuthType=shib&db=f-6h&AN=24660725&site=eds-live&scope=site.

Cottom, Tressie McMillan. "The Dolly Moment: Why We Stan a Post-Racism Queen." *Essaying* (website), February 24, 2021; https://tressie.substack.com/p/the-dolly-moment.

Country Music Hall of Fame, *Suiting the Sound* (website and online exhibit dedicated to country music fashion), accessed October 21, 2022; https://countrymusichalloffame.org/exhibit/suiting-the-sound.

Daly, Sean. "Dolly Parton recalls brother's death: 'There is a lot of heartache.'" *Fox News* (website), May 2, 2016; https://www.foxnews.com/entertainment/dolly-parton-recalls-brothers-death-there-is-a-lot-of-heartache.

Davey, Emma. "Dolly Parton Lookalike Contest Returns to Mable's Smokehouse." *Greenpointers* (website), March 1, 2022; https://greenpointers.com/2022/03/01/dolly-parton-lookalike-contest-returns-to-mables-smokehouse.

Dezeen. "Heather Colbert's stop-motion animation of Dolly Parton is a "tale of female confidence." *YouTube*, March 7, 2018; https://youtu.be/wp0B-9yeAGzE.

Dolly Parton Interview. Library of Congress, February 28, 2018. Video. https://www.loc.gov/item/webcast-8329.

Drury, Sharareh. "How 'Odd Couple' Linda Perry and Dolly Parton Created Grammy-Nominated Song 'Girl in the Movies.'" *The Hollywood Reporter* (blog), December 19, 2019; https://www.hollywoodreporter.com/news/music-news/how-linda-perry-dolly-parton-created-grammy-nominated-girl-movies-1264217.

Dukes, Billy. "How Dolly Parton Saved Kenny Rogers from Passing on a Career Hit." *Taste of Country* (website), August 19, 2022; https://tasteofcountry.com/remember-when-kenny-rogers-almost-passed-on-islands-in-the-stream.

"Dunmow Flitch Trials: Come and Claim the Bacon!" Accessed July 1, 2022; https://www.dunmowflitchtrials.co.uk.

Entertainment Tonight website. February, 11, 2019; https://www.etonline.com/media/videos/grammys-2019-watch-dolly-partons-big-performance-with-her-girl-power-entourage-119427.

Galantis. "Galantis & Dolly Parton: Faith feat. Mr. Probz [Official Music Video]." *YouTube*, October 25, 2019; https://youtu.be/KA07g2lvgbo.

Garner, George. "Dolly Parton: The Music Week Interview." *Music Week*, December 7, 2020; http://www.musicweek.com/interviews/read/dolly-parton-the-music-week-interview/082141.

Gleason, Holly. "Why Dolly Parton Belongs in the Rock Hall." *PollStar* (website), October 27, 2022; https://news.pollstar.com/2022/10/27/why-dolly-parton-belongs-in-the-rock-hall.

Goldstein, Tiffany. "Dolly Parton Opens Up About An Unreleased Song That She Was Asked To Bury: "Burning Me Up Inside." *cmt.com* (website), December 21, 2022; https://www.cmt.com/news/20jc66/dolly-parton-opens-up-about-an-unreleased-song-that-she-was-forced-to-bury-burning-me-up-inside.

"Goodnight with Dolly." *Imagination Library* (website); https://donate.imaginationlibrary.com/goodnight-with-dolly.

Graham, Sonny. "Dolly Parton - Rock & Roll Hall of Fame Induction – 2022." *YouTube*, November 26, 2022; https://youtu.be/eR3awRAZiko.

Green, Kai, "50 Quotes From Gloria Steinem, the 'World's Most Famous Feminist,' That Are Perfect for Women's History Month," *Parade* (website), March 24, 2022; https://parade.com/1351660/kaigreen/gloria-steinem-quotes.

Gross, Terry. "Dolly Parton: Singing Songs from the Heart and Soul." *Fresh Air* [transcript], NPR, 2010; archival material from 2001; https://www.proquest.com/other-sources/dolly-parton-singing-songs-heart-soul/docview/856351198/se-2.

Hocter, Matthew. "Dolly Parton's 'The Bargain Store' Turns 45 | Anniversary Retrospective," *Albumism* (website), February 16, 2020; https://albumism.com/features/dolly-parton-the-bargain-store-turns-45-anniversary-retrospective.

Iahn, Buddy. "Episode 134 with Bill Anderson." *The Music Universe* [podcast], June 10, 2022; https://themusicuniverse.com/episode-134-with-bill-anderson.

Jacobson, Kevin, and Chris Beachum. "Dolly Parton ('Heartstrings') on how Netflix inspired her to 'really give everything that I had," *Gold Derby* (website), July 15, 2020; https://www.goldderby.com/article/2020/dolly-parton-heartstrings-netflix-video-interview-transcript.

Jocar Productions, "Dolly and Carol in Nashville," February 14, 1979; accessed July 28, 2022; "VHS Vault Collection"; *Internet Archives*, https://archive.org/details/dolly-carol-in-nashville-1979.

Kabota, Samantha. "Dolly Parton turned down the Presidential Medal of Freedom twice." NBC *Today* (website), February 1, 2021; https://www.today.com/popculture/dolly-parton-turned-down-presidential-medal-freedom-twice-t207752?cid=sm_npd_td_tw_ma.

Keeley, Pete. "Dolly Parton on Creating Tunes for 'Dumplin': 'I Was Playing Off a Lot of My Own Emotions.'" *The Hollywood Reporter* (blog), December 12, 2018. https://www.hollywoodreporter.com/news/music-news/dolly-parton-creating-tunes-jennifer-aniston-movie-dumplin-1167900.

Kelly Clarkson Show. "Dolly Parton Has a Secret Song Buried in a Time Capsule & She Wants to Dig It Up." *YouTube*, December 20, 2022; https://youtu.be/1NHV3lvyBfM.

Kelly, Mary Louise, and Ari Shapiro. "Dolly Parton Donations Helped in Developing Coronavirus Vaccine," *NPR's All Things Considered*, November 18, 2020; https://www.npr.org/2020/11/18/936342881/dolly-parton-donations-helped-in-developing-coronavirus-vaccine.

Ketar, Tahir. "Dolly Parton Honoree (Complete) 29th Kennedy Center Honors, 2006 (150)." *YouTube*, September 20, 2016; https://youtu.be/efujlvF9SQI.

Konc, Riane. "Interview: Emmylou Harris, Dolly Parton and Linda Ronstadt Reflect on 'Trio' Projects." *The Boot* (website), September 9, 2016; https://theboot.com/trio-dolly-parton-emmylou-harris-linda-ronstadt-interview-2016.

Lunden, Jeff. "Dolly Parton, Working '9 to 5' to Get to Broadway." *National Public Radio, Weekend Edition*, September 20, 2008; https://www.npr.org/2008/09/20/94823815/dolly-parton-working-9-to-5-to-get-to-broadway.

Martinez, Amanda Marie. "Why Do We Need Dolly To Be A Saint?" *NPR* (website), August 20, 2021; https://www.npr.org/2021/08/20/1029306864/dolly-parton-nashville-sevier-park-real-estate-why-need-be-saint.

Mayer, Petra. "Dolly Parton Says She Turned Down Presidential Medal Of Freedom — Twice." *NPR* (website), February 2, 2021; https://www.npr.org/2021/02/02/963172542/dolly-parton-says-she-turned-down-presidential-medal-of-freedom-twice.

McKenzie, Angela. "Al Cecere, American Eagle Foundation," *Initiative Radio*, 2011; https://archive.org/details/Ir-11-13AlCecereAmericanEagleFoundation.

McMahan, Carroll. "Dolly Parton Statue Has Become Iconic Symbol." *Sevierhistory.com* (website), 2016; http://sevierhistory.com/PDFs/Dolly-Statue.pdf.

MegaKal13. "He's Alive: Dolly Parton – 1989." *YouTube*, July 16, 2011; https://youtu.be/05W4OX7WrJU.

n.a. "Nomination for Hollywood Walk of Fame 2023 Selection." *walkoffame.com* (website); https://walkoffame.com/nomination-procedure.

O'Connor, Roisin. "Dolly Parton Reveals the Meaning Behind Her Butterfly Tattoos." *Independent*, October 7, 2021; independent.co.uk/arts-enterntainment/music/news/dolly-parton-tattoos-meaning-surgery-b1933914.html.

Parton, Dolly. "Dolly Parton with Little Tiny Tassletop on *The Dolly Show* 1987/88 (Ep 10, Pt 6)," February 11, 2014; https://www.youtube.com/watch?v=TthyDduiSKg.

Price, Deborah Evans. "Dolly Parton: How She Fell in Love All Over Again With 'Pure and Simple,'" *Rolling Stone*, August 19, 2016; https://www.rollingstone.com/music/music-country/dolly-parton-how-she-fell-in-love-all-over-again-with-pure-and-simple-248241.

Price, Deborah Evans. "Dolly Parton Interview." American Songwriter, March/April 1990, in Song: The World's Best Songwriters on Creating the Music That Moves Us, edited by J. Douglas Waterman. Cincinnati, OH: Writer's Digest Books, 2007.

Price, Deborah Evans. "Dolly Parton Q&A: The Country Legend on 50 Years in Nashville and Why She Supports Her Gay Fans." Billboard (blog), October 24, 2014; https://www.billboard.com/music/country/dolly-parton-talks-50-years-in-nashville-and-supporting-gay-fans-6296620.

Radar, Dotson. "Dolly Parton on Coat of Many Colors, Faith and Marriage." Parade (online), December 4, 2015; https://parade.com/440805/dotson-rader/dolly-parton-on-coat-of-many-colors-faith-and-marriage.

raredolly. "Little Tiny Tassletop - Dolly Parton," September 30, 2010; https://www.youtube.com/watch?v=XVcu4pbtjQo.

Roberts, Robin. Interview with Dolly Parton for ABC Nightline, November 12, 2019; https://abc.com/shows/nightline/episode-guide/2019-11/12-tuesday-nov-12-2019.

Rose, Charlie. "Dolly Parton Discusses Her Music and Career Choices. Director Sam Mendes Discusses New Movie and Artistic Process." Charlie Rose Show [MSNBC; transcript], June 5, 2009; https://search.ebscohost.com/login.aspx?direct=true&AuthType=shib&db=pwh&AN=32U3334218582MS8&site=eds-live&scope=site.

Sexton, Cindy. "Dolly Parton: 'So we thought Ringgold.'" Local 3 News (Chattanooga, TN; website), May 18, 2012; updated December 2, 2021; https://www.local3news.com/dolly-parton-so-we-thought-ringgold/article_19d09b19-ec6b-570c-9ff6-81791a464969.html.

Shelburne, Craig. "Gender Identity and Country Music Merge in 'Transamerica.'" CMT (website), March 3, 2006; https://www.cmt.com/news/2fy4as/gender-identity-and-country-music-merge-in-transamerica.

Smith, Jules. "TACF presents the Chestnut Conservation Champion Award to Dolly Parton on behalf of her late uncle, Bill Owens." American Chestnut Foundation (website), July 11, 2022; https://acf.org/tacf-presents-the-chestnut-conservation-champion-award-to-dolly-parton-on-behalf-of-her-late-uncle-bill-owens.

Sutton, Amber. "36 sad songs that make us cry every time we hear 'em." It's a Southern Thing (website), February 28, 2020; https://www.southernthing.com/36-sad-songs-that-make-us-cry-every-time-2645330345.html.

Thompson, Gayle. "Bill Anderson Praises Dolly Parton: 'She's Amazing.'" Everything Nash (website), February 3, 2023; https://www.everythingnash.com/bill-anderson-praises-dolly-parton-shes-amazing.

The Tonight Show Starring Jimmy Fallon. Dolly Parton's Husband Wants a Threesome with Jennifer Aniston, 2018; https://www.youtube.com/watch?v=1P-KEZ-BJX6s.

Torchinsky, Rina. "People who work at Dollywood will soon be eligible for free tuition," NPR (website), February 9, 2022; https://www.npr.org/2022/02/09/1079606811/dolly-parton-dollywood-free-tuition.

Vandergriff, Maranda. "Dr. Robert F. Thomas: The Great Smoky Mountain Horseback Healer of Body and Soul." YouTube, April 7, 2009; https://youtu.be/_PpaoaJ-XBk.

Vera, Kelby. "Dolly Parton says that goddaughter Miley Cyrus was always bound for stardom: 'I Knew She Was Special," Daily Mail (website), December 7, 2020; https://www.dailymail.co.uk/tvshowbiz/article-9027019/Dolly-Parton-says-goddaughter-Miley-Cyrus-bound-stardom.html.

VHS Archives. "Dolly Parton and Jimmy Stewart Interview – Barbara Walters." YouTube, June 17, 2022; https://youtu.be/OLMR4LcF8us.

Vitale, Tom. "Dolly Parton's 'Jolene' Still Haunts Singers." NPR (website), October 9, 2008; https://www.npr.org/2008/10/09/95520570/dolly-partons-jolene-still-haunts-singers.

Wade, Gary. "A Country Doctor." CityView (web magazine), n.d.; https://cityviewmag.com/fact-and-fiction.

WBIR. "Dolly Parton and Kenny Rogers Reveal Why They Never Became a Couple." WWLTV (website), October 25, 2017; https://www.wwltv.com/article/news/entertainment-news/dolly-parton-and-kenny-rogers-reveal-why-they-never-became-a-couple/51-485964818.

Wilkerson, Jessica. "Living With Dolly Parton." Longreads (website), October 2018; https://longreads.com/2018/10/16/living-with-dolly-parton.

Windsor, Amie. "Dear Readers: Love is Love." Sonoma County Gazette, June 1, 2022; https://www.sonomacountygazette.com/sonoma-county-news/dear-readers-love-is-love.

Woods, Cat. "Meet Steve Summers, From Dancer to Dolly Parton's Creative Director." partonandpearl.com (website), March 8, 2021; https://www.partonandpearl.com/blog/meet-steve-summers-from-dancer-to-dolly-partons-creative-director.

Young, Casey. "Dolly Parton Recalls Actually Losing A Dolly Parton Look-Alike Contest: "I Got the Least Applause But I Was Dying Laughing Inside." Whiskeyriff (website), April 7, 2022; https://www.whiskeyriff.com/2022/04/07/dolly-parton-recalls-actually-losing-a-dolly-parton-look-alike-contest-i-got-the-least-applause-but-i-was-dying-laughing-inside.

NEWS AND NEWSPAPERS

Adamson, Lesley. "Country Comes to Town: Lesley Adamson Meets Dolly Parton, Just a Girl from Smoky Mountain, Whose European Tour Brings Her to the Rainbow on Saturday." The Guardian, May 25, 1977.

AP. "Right from the Heart to the Bank with Dolly." Toronto Star, March 13, 1993.

Bailey, Jerry. "Porter Pushes Dolly's Bandwagon." The Tennessean, December 2, 1973.

Barnes, Brooks. "Hollywood's Queen of Reinvention Takes on 'Rocky Horror'." New York Times, October 9, 2016.

Blowen, Michael. "Review Movie; They Took The Texas Out Of, Whorehouse'; The Best Little Whorehouse In Texas." Boston Globe, Jul 24, 1982.

Brady, James. "In Step with Dolly Parton." Newsday/Parade, October 10, 1999, Combined editions.

Brasch, Ben. "From '9 to 5' to $100 Million, Dolly Parton Receives Bezos Charity Award." The Washington Post, November 14, 2022.

Brown, Ellen. "Gatlinburg youth headed to National History Day - First in a series." The Mountain Press, May 6, 2009: A1, A4.

Campbell, Mary. "Dolly Parton: Individual Voice, Individual Style and a Dream Come True." The Austin American Statesman, May 4, 1975.

Chamberlain, Chris. "White Limozeen Restaurant Coming Soon to the Graduate Nashville: Rooftop-pool dining spot and bar will be the latest project at the Midtown hotel." Nashville Scene (TN), July 7, 2020.

Chase, Chris. "The Country Girl." New York Times, May 9, 1976.

Churchill, Bonnie. "With Dolly, Somethin's Always Cookin': [Chicagoland Final Edition]." Chicago Tribune, October 02, 1999.

Clouse, Allie. "Dolly Parton helped fund 95% effective Moderna COVID-19 vaccine that could end pandemic." Knoxville News Sentinel, November 17, 2020.

Cooper, Peter. "Dolly Knows What Outcasts Feel." *The Tennessean*, February 23, 2006.

Edelstein, Andy. "Dolly Parton's '80s Variety show: 5 Memories from a Rare Failure." *Newsday*, November 27, 2016, Combined editions.

Edwards, Joe. "First, Dolly Dolls; and Now, A Song." *The Atlanta Constitution*, November 25, 1978.

Freeman, Hadley. "The Guardian: G2 interview: 'Oprah and I share many very special bonds': Dolly Parton talks to Hadley Freeman." *The Guardian*, August 22, 2011.

Freeman, Hadley. "The Guardian: G2: The Muppets and moi: Kermit, Miss Piggy and pals are back with a new film and a TV series in the works. Hadley Freeman fondly remembers the satirical puppets and the massive role they played in her childhood." *The Guardian*, November 24, 2011.

Friskics-Warren, Bill. "The Other Dolly Parton, the Songwriting One." *New York Times*, July 21, 2002, Late Edition (East Coast).

Friskics-Warren, Bill. "Paisley's Pattern; on 'Time Well Wasted,' the Country Showman Offers More Beef, Less Corn [Final Edition]." *The Washington Post*, August 17, 2005.

Frost, Caroline. "Dolly Parton On Getting To Grips With Queen Latifah In 'Joyful Noise' (Interview)." *Huffington Post—UK Edition*, June 29, 2012; https://www.huffingtonpost.co.uk/2012/06/29/dolly-parton-queen-latifah-joyful-noise-dollywood_n_1638463.html.

Gamboa, Glenn. "Dolly Parton Donation Strategy: 'I Just Give from My Heart.'" *The Independent*, October 14, 2022.

Gamboa, Glenn. "Dolly Parton Receives Philanthropy Award for Children's Book Programme." *Irish Examiner*, October 14, 2022.

Gleason, Sinead. "Hello Dolly!" *Irish Times*, September 2, 2011.

Grobel, Larry. "The LI Interview: Dolly Parton." *Newsday*, January 14, 1979.

Gross, Michael Joseph. "Music; St. Dolly and Her Flock." *New York Times*, January 26, 2003; https://www.nytimes.com/2003/01/26/arts/music-st-dolly-and-her-flock.html.

Guerrero, Gene. "Porter Wagoner and Dolly Parton." *The Great Speckled Bird*, May 17 and May 24, 1971. In Randy Schmidt, *Dolly on Dolly*, pp. 33-45.

Hance, Bill. "Sour Notes for Three Country Queens." *Newsday*, September 7, 1976.

Heathcote, Elizabeth. "Q the Interview: Dolly Parton [Foreign Edition]." *The Independent*, June 30, 2002.

Holden, Stephen. "For Linda Ronstadt, The Past Continues To Inspire." *New York Times*, Sep 14, 1986, Late Edition (East Coast).

Holden, Stephen. "Recordings: Laurie Anderson Unfurls A Pop Opera About America [Review]." *New York Times*, January 20, 1985, Late Edition (East Coast).

Hurst, Jack. "Shoestring TV." *Chicago Tribune*, May 29, 1990; https://www.chicagotribune.com/news/ct-xpm-1990-05-29-9002130667-story.html.

Hurst, Jack. "Shopping in Antique Store, Dolly Found a Big New Hit." *Detroit Free Press*, March 31, 1975.

Jackson, Leigh-Ann. "If You Thought Fringe Was Just for Gussying…" *Austin American Statesman*, February 20, 2003.

Kempley, Rita. "Dolly Parton Going for Glitter; from Mountain Roots to Hollywood Hills." *The Washington Post*, November 17, 1989.

King, Larry L. "The Buck Stops at Burt: Hollywood Egos Run Amok with Larry L. King's Best Little Whorehouse. The Whorehouse Papers: Last of a Series." *Newsday*, July 15, 1982, Nassau ed.

King, Larry L. Third of a series. "Tinsel Town Moves In: Larry L. King's 'The Best Little Whorehouse in Texas' Stumbles Toward Film. The Whorehouse Papers." *Newsday*, July 14, 1982, Nassau ed.

Kolata, Gina. "First Mammal Clone Dies; Dolly Made Science History." *New York Times*, February 15, 2003, Late Edition (East Coast).

Lipper, Hal. "Women of Steel: 'Magnolias' Stars Found Strength in Each Other [City Edition]." *St. Petersburg Times*, November 19, 1989.

Litsch, Joseph. "A Pair to Remember: Dolly Parton and Carol Burnett." *The Atlanta Constitution*, February 10, 1979.

Litsch, Joseph. "Dolly!" *The Atlanta Constitution*, May 20, 1978.

Lordi, Emily. "Working Girl." *New York Times Magazine*, December 6, 2020, 70-75.

Lowman, Rob. "From Dollywood To Hollywood Parton Keeps On Pushing For 'Transamerica' Oscar [Valley Edition]." *Daily News*, February 19, 2006.

Maslin, Janet. "Film: 'Whorehouse in Texas,' Reynolds-Parton Version." *New York Times*, July 24, 1982.

Merrill, James. "Dazzling Dolly takes minds off the mud at Glastonbury - Last Night Glastonbury: Festival Worthy Farm, Somerset ****." *The Independent*, June 30, 2014, 4, 5.

Morrow, Terry. "'It's all Good'; Dolly Takes Time from Bluegrass & BBQ Fest to Banter about Love [Five-Star Edition]." *News Sentinel*, September 16, 2006.

n.a. "Bill Anderson & Dolly Parton unleash bluegrass version of 'Someday It'll All Make Sense.'" *Lewiston-Porter Sentinel*, August 19, 2022.

n.a., "Dolly Parton benefit concert helps hometown hospital." *The Times Union*, May 22, 2007, A2.

n.a. "Dolly Parton: My talented goddaughter Miley is just trying to find her way." *Evening Standard* November 1, 2013; https://www.standard.co.uk/showbiz/dolly-parton-my-talented-goddaughter-miley-is-just-trying-to-find-her-way-8918083.html.

n.a. "Dolly Parton On 'Going Home.'" *St. Louis Post-Dispatch*, May 27, 1987.

n.a. "Country Icon Parton Sets 19th Amendment to Song." *Washington Post*, September 17, 2018.

n.a. "From Metallica to Dolly, Glasto is all set to rock Screen Small." *Birmingham Post*, June 26, 2014, 11.

n.a. "Music interview: Mark E Nevin on 'Dolly Said No to Elvis' and working with Morrissey." *Yorkshire Evening Post*, March 8, 2018; https://www.yorkshireeveningpost.co.uk/arts-and-culture/music-interview-mark-e-nevin-dolly-said-no-elvis-and-working-morrissey-330669.

n.a. "Parton Wins Top C&W Award." *The Austin American Statesman* (evening ed.), October 10, 1978.

n.a. "Porter Wagoner Sues Dolly Parton." *The Austin American Statesman* (evening ed.), March 22, 1979.

n.a. "The Queen of Country Meets the King Of Crime." *Daily Mail*, March 12, 2022.

n.a. "Dr. Robert F. Thomas Foundation joins Covenant, Essary named as development manager." *The Mountain Press*, April 23, 2021.

Nazzari, Natalie. "10 Things You Didn't Know About Dolly Parton." *STM Entertainment Magazine*, June 19, 2011 12.

"NEA Honors Dolly Parton with Friend of Education Award." *Targeted News Service*, July 6, 2022.

Nicholson, Rebecca. "Hear me out: why, Joyful Noise, isn't a bad movie." *The Guardian*, June 1, 2021; https://www.theguardian.com/film/2021/jun/01/joyful-noise-dolly-parton-queen-latifah."The Nominees." *Billboard* 134, no. 17 (December 17, 2022): 133–56.

Otis, James. "Oh... Oh, what a Gal; She Likes to Keep 'Em Guessing." *The Atlanta Constitution*, October 22, 1978.

Ouzounian, Richard. "Life Begins at 'Sexty'; at a Point in Life Where Some Might Think about Slowing Down, Dolly Parton Remains a 'Busy Little Bee,' Writes Richard Ouzounian [ONT Edition]." *Toronto Star*, November 20, 2006.

Pareles, Jon. "Dolly Parton Heads from the Mountains Up to Carnegie Hall." *New York Times*, May 17, 1993.

PR Newswire. "Bill Anderson to Release New Album, 'As Far as I Can See: The Best Of,' on June 10." *PR Newswire*, April 26, 2022.

Pyle, Sheila Joyce. "Did Dolly Parton Cheat This Woman's Man?" *The Courier-Journal*, February 26, 1978.

Rockwell, John. "Pop Life: 'I Am Dolly Parton From the Mountains . . . I Am Country.'" *New York Times*, November 19, 1976.

Rockwell, John. "The Pop Life: Why Garland Jeffreys Says He Now Knows the Score." *New York Times*, 1977, sec. New Jersey Weekly.

Rockwell, John. "Three of Pop's Best Go Romping in the Country [Review]." *New York Times*, March 1, 1987.

Rousack, J. Wynn. "Here She Comes Again." *The Baltimore Sun*, November 26, 2006.

Rush, George, and Joanna Rush Molloy with Jo Piazza and Chris Rovzar. "Crossover Hit: Dolly's Tune Owes a Lot to Transsexual." *New York Daily News*, December 14, 2005.

Saad, Nardine. "Dolly Parton Tells Lawmakers She Doesn't Want a Statue of Herself — but Maybe Later." *Los Angeles Times*, February 18, 2021.

Schwed, Mark. "Dolly Brings Country Out of the Closet." *The Atlanta Constitution*, October 13, 1978.

Scott, Jay. "Dolly Parton Transcendent." *The Globe and Mail*, August 23, 1978, C11.

Scott, Jay. "'You Gotta Do What You Gotta Do': Crossing Paths with Dolly Parton Is a Mind-Boggling Experience; She's One Shrewd, Sexy Lady." *The Globe and Mail*, July 17, 1982.

Smyth, David. "Dolly's Novel Album Is Rosy." *Evening Standard*, March 4, 2022.

Snyder, Patrick. "Dolly's Gamble." *The Globe and Mail*, July 22, 1978.

Stevens, Heidi. "Add Vaccine to Reasons We'll Always Love Dolly Parton." *Chicago Tribune*, November 19, 2020.

Strauss, Neil. "Countrified and Dignified." *New York Times*, June 23, 1999.

Strauss, Neil. "Shania Twain Is Top Country Music Entertainer." *New York Times*, September 23, 1999.

Strickler, Jeff, and Staff Writer. "Doors Open for 'Little Movie That Could.'" *Star Tribune*, February 03, 2006.

Thomas, Bob. Associated Press. "Parton Says, Whorehouse' May Be Her Last Film." *Boston Globe*, December 30, 1981.

Trescott, Jacqueline. "Duvall, Marsalis among Arts Medalists." *The Washington Post*, November 9, 2005.

Trescott, Jacqueline. "The Kennedy Center Honor Roll: Five A." *The Washington Post*, September 7, 2006.

Valdesolo, Fiorella. "Dolly Parton Still Swears by Cheap Makeup; the Cultural Icon, Pandemic Hero and Newly Minted Beauty-Brand Mogul Hates Exercise, Loves Food and Is Thrilled by Cheap Makeup." *Wall Street Journal* (Online), May 31, 2021.

Vasquez Russell, Melanie. "'Goodnight with Dolly' wins multiple Telly Awards," *WATE* (website), July 13, 2021; https://www.wate.com/news/all-about-dolly-parton/goodnight-with-dolly-wins-multiple-telly-awards.

Waddell, Ray. "Barbie for a Whole New Generation; Dolly Parton Looks to Outlast Industry That Forgot Her." *Calgary Herald*, April 23, 2008.

Walburn, Lee. "Please, Dolly, Don't Sacrifice The Pure Sound." *The Atlanta Constitution*, February 26, 1977.

Watts, Cindy. "Dolly Parton's Smoky Mountains Rise telethon raises nearly $9M." *The Tennessean*, December 14, 2016; https://www.tennessean.com/story/entertainment/music/2016/12/14/dolly-partons-smoky-mountains-rise-telethon-raises-nearly-9m/95453636.

White, Chloe. "With Laughter and Song, Parton Urges UT Graduates to Dream." *McClatchy: Tribune Business News*, May 8, 2009.

Wilson, Robert L. "Maintaining His Medical Mission." *Knox News*, December 1, 2008; https://archive.knoxnews.com/news/local/maintaining-his-medical-mission-ep-410681416-359685021.html.

Zimmerman, David. "Country Angels: A Trio of Heavenly Voices in a Down-to-Earth Collaboration" 'Honky Tonk' Sisterhood of Grit and Glory." *USA Today*, October 29, 1993.

Zoladz, Lindsay. "Is There Anything We Can All Agree On? Yes: Dolly Parton." *New York Times*, November. 21, 2019; https://www.nytimes.com/2019/11/21/arts/music/dolly-parton.html.

MAGAZINES AND JOURNALS

Bellows, Keith. "Down Home with Dolly." *National Geographic Traveler* 26, no. 5 (July 2009): 20–26.

Berman, Judy. "Welcome to the Golden Era of Livestreaming." *Time* 195, no. 14 (April 20, 2020): 47–49.

Betts, Stephen L. "Dolly Parton on Children's Album, Miley Cyrus Duet, Emmys Controversy." *Rolling Stone*, October 13, 2017; https://www.rollingstone.com/music/music-country/dolly-parton-on-childrens-album-miley-cyrus-duet-emmys-controversy-117285.

Bragg, Rick. "Dolly Parton's Generosity Made Rick Bragg a Lifelong Fan." *Southern Living*, May 19, 2022; https://www.southernliving.com/culture/celebrities/rick-bragg-fan-letter-to-dolly-parton.

Briese, Nicole. "Dolly Parton and Carl Thomas Dean's Relationship Timeline." *People*, last updated on October 27, 2022; https://people.com/music/dolly-parton-carl-thomas-dean-relationship-timeline.

Charles, RuPaul. "Dolly: Patron Saint of 2020 in Conversation With the Blessed RuPaul." *Marie Claire*, October 20, 2021; https://www.marieclaire.com/celebrity/a34688302/dolly-parton-december-2020-interview.

Collins, Lauren. "Looking Swell." *New Yorker* 85, no. 12 (May 4, 2009): 19–20.

Daniel, Drew. "Not Home Right Now." *Art in America* 109, no. 2 (March 2021): 50–55.

Dowling, Marcus K. "Why Dolly Parton Doesn't Deserve a Nashville Statue—Yet." *Rolling Stone*, January 20, 2021; https://www.rollingstone.com/music/music-country/dolly-parton-statue-tennessee-capitol-1114864.

Dunn, Jancee. "Dolly Parton." *Rolling Stone*, no. 934 (October 30, 2003): 51–56.

East, Elyssa. "Nudie and the Cosmic American." *Oxford American* 91 (Winter 2015). Online. https://main.oxfordamerican.org/magazine/item/744-nudie-and-the-cosmic-american.

Eells, Josh. "The Last." *Rolling Stone*, no. 1210 (June 2014): 57–61.

Espen, Hal, Cynthia Sanz, and David Hiltbrand. "Song." *People* 39, no. 14 (April 12, 1993): 21.

Exposito, Suzy. "See Dolly Parton Join the Highwomen, Linda Perry at Newport Folk Festival." *Rolling Stone*, July 28, 2019; https://www.rollingstone.com/music/music-country/dolly-parton-brandi-carlile-highwomen-newport-folk-festival-2019-864399.

Flippo, Chet. "Interview: Dolly Parton." *Rolling Stone*, August 25, 1977; in Schmidt, 2017.

Garner, Glenn. "Dolly Parton Coming to Netflix Again with Star-Studded MusiCares Person of the Year Tribute Concert." *People.com*, March 26, 2021.

Gold, Adam. "Dolly Parton Unveils Children's Album, Talks Kesha Collaboration." *Rolling Stone*, August 16, 2017; https://www.rollingstone.com/music/music-country/dolly-parton-unveils-childrens-album-talks-kesha-collaboration-204861.

Gordon, Mel. "Laurie Anderson: Performance Artist." *The Drama Review*: TDR 24, no. 2 (1980): 51–54; https://doi.org/10.2307/1145281.

Grobel, Lawrence. "Playboy Interview: Dolly Parton: A Candid Conversation with the Curvaceous Queen of Country Music." *Playboy*, October 1978; in Schmidt, 2017, pp. 79-126.

Hirschberg, Lynn. "Dolly Parton Simply Doesn't Stop." *W Magazine*, October 6, 2021; https://www.wmagazine.com/life/dolly-parton-interview-2-21/amp.

Hirshey, Gerri. "Dolly Parton: Doin' What Comes Naturally." *Family Circle*, January 9, 1979; in Schmidt, pp. 144-55.

Jackson, Lauren Michele. "The United States of Dolly Parton." *The New Yorker*, October 12, 2020; https://www.newyorker.com/magazine/2020/10/19/the-united-states-of-dolly-parton.

Jaehne, Karen. "CEO and Cinderella." *Cineaste* 17, no. 4 (1990).

Jefferson, Margo. "Dolly Parton: Bewigged, Bespangled . . . and Proud." *Ms.* 7, no. 12 (June 1979): 14-16, 20-22.

Jones, Nicole. "Dolly Parton's Latest Act of Reinvention: A Dull TV Movie About Her Childhood." *Vanity Fair*, December 11, 2015; https://www.vanityfair.com/hollywood/2015/12/dolly-parton-coat-of-many-colors.

Kavehkar, Kimya. "Dearest Dumplin': YA Novelist Julie Murphy Talks Teen Empowerment, Dolly Parton, and Her Netflix Movie." *Texas Highways* (website), March 26, 2019; https://texashighways.com/culture/people/dearest-dumplin-ya-novelist-julie-murphy-talks-teen-empowerment-dolly-parton-and-her-netflix-movie.

Levins, Harry [compiler]. *St. Louis Post-Dispatch*, October 3, 1993.

Lewis, Randy. "Dolly Parton Covers a Lot of Ground; the Singer is Busy with a New Album, Tour Dates, Dollywood Expansion and More." *Los Angeles Times*, May 14, 2014.

McHenry, Susan "Positively Parton." *Ms.* 15, no. 1 (July 1986): 14.

McQuaid, Peter. "The Cowboy Couturier." *New York Times Magazine*, March 19, 2000, 86-94.

n.a. "Exhibit Marks 30th Anniversary of Dolly Parton Statue." *Southern Jewish Life* 27, no. 5 (May 2017): 27.

n.a. "'I Will Always Love You.'" *Woman's Day* (Australia Edition), no. 2015 (April 6, 2020): 32–33.

Newman, Melinda. "Barry Gibb on Reuniting with Dolly Parton & Who He 'Freaked Out' Over While Recording New Country Duets Album." *Billboard*, January 5, 2021; https://www.billboard.com/music/country/barry-gibb-interview-duets-album-dolly-parton-9507251.

Ray, Linda. "Dolly Parton—The Smartest Working Woman in Show Business." *No Depression*, November/December 1999; in Schmidt, 2017, pp. 308-23.

Roberts, Dave. "Royal Parton." *Music Week*, no. 74 (June 27, 2014): 27–37.

Sachs, Andrea. "Q & A: Dolly Parton." *Time*, June 22, 2009; https://content.time.com/time/arts/article/0,8599,1906079,00.html.

Simpson, George. "Led Zeppelin Reunion with Robert Plant and Jimmy Page Being Orchestrated by Dolly Parton." *Express* (Online), October 31, 2022.

Smith, Nasha. "21 Things You Probably Didn't Know about Dolly Parton." *Insider*, US edition, January 19, 2021.

Spanos, Brittany. "After Galantis' 'Faith,' Dolly Parton Ready to Make More Dance Music." *Rolling Stone*, October 25, 2019; https://www.rollingstone.com/music/music-features/dolly-parton-galantis-mr-probz-interview-faith-new-song-902765.

Stadiem, William. "Daisy Mae in Hollywood." *Interview*, July 1989; in Schmidt, pp. 269-93.

Steinem, Gloria. "Dolly Parton." *Ms.* 15, no. 7 (January 1987): 66-68.

Steinfeld, Dave. "Country Outing." *Curve*, September, 2016, 59.

Tirella, Joseph V. "Talking with . . . Dolly Parton." *People* 55, no. 4 (January 29, 2001): 38.

Weiss, Rick. "In Dollywood; Dolly Sheepish about Appearing." *Edmonton Journal*, April 5, 1999.

Wilson, Pamela. "Mountains of Contradictions: Gender, Class, and Region in the Star Image of Dolly Parton." *The South Atlantic Quarterly* 94, no. 1 (Winter 1995): 109-34.

Wootton, Dan. "I'm very worried about Miley. She told me she needed to murder Hannah Montana: Country Music Legend on the Perils of Showbiz Says Dolly Parton (Star's godmother)." *The Sun*, April 19, 2014: 12, 13.

MEDIA

Dolly & Friends: The Making of a Soundtrack. Directed by Justine Feldt. Minneapolis, MN: Mill Creek Entertainment, 2018.

Dolly Parton: Here I Am. 2019 BBC documentary; originally broadcast on PBS December 25, 2019. Time-Life DVD, 2021.

Dolly: The Ultimate Collection. 2020 Time-Life (Time Warner, Inc.), DVD.

UNPUBLISHED INTERVIEWS

Nichols, Leslie. Interview by Emily Wilkinson, April 11, 2007, Austin. *Austin City Limits Oral History* Project Records, 2007, Dolph Briscoe Center for American History; DVD copy in author's files.

INDEX

Page numbers in **bold** indicate illustrations

9 to 5 (movie), 12, 72, 82–83, 97–99, **97**, **98**, 104, 137, 177, 224
9 to 5: The Musical, 184, 198–199, **199**

A

Abumrad, Jad, 40, 47, 55, 124, 224
Abumrad, Naji, 233, 234
Academy Awards, 185, **186**, **193**
Academy of Country Music, 127, 214
Acuff, Roy, 79, 149, 162
Aguilera, Christina, 220
Album of the Year award (ACM), 127
Album of the Year award (International Bluegrass Music Association), 160, 174
albums
    27: The Most Perfect Album (2018), 223–224
    All I Can Do (1976), 176
    Backwoods Barbie (2008), **156**, 196, 198
    The Bargain Store (1975), 64
    Best of Dolly Parton, Vol. 2 (2011), 66
    Better Day (2011), 208
    Blue Smoke (2014), 208, **209**
    Coat of Many Colors (1971), 173
    The Complete Trio Collection (2016), 116
    Dolly, Dolly, Dolly (1980), 218
    Eagle When She Flies (1991), 142–143, 176
    The Fairest of Them All (1970), 47
    For God and Country (2003), 177
    The Golden Streets of Glory (1971), 14, 65
    The Grass Is Blue (1999), 159–160, 162, 173, 174
    Halos & Horns (2002), 174
    Heartbreaker (1978), 79, 96
    Heartbreak Express (1982), 83
    Hello, I'm Dolly (1967), 26, 33, **33**, 34
    Here You Come Again (1977), 79, 84–85, 86, 87, 88, 92
    A Holly Dolly Christmas (2020), 147
    Honky Tonk Angels (1993), 148–149, 161
    Hungry Again (1998), 153, 159, 168
    I Believe In You (2017), 203, 234, 235
    Jolene (1974), 53
    Jolene (1984), 173
    Joshua (1971), 50, **50**
    Joyful Noise (2012), 235
    Just Between You and Me (1968), 43
    Little Sparrow (2001), 48, 168, **169**, 172, 173
    Live and Well (2004), 200
    Love Is Like a Butterfly (1974), 61–62
    My Blue Ridge Mountain Boy (1969), 159
    My Favorite Songwriter, Porter Wagoner (1972), 27
    My Tennessee Mountain Home (1973), 8, 24, 107
    New Harvest . . . First Gathering (1977), 77, 79, 84
    Porter 'n' Dolly (1980), 44
    Pure & Simple (2016), 216
    Run, Rose, Run (2022), 239
    Slow Dancing with the Moon (1993), 150–151
    Something Special (1995), **140**, 152, 168
    The Best of Dolly Parton (1970), 173
    Those Were the Days (2005), 185, 192
    Treasures (1996), 152–153
    Trio (1987), 74, 115–116, 125, **126**, 127, 131
    Trio II (1999), 116, 161
    White Limozeen (1989), 135, 137, 143
    The Winning Hand (1982), 27
Ali, Muhammad, 184
Allen, Debbie, 237
"Alligator Girl from the Nile" sideshow, 18

American Chestnut Foundation, 212
American Eagle Foundation (AEF), 118, 180–181
American Red Cross, 151
Anderson, "Whispering" Bill, 241, **242**, 243
Andrés, José, 245
Andrews, Courtney Marie, 231
Andrews, Julie, 96
Aniston, Jennifer, 220, 222
Anthony, Susan B., 223
Applebaum, Ralph, 162
Archuleta, David, 198
Arnold, Eddy, 19
Atkins, Chet, **12**, 19, 23, 79

B

Back Porch Theater (Dollywood), 118
Baez, Joan, 159, 168
Ballas, Mark, Jr., 196, **197**
Batiste, Jon, 225
Beach Boys, 135
Bee Gees, 109, 110
Benatar, Pat, 246
Bennett, Tony, 182
Bentley, Dierks, 214
Berman, Gail, 122
Big and Rich, 214
Bird, Jade, 231
Blackfoot, 162
Blackwood, R.W., Jr., 87
Block, Stephanie J., 198–199, **199**
Blue Eye Records, 35, 152
Boden, Jack, **156**
Bond, Johnny, 162
Bon Jovi, 208–209, 210
Bradley, Owen, 31
Bradley's Barn studio, 243
Bragg, Rick, 234
Bread, 176
Bridges, Leon, 225
Broadcast Music, Inc. (BMI), 28, 31, 45, 50
Brooks, Garth, 149
Brother Records, 135
Brubeck, Dave, 182
Bryant, Boudleaux, 200
Bryant, Felice, 200
Bublé, Michael, 147
Buckingham, Steve, 143, 148, 150, 152, 153, **153**, 159, 160, 166, 168, 190
Buddy Program, 155
Burke, Cheryl, 196
Burnett, Carol, 94, **95**, **96**, 131
Bush, George, 190, **191**
Bush, Laura, 190, **191**
Butler, Carl, 16, 79
Butler, Pearl, 16, 79
Butterfly Records, 239

C

Campbell, Glen, **12**, 73, 84
Campbell, Mary, 64
Capitol Records, 135
Captain Kangaroo, 75–76, **76**
Cardwell, Nancy, 135
Care More Initiative, 245
Carlile, Brandi, 225, 231, **232**, 246, 248
Carlisle, Bob, 137
Carnegie Medal of Philanthropy, 244–245
Carpenter, Candi, 231
Carpenter, Mary Chapin, 150
Carson, Johnny, 82–83, **83**, 127
Carter, Maybelle, 149
Cash, John Carter, 189
Cash, Johnny, **12**, 19, 23, 66, 79, 149, 182, 189

Cash, June Carter, 189
Cason, Buzz, 87
Cecere, Al, 180, 181
Chandaria, Manu, 244
Charles, Ray, 170, 182
Chase, Chris, 73
Chávez, Hugo, 147
Chavis, Boozoo, 17
Cher, 67, 72, 79, 90
Chesney, Kenny, 214
Chestnut Champion Award, 212
Christ Church Pentecostal Choir, 137
Churchill, Bonnie, 192
Citizen of the Year award, 128
Clark, Roy, **42**, **49**
Clarkson, Kelly, 212
Cline, Patsy, 148, 149, 251
Clinton, Bill, 157
Coat of Many Colors (book), 52, **155**
Cohn, Nudie, 66–67, **67**, 127, 172
Colbert, Stephen, 184, 235–236
Coleman, Dabney, **97**, 98, 197, **197**
Collins, Judy, 231
Columbia Records, 19
Combine Music, 26, 35
Cook, David, 198
Corbin, Everett, 20, 21, 26, 34, 51
Costello, Elvis, 166
Costner, Kevin, 144
Cottom, Tressie McMillan, 118, 145
Country Music Association (CMA), **12**, 65, 86, 127, 137, **149**, 160, 161, **163**, 188, 214, **230**
Country Music Hall of Fame and Museum, 161–162, **161**, 177, 190, **215**, 241
Courage and Civility Award, 245
COVID-19 pandemic, 91, 203, 233–234, **234**, 235–236, 241, 244
Cowell, Simon, 196
Cox, Suzanne, 190
CoZmo, Jason, **91**
Cramer, Floyd, 23
Croce, Jim, 73
Cronin, Kevin, 137
Crow, Sheryl, 231, 246, 248
Cuevas, Manuel, 127, 172
Curtis, Tony, 127
Cyrus, Billy Ray, 146, 147, 150, 151, **151**
Cyrus, Miley, 146, **147**, 218, **219**, 225, 226, 248, 249, **250**, 251

D

Dacus, Lucy, 231
Daigle, Lauren, 226
Daly, Tyne, **124**
Daniels, Charlie, 62
Darrell, Johnny, 33
Darton, Polly, 102–103
David M. Rubenstein Prize, 156
Davis, Mac, 70, 85, 137, 143, 150, 162
Davis, Skeeter, 34
Day on the Green concert, **71**, **87**
Dean, Carl (husband), 28, 30, 80, 92–93, 99, 176, 192, 209, 216–217, 222
Dean, Eddie, 148
Decca Records, 31, 153
DeMain, Bill, 58
Dennison, Hannah (niece), 234
DePreist, James, 182
Devey, Jake, **156**
Devey, Josh, **156**
Dion and the Belmonts, 21
Dirty Dozen Brass Band, 241
Dixie Pixie Productions, 122, 227
D-Nice, 235

Dolly (cloned sheep), 157–158, **158**
Dolly Lookalike Beauty Pageant, 129
Dolly: My Life and Other Unfinished Business (memoir), 8, 25, 97, 99, 130, 148
Dolly on Dolly (Randy Schmidt, editor), 54
Dolly Parton: A Personal Portrait (James Otis), 86
Dolly Parton Center for Women's Services, 108
Dolly Parton COVID-19 Research Fund, 233
"Dolly Parton Day" (Sevierville, Tennessee), 45, 128
Dolly Parton: Here I Am (documentary), 47, 48, 58, 72, 85, 97, 99, 144
Dolly Parton (Maria Isabel Sanchez Vegara and Daria Solak), 203
Dolly Parton Parkway., 87
Dolly Parton's America (podcast), 40, 47, 55, 57, 124, 224
Dolly Parton, Songteller: My Life in Lyrics (with Robert Oermann), 23, 27, 65, 207, 209, 212
Dolly Parton's Southern Light Productions, 122
Dolly Parton Wellness and Rehabilitation Center, 128
Dolly Records, 35, 152, 208, 216
"Dolly" (R.W. Blackwood, Jr.), 87
Dolly Said No to Elvis (Mark E. Nevin), 60
Dolly's Dixie Fixin's (cookbook), 13, 192–193
Dollywood, 4, 15, 36, 117–118, **119**, 158, 174, 180, 181, 196, 212, **213**, **228**, 245, 251
Dollywood Foundation, 118, 154–155
Domino, Fats, 170
Doobie Brothers, 73
Dove Awards (Gospel Music Association), 14
Dowell, Joe, 21
DreamMore Resort, 108, 212, **213**
Dr. Robert F. Thomas Foundation, 107, 108
Dukakis, Olympia, 132, **133**
Dunmow Flitch Trials, 30
Dunn, Jancee, 115, 122, 142, 143, 176
Dunn, Nora, 138, **139**
Duvall, Don, 28, 217
Duvall, Robert, 182
Dylan, Bob, 168, 176, 208

E

Eagle Mountain Sanctuary, 181
the Eagles, 72
Eavis, Emily, 210
Eavis, Michael, 210
Edwards, Leigh, 36, 157
Eklöw, Linus, 229
EmArcy label, 21
Emery, Ralph, 73
Engine Company No. 7 (Nashville), **25**
Entertainer of the Year award (CMA), 86
Etheridge, Melissa, 178
Evans, Dale, 66
Evans, Deborah Price, 216
Exposito, Suzy, 231–232

F

Fallon, Jimmy, 147, **217**, 222
Fanjoy, Trey, 243
Female Vocalist of the Year Award (CMA), 65
Ferguson, Bob, 43, 64
Field, Sally, 132
Fineman, Chloe, 249
First Ladies of Bluegrass, 231
Fleck, Béla, 135
Fletcher, Anne, 220
Flying Burrito Brothers band, 67
Foley, Red, 40

Fonda, Jane, **97**, 98–99, **98**, 137, 177, 199, **199**
For King & Country band, 14
Foster, Fred, 26, 27, 31, 33, 35, **37**
Frances Lincoln Children's Books, 203
Franklin, Aretha, 67, 231
Francisco, Don, 137
Freeman, Hadley, 28
Friend of Education award, 156
Friskics-Warren, Bill, 176, 189
Frizzell, Lefty, 66, 127
Frost, Caroline, 26, 205

G
Galantis, 229
Gallin, Sandy, 36, 70, 72, 79, 84, 92, 112, 114, 120–121, 121–122
Garment, Leonard, 182
Garner, George, 167, 194
Gellar, Sarah Michelle, 122
Georgia Campaign for Adolescent Power and Potential (GCAPP), 177
Gibb, Barry, 109, 110
Gibb, Maurice, 109
Gibb, Robin, 109
Giddens, Rhiannon, 231
Gill, Vince, 135, 145, 149, 152, 162, **163**, 173, 190
Gioia, Dana, 184
Glastonbury Festival, 209, 210–211, **211**
Gleason, Holly, 248
Gless, Sharon, **124**
Goldband Records, 17
Golden Globe Awards, 185, 222
Goldrush Junction, 117
"Goodnight with Dolly" web series, 235, 236
Gospel Music Association, 14
Graff, Todd, 204
Graham, Bill, 73
Grammy Awards, 14, 50, 52, 77, 99, 127, 160, 168, **189**, **219**, 222, 241, 243
Grand Ole Opry, 19–20, **20**, 21, 45, 94, 96, 177, 189, 190, 241, **242**
Gray, Jim, 129
Great Smoky Mountains, **6**, 118, 214
Greenblatt, Robert, 198
Green, Lloyd, 58, 135
Griffith, Nanci, 170
Griles, Steve, 180
Grobel, Lawrence, 65, 84, 88, 92
Gross, Terry, 13
Guerrero, Gene, 50
Guest, Steve, 211
Guyton, Mickey, 232
Gypsy Fever band, 65, 79, 84

H
Haggard, Merle, **42**, 149
Halford, Rob, 248
Hamessley, Lydia, 51, 127, 160, 168
Hamilton, Scott, 188
Hannah, Daryl, 132
Hardy, Tom, 236
Harling, Robert, 134
Harmonia Mundi, 77
Harris, Emmylou, **67**, 72, 74, 115–116, 125, **126**, 127, 131, 161, 226
Harrison, George, 115
Hartman, Phil, 138, **139**
Heart, 248
Hemby, Natalie, 231, **232**
Henderson, Florence, 72
Herlihy, Martin, 249
Herman, Pee-wee, 130
Hiatt, John, 229

Higgins, Colin, 104
Higgins, John, 249
The Highwomen, 231
Hill, Lyda, 244
Hilty, Megan, 198, **199**
Hirschberg, Lynn, 4
Hocter, Matthew, 65
Hogan, Hulk, 130
Holder, Stephen, 127
Hollywood Walk of Fame, 115–116, **116**
Hope, Dorothy Jo (aunt), 13, 18, 65
Horton, Johnny, 23
Hough, Derek, 196, **197**
Houston, David, 33
Houston, Whitney, 60, 144, 145, **145**
Howard, Jan, 34, 243
Huffman, Felicity, 187
Hull, Sierra, 241
Hurst, Jack, 33, 45, 46, 64

I
I Am a Rainbow (children's book), 202–203, **202**
Imagination Library, 75–76, 154–156, **156**, 200, 209, 235, 236, 245
Independence Day performance, 177, 180
Indigo Girls, 231
Ingrooves/UMG, 239
International Bluegrass Music Association (IBMA), 160, 174
Ivanhoe Theater (Chicago), 68

J
Jackson, Michael, 110, 115
Jaehne, Karen, 101
Jahr, Cliff, 54
Janney, Allison, 199, **199**
Jean, Norma, 40, 42
Jefferson, Margo, 123
Jennings, Waylon, 135, 170
Jerome, Jim, 141
Jett, Joan, 249
Joe Layton Dancers, 96
Joel, Billy, 166
John, Elton, 67
Johnny Mercer Award, 167
Johns, Michael, 198
Johnson, Craig Hella, 77
Johnston, Ollie, 182
Jones, George, 15, 20, 21, 33
Jones, Grandpa, 79
Jones, Marie, 23
Jones, Norah, 177, 225
Jones, Ramona, 79
Jones, Tom, 33, 70
Jones, Van, 245
Judas Priest, 248
the Judds, 149

K
Karlsson, Christian, 229
Katrina and the Waves, 153
Katz-Gallin-Cleary agency, 70
Kempley, Rita, 82, 90, 132
Kennedy Center Honors, 190–191
Kennedy, Jerry, 23
Kermit the Frog, 130
Kesha, 218
Kiah, Amythyst, 231
Killen, William Doyce "Buddy," 21
Kimmel, Jimmy, 129
King, Elle, 221
King, Gayle, 10
King, Larry, 177, 178, 202, 218, 219, 224
King, Larry L., 104, 106
Klein, Gary, 79, 84–85

Koch, Ed, 130
Krauss, Alison, 162, 190, 214, 222
Kristofferson, Kris, 15, 27, 204, 209
Krugman, Paul, 156
Kudisch, Marc, 197, **197**

L
Ladysmith Black Mambazo, 152–153
Lake Street Dive, 231
Lambert, Miranda, 222
Langdon, Harry, 92
Larkins, Ryan, 241
Lauper, Cyndi, 214
Lawrence, Vicki, 146
Le Bon, Simon, 246
Led Zeppelin, 176, 248
Lee, Brenda, 21, 27
LeJeune, Iry, 17
Lennon, John, 67, 115, 185
Lennox, Annie, 231, 246
Lewis, Jerry Lee, 21, 35
LGBTQ+ community, 185, 187, 219
Liberace, 67
Library of Congress, 155–156, **155**, 156, 182, 190
Lickona, Terry, 170, 172
Lifetime Achievement Award (Recording Academy), 226
Lil Nas X, 54
Litsch, Joseph, 8, 11, 12, 94
The Little Engine That Could (Watty Piper), 154, 203, 235
Little Big Town, 225
Little People, Big Dreams (book series), 203
Living Legend Award (Library of Congress), 182, 190
Llama Llama, Red Pajama (Anna Dewdney), 235
Long, Loren, 235
Looby, Z. Alexander, 129
Lordi, Emily, 166, 187
Los Angeles House of Blues, 54
Loveless, Patty, 162
Lovitz, Jon, 138, **139**
Lynn, Loretta, 15, 86, 148, 149, **149**, 161, 215

M
Mable's Smokehouse, 91
MacLaine, Shirley, 132, 134
Maddox, Rose, 20, 23
Majors, Lee, 120
Mann, Barry, 85
Mantello, Joe, 198
Manuel (tailor), 127, 172
Marcus, Greil, 159
Marsalis, Wynton, 182
Marshall, Ben, 249
Martin, Steve, 122
Mattea, Kathy, 150
McCalla, Leyla, 231
McCartney, Paul, 110, 115, 243
McDowell, Roddy, 208
McEntire, Reba, 149, **161**, 190, 214, 241, 243
McLean, Don, 214
Mehta, Zubin, 190, **191**
Mellard, Jason, 104
Mendes, Shawn, 225
Mercer, Johnny, 167
Mercury Records, 21
Meyers, Seth, 235
Mighty Fine Band, 138, 150, 198
Mikulski, Barbara, **124**
Miller, Roger, 21, 149
Mills, Irving, 148
Miss Piggy, 103, **103**, 130

Mitchell, Joni, 73, 185, 231
Moderna, 233
Monroe, Bill, 46
Montgomery, Earl, 43
Monument Records, 26, **27**, 31, 33, 35, 43, 56, 87
Moore, Dudley, 130
Morgan, Lorrie, 142
Morricone, Ennio, 77
Morris, Maren, 231, 232, **232**
Morris, Mitchell, 54, 70
Moses, Justin, 241
Moss, Marissa R., 231, 232
movies
   The Best Little Whorehouse in Texas, 83, 90, 104, **105**, 106, **106**, 112, 144, 173
   Blue Valley Songbird, 122, 159
   The Bodyguard, 144
   Buffy the Vampire Slayer, 122
   Christmas of Many Colors: Circle of Love, 52, 227
   Christmas on the Square, 237–238, **238**
   Coat of Many Colors, 52, 122, 227
   Dolly Parton: Here I Am, 47, 48, 58, 72, 85, 97, 99, 144
   Dolly Parton's Heartstrings, 54, 122, 227, **228**
   Dolly Parton's Mountain Magic Christmas, 236, **236**
   Dumplin', **91**, 220, **221**
   Father of the Bride, 122
   Joyful Noise, 204–205, **205**, 209
   The Library that Dolly Built, 236
   Live . . . And in Person, 111
   Live From London, 53
   The Mountain King, 185
   Rhinestone, 15, 83, 112, 115, 176
   A Smoky Mountain Christmas, 120, **121**
   Steel Magnolias, 132, **133**, 134
   Straight Talk, 122
   Transamerica, 185, 187
   Unlikely Angel, 208
   Urban Cowboy, 104
Musgraves, Kacey, 225, 231, 232
MusiCares, 225, 226, **226**
Myers, Mike, 138, **139**
My Life and Other Unfinished Business (memoir), 8, 25, 97, 99, 130, 148
My People Fund, 214–215

N
Nash, Alanna, 62, **63**, 72
National Assembly of State Arts Agencies, 184
National Educators Association, 156
National Endowment for the Arts (NEA), 182, 184
National Endowment for the Humanities (NEH), 184
National Humanities Medal, 182
National Medal of Arts, 182
National Medal of Freedom, 184
National Museum of Scotland, 158
National Recording Registry, 184
National Wildlife Refuge System, 181
National Woman Suffrage Association (NWSA), 223
National Zoo, 180, 181
Nealon, Kevin, 138
Nelson, Willie, 27, 106, 131, 149, 162, 166, **167**, 209, 225
Nettles, Jennifer, 52
Neville, Aaron, 241
Nevin, Mark E., 60
Newman, Jimmy C., 19
Newman, Melinda, 234

Newport Folk Festival, 231–232, **232**
Newton-John, Olivia, 72
New Year's Day Bum Steer Awards, 90
Nichols, Leslie, 172
Nicholson, Rebecca, 204
Nixon, Richard, 187
Norma Jean, 40, 42
Norton, Gale, 180
Nozell, Danny, 194–195, **195**, 208, 211

O

Oak Ridge Boys, 131
Obama, Barack, 184
Obama, Michelle, 236
O'Connor, Mark, 125
Oermann, Robert, 23
Ogle, Judy, 99, 162
Opryland, 94
Orbison, Roy, 77
Orlando, Tony, 72, 73
Osborne Brothers, 200
Oscars. See Academy Awards
the Osmonds, 72
Otis, James, 86
Our Native Daughters, 231
Ouzounian, Richard, 216
Owens, Bill (uncle), 15–16, 18, 19, 21, 26, 28, 31, 34, 35, **36**, **37**, 43, 44, 55, 56, 143, 162, 212
Owens, Henry (uncle), 17
Owens, Jake (grandfather), 13, 65, 106, 188
Owens, Kathy (aunt), **37**
Owens, Louis (uncle), 35, 45–46, 79
Owens, Richie (cousin), 153
Owens, Robert (uncle), 31
Owens, Sandy (aunt), 212
Owe-Par Publishing Company, 34, 35, 36, 45, 58

P

Page, Jimmy, 248
Paisley, Brad, 188, 189, **189**
Parker, Tom, 58, 67
Parsons, Gram, 67, 127
Partnership Award (US Fish and Wildlife Service), 180
Parton, Avie Lee Owens (mother), **5**, 8, **9**, 21, 28, 52, 74, 79, 106, 162, 166, 192, 217
Parton, Cassie (sister), **5**, 74
Parton, Floyd (brother), **5**, 74, 142
Parton, Freida (sister), **5**, 74
Parton, Rachel (sister), **5**, 74, 159, 162
Parton, Randy (brother), **5**, 65, 70, 74, 147, 162
Parton, Robert Lee (father), **5**, 8, **9**, 21, 42, 74, 79, 120, 123, 129, 154, 162, 166, 193
Parton, Stella (sister), **5**, 74
Parton, Willadeene (sister), **5**, 74, 192
Patterson, James, 239–240, **240**, 251
Paxton, Tom, 43
Peaches Records (Atlanta), **85**
Pearl, Minnie, 149
Pentatonix, 146
Perkins, Carl, 35, 143
Perry, Gregg, 84
Perry, Katy, 225
Perry, Linda, 220–221, **221**, 226, **226**, 231
Person of the Year Award (MusiCares), 225
Philips, Lewis, 96
Phillips, Bill, 31, 33, 43
Pierce, Webb, 66, 127
Pink, 220, 246, 248
Piper, Watty, 154, 203, 235
Plant, Robert, 248

Presidential Medal of Freedom, 184
Presley, Elvis, 35, 58, 60, 67, 70, 146, 149
Price, Deborah Evans, 14, 210
Prince, 110
Puckett, Dwight (cousin), 65, 70
Puss N Boots, 225
Putman, Curly, 33

Q

Queen Latifah, 204, **205**

R

radio shows
 Cas Walker Farm and Home Hour, 15, 16, 200
 Friday Night Opry, 19–20
 Louisiana Hayride, 23
Rag Time Follies fundraiser, 90
Ramirez, Tina, 182
Ray, Amy, 231
Raye, Martha, 96
Ray, Linda, 153
RCA Records, 42, 43–44, 55, 64, 66, 135
Reagan, Ronald, 187
Recording Academy, 225, 226
Rehrig, Bill, 65
REO Speedwagon, 176
Resnick, Patricia, 198, 199
Rew, Kimberley Charles, 153
Reynolds, Burt, 104, **105**
Rhino Records, 127
Rhodes, Speck, **44**, **57**
Riddle, Cheryl, 241
Riley, Jeannie C., **12**
Riley, Robert, 23
Ringgold, Georgia, 217
Rising Tide Records, 153
Ritter, John, 120
Ritter, Tex, 149
Robbins, Marty, 149
Robert F. Thomas Foundation, 107, 108
Roberts, Austin, 87
Roberts, Julia, 132, 134
Robinson, John, 67
Robinson, Smokey, 115, 190, **191**
Rock and Roll Hall of Fame, 172, **206**, 246, **247**, 249
Rockwell, John, 55, 79, 125, 127
Rodgers, Jimmie, 46, 149, 161, 170
Rogers, Kenny, 73–74, 109, 110, **111**, 161, 162, 190, 209, 214
Rogers, Maggie, 231
Rogers, Roy, 66
Rogers, Will, 149
Ronson, Mark, 225
Ronstadt, Linda, 72, 74, 115–116, 125, **126**, 127, 131, 161, 226
Rose, Fred, 161
Rose, Marc, 135
Roslin Institute (Edinburgh), 157, 158
Ross, Diana, 109, 115
Ross, Herb, 132
Rousuck, J. Wynn, 166
Run, Rose, Run (Dolly Parton and James Patterson), 239–240, **240**, 251
RuPaul, 147
Russell, Allison, 231
Russell, Bobby, **12**
Russell, Johnny, **37**
Rutherford, Rivers, 188
Ryman Auditorium (Nashville), 19–20

S

Sambora, Richie, 208–209, 210

Sanchez, Lauren, 245
Sanchez Vegara, Maria Isabel, 203
Sandollar Productions, 35–36, 120–121, 122
Savoy Hotel (London), **156**
Schlapman, Kimberly, 225
Schmidt, Randy, 54
Schusterman Family Philanthropies, 244
Schwed, Mark, 86
Scott, Jay, 30, 79, 106
Seals and Crofts, 72
Sebert, Pebe, 218
Sevier County High School, **22**, 24, 45
Sevier County, Tennessee, 128, 154, 155, 162, 214
Sha-Kon-O-Hey! (Land of Blue Smoke) stage show, 118
She Come By It Natural (Sarah Smarsh), 5, 99, 134, 146, 211, 224
Sheeran, Ed, 248
Shepard, Sam, 134
Sherman, Sarah, 249
Shires, Amanda, 231, **232**
Shuler, Eddie, 17
Shuler, Johnny, 17–18, 18
Sia, 221
Sills, Beverly, 96
Simon, Paul, 153, 214
Skaggs, Ricky, 15, 135
Smarsh, Sarah, 5, 99, 127, 134, 142, 146, 182, 211, 215, 224
Smithson, Carly, 198
Smithsonian Institution, 184
Smoky Mountain Music Barn, **37**
Smoky Mountains Rise: A Benefit for the My People Fund, 214–215
Snow, Hank, 66
Snyder, Patrick, 7, 84
Solak, Daria, 203
Song of the Year Award (BMI), 28
songs
 "9 to 5," 97, 99, 196, 210, 225, 231, 245, 246
 "After the Goldrush," 153
 "Applejack," 79
 "Baby I'm Burnin'," 229
 "Backwoods Barbie," 198
 "Banks of the Ohio," 209
 "The Bargain Store," 64–65
 "Best Woman Wins," 142
 "Better Get to Livin'," 196
 "Blackie, Kentucky," 61–62
 "Blue Smoke," 208
 "Book of Life," 65
 "Both Sides Now," 185
 "The Bridge," 48
 "Can't Be That Wrong," 216
 "Chemo Hero," 234
 "Chicken Every Sunday," 50
 "Christmas Is," 147
 "Coat of Many Colors," 35, 51–52, 173, 177, 184, 190, 226, 246
 "Come Ye Fair and Tender Maidens," 168
 "Cracker Jack," 75
 "Daddy Was an Old Time Preacher Man," 13, 45, 50, 65
 "Dagger Through the Heart," 174
 "Do I Ever Cross Your Mind," 225–226
 "Don't Drop Out," 87
 "Don't Think Twice, It's All Right," 208
 "Down from Dover," 47, 48
 "Dreams Do Come True," 143
 "Dr. Robert F. Thomas," 107
 "Dumb Blonde," 33, 40, 222
 "Eagle When She Flies," 142, 231

 "Everything is Beautiful (In Its Own Way)," 26–27, 225
 "Faith," 229
 "Family," 143
 "Farther Along," 125
 "Forever Love," 216
 "Four O'Thirty Three," 43
 "From Here to the Moon and Back," 209, 235
 "Get Out and Stay Out," 197
 "Gettin' Happy," 62
 "Girl in the Movies," 222
 "Girl Left Alone," 18
 "God Only Knows," 14
 "The Grass is Blue," 177, 225
 "Halos & Horns," 174
 "Happy, Happy Birthday, Baby," 31
 "Hello God," 176
 "Here I Am," 221
 "Here You Come Again," 85, 86, 87, 196, 225
 "He's Alive," 137
 "He's Got a Headlock on My Heart," 130
 "He's Got the Whole World In His Hands," 83
 "Highway Headin' South," 62
 "Holding on to Nothing," 44
 "Holdin' on to You," 221
 "Home," 209
 "I Am a Rainbow," 202–203
 "I Am Ready," 159
 "I Don't Believe You've Met My Baby," 173
 "I Dreamed of a Hillbilly Heaven," 148–149
 "If," 176
 "If I Cross Your Mind," 61
 "If I Had Wings," 209
 "If It Is All The Same To You," 243
 "If We Don't," 222
 "If We Never Meet Again," 62
 "Imagine," 185
 "I'm a Hog For You," 103
 "I'm Gone," 176
 "I'm Here," 235
 "I'm Sixteen," 216
 "In the Good Old Days (When Times Were Bad)," 8
 "In the Pines," 74
 "I Remember," 8
 "Islands in the Stream," 74, 109–110, **109**, 190, 214, 225
 "(It May Not Kill Me but) It's Sure Gonna Hurt," 21, 23
 "It's All Wrong, but It's All Right," 196
 "I Wasted My Tears," 31
 "I Will Always Love You," 55, 58, 60, 69, 106, 134, 144–145, 152, 173, 177, 190, 199, 226, 231, 249, 251
 "Jesus & Gravity," 196
 "J. J. Sneed," 50
 "John Daniel," 176
 "Jolene," 53–54, 70, 146, 147, 190, 211, 218, 220–221, 227, 229, 231, 233, **234**, 246, 248, 251
 "Joshua," 35, 50
 "Just Because I'm a Woman," 231
 "The Last Thing on My Mind," 43
 "Lay Your Hands On Me," 208–209, 210
 "The Letter," 24
 "Letter to Heaven," 50
 "Light of a Clear Blue Morning," 77, 79, 142
 "The Little Things," 31
 "Little Sparrow," 173, 196

"Little Tiny Tasseltop," 10, 202
"The Love You Gave," 23
"Love Is Like a Butterfly," 61, 73
"Lovesick Blues," 148
"Makin' Fun Ain't Funny," 52
"Marry Me," 173
"Mommie, Ain't That Daddy," 43
"Mountain Angel," 172, 173
"Mule Skinner Blues (Blue Yodel No. 8)," 45, 46, 170, 173
"My Eyes Can Only See You," 61
"My Mountains, My Home," 214
"Nineteenth Amendment," 223–224
"No One Kicks Like a Nashville Kicker Kicks," 96
"No One Picks Like a Nashville Picker Picks," 94
"Not Enough," 225
"Not for Me," 174
"Old Black Kettle," 8
"Old Flames Can't Hold A Candle to You," 218
"Once Upon a Memory," 61
"Orange Blossom Special," 94
"Outside Your Door," 216
"Pretty Is As Pretty Does," 120
"Puppy Love," 18
"Put It Off Until Tomorrow," 28, 43
"Rainbowland," 218
"Raven Dove," 176
"Real Love," 110
"Rockin'," 246
"Rockin' Years," 142, 188
"Rocky Top," 200
"Romeo," 150, 151
"Rosewood Casket," 127
"Sacred Memories," 62
"Sandy's Song," 168
"Say Forever You'll Be Mine," 216
"The Seeker," 226
"Shattered Image," 174, 176
"Shine," 168, 173
"Shine On," 168
"Silver Dagger," 159, 168
"Silver Threads," 74
"Singing His Praise," 65
"Slow Dancing with the Moon," 150
"Smoky Mountain Memories," 196, 214
"Someday It'll All Make Sense," 241, 243
"Someone to Watch Over Me," 131
"Something Fishy," 34, 40
"Sorrow's Tearing Down the House (That Happiness Once Built)," 43
"Stairway to Heaven," 176, 248
"Sugar Hill," 174
"Take Me Back," 62
"A Tender Lie," 173
"Tennessee Homesick Blues," 83
"There Was Jesus," 14
"These Old Bones," 174
"Time for Me to Fly," 137, 176
"Tomorrow Is Forever," 216
"Train, Train," 162, 170, 173
"Travelin' Prayer," 159, 176
"Travelin' Thru," 185, 186, 187
"Try," 209
"Turn Around (Where Are You Going, My Little One?)," 96
"Two Doors Down," 87, 88, 222, 227
"Two Sides to Every Story," 44
"Unlikely Angel," 208
"Wait 'Til I Get You Home," 137
"Walking on Sunshine," 153
"Wayfaring Stranger," 187

"What A Heartache," 174, 176
"What Am I Doing Up Here?", 94
"What Do You Think About Lovin'?", 31
"When I Get Where I'm Going" (Brady Paisley), 188–189
"When Life Is Good Again," 233–234
"White Limozeen," 137, 138
"Why," 221–222
"Why'd You Come in Here Looking Like That," 137, 138
"Wildest Dreams," 143
"Wildflowers," 127
"Words," 110
"Yakety Sax," 210
"Yellow Roses," 137
"You Can't Make Old Friends," 209
"You Gotta Be My Baby," 15, 20
"You're Known by the Company You Keep," 31
"You're the One That Taught Me How to Swing," 61, 62
Songwriters Hall of Fame, 153, 166–167, 167, 190
Sonnier, Jo-El, 137
Sonny and Cher, 67
Sothern, Hal, 148
SoundCloud, 235
Spelman, Lucy, 180
Spielberg, Steven, 190, 191
Spiva, Sidney (cousin), 65, 70
Stadiem, William, 121
Stallone, Sylvester, 15, 83, 112, 115, 176
Staples, Mavis, 221–222, 225
Stapleton, Chris, 214, 225
Starday Records, 21
Starling, John, 125
Starr, Ringo, 115
statue, 128–129, 128
Stehr, Dennis Princewell "Mr. Probz," 229
Steinem, Gloria, 123
Stevens, Ray, 21, 26, 27
Stiller, Ben, 138, 139
Stone, Lucy, 223
Stone, Sly, 67
Streisand, Barbra, 79, 84, 109
Stuart, Marty, 161
Studio 54 disco, 112, 113
Sugar Hill Records, 153, 159
Summer, Donna, 70
Sun, Joe, 218
Sun Records, 19, 35
Sutton, Judith, 52
Sweet, Jay, 231
Sweet, Philip, 225
Swift, Taylor, 214, 243

T
The Teeny Tiny Woman (children's book), 75
television
  American Bandstand, 35, 56
  Austin City Limits (ACL), 69, 170, 172–173
  The Carol Burnett Show, 94
  CBS This Morning, 10
  Cher . . . Special, 79
  Dancing with the Stars, 198, 199
  David Letterman Show, 181
  Dolly!, 10, 73–74, 74, 125
  The Dolly Show, 103, 103, 130–131, 178, 179
  Dolly Parton Meets the Kids, 10
  The Eddie Hill Show, 24, 34, 35
  Good Morning America, 181
  Great American Country network, 182
  Hannah Montana, 146, 147, 151, 249

  Hee-Haw, 131
  Hollywood Squares, 72
  Larry King Live, 177, 178, 180, 202, 218, 219, 224
  The Late Show with Stephen Colbert, 184
  The Mac Davis Show, 70
  Miley's New Year's Eve Party, 249, 250
  Nightline, 90
  The Oprah Winfrey Show, 143, 144
  Ozark Jubilee, 40
  The Porter Wagoner Show, 27, 35, 40, 42, 42, 44, 45–46, 46, 51, 53, 55–56, 57, 73, 77, 81, 82, 142, 189
  The Ralph Emery Show, 35
  Saturday Night Live (SNL), 138–139, 139, 249
  Sesame Street, 102
  Song by Song, 13
  The Tonight Show with Jay Leno, 160
  The Tonight Show with Jimmy Fallon, 217, 222
  The Tonight Show with Johnny Carson, 72, 82–83, 83, 115, 127
  Valentine's Day special, 94, 95, 96, 96
  The Voice, 146
Telly Awards, 236
Teren, George, 188
Texas Monthly, 90
There's a Hole in the Log on the Bottom of the Lake (Loren Long), 235
Thomas, Bob, 106
Thomas, Randy, 137
Thomas, Robert F., 107–108, 117
Thompson, Gayle, 241, 243
Tillis, Mel, 82, 102
Tomberlin, Bobby, 241
Tomlin, Lily, 97, 98–99, 98, 137, 199, 199
Tony Awards, 197
Tony Orlando and Dawn, 73
Travelin' Family Band, 65, 70, 79, 81
Travis, Randy, 149
Treasure Isle Studios, 135
Tree Publishing, 21
Trescott, Jacqueline, 191
Tubb, Ernest, 79, 149
Tucker, Duncan, 185
Tucker, Tanya, 149, 150
Tuttle, Molly, 231
Twain, Shania, 177, 178, 190
Twitty, Conway, 149, 162
Tyler, Steven, 243

U
Underwood, Carrie, 190
Universal Records, 153
US Highway 411 (Dolly Parton Parkway), 87

V
Vail, Fred, 135, 137
Vanderbilt University, 233, 234, 240
Van Dyke, Leroy, 21
Vanguard Records, 153
Van Halen, Eddie, 110
Van Shelton, Ricky, 142
Velvet Apple Music, 35, 58, 60, 112
Vincent, Rhonda, 222
Vocal Event of the Year award (CMA), 127, 161

W
Wagoner, Porter, 12, 13, 15, 33, 35, 38, 40, 41, 42, 43, 44, 45, 46, 47, 51–52, 53, 55, 56–57, 56, 57, 61, 62, 64, 65, 66, 79, 149, 162, 177, 243
Wagonmasters, 44, 47, 52, 57, 66

Walburn, Lee, 72, 79
Walker, Cas, 16, 128
Walters, Barbara, 80–81, 81, 117
Warden, Ann, 162
Warden, Don, 79, 162
Warhol, Andy, 112, 113, 114, 114
Warnock, Neil, 208
Warwick, Dionne, 166
Watson, Dot (uncle), 16
Watson, Estelle Owens (aunt), 16
Webber, Andrew Lloyd, 77, 190, 191
Weil, Cynthia, 85
Wells, Ida B., 129
Wells, Kent, 209
Wells, Kitty, 34, 65, 79, 148
West, Dottie, 149
White, Cheryl, 190
White Limozeen bar, 135, 137
Whitman, Slim, 23
The Whorehouse Papers (Larry L. King), 106
Wild Possums Band, 15
Williams, Hank, Jr., 34
Williams, Hank, Sr., 15, 66, 148, 149, 161
Williams, Paul, 166, 167
Williams, Tex, 66
Williams, Zach, 14
Willis, Bruce, 130
Wilmut, Sir Ian, 157
Wilson, Ann, 248
Wilson, Brian, 135
Wilson, Nancy, 248
Windle, John Mark, 129
Windsor, Amie, 218
Winfrey, Oprah, 130, 178, 179
Winkler, Henry, 120
Winslet, Kate, 236
Wiseman, Craig, 196
Wishy Washy Laundromat, 28, 216–217
Witherspoon, Reese, 190
Woman of the Year award (Ms. magazine), 123, 124, 124
Wooley, Sheb, 12
Wright, Johnny, 79
Wynette, Tammy, 12, 33, 148, 149, 149, 161

Y
Yola, 231
Young, Chris, 214
Young, Faron, 21
Young, Neil, 153
Yousafzai, Malala, 156

Z
ZZ Top, 67

ACKNOWLEDGMENTS

I would like to thank the editors and other creative team members at Quarto for their work in seeing this project through over a relatively short time frame. The library staff at Agnes Scott College is a powerful resource for any kind of project, and I am grateful for all my colleagues there. I also thank Kathleen Campbell, archivist at the Country Music Hall of Fame. My faculty and staff colleagues are lovely and supportive, and I am blessed to work alongside such fantastic people: that includes Journeys and Summit colleagues, music and creative arts colleagues, friends, as well as students from whom and with whom I learn every day. Here's a shout-out to Epiphany friends and neighbors . . . I'm glad to know you. I am grateful to my family for their love and support, and for anyone and everyone in my life with ears to listen to music, thoughts, stories, ideas, and words about Dolly when and where they have poured forth these past months. I thank the scholars, music writers, journalists, interviewers, novelists, podcasters, and everyone who has spent time exploring Dolly Parton's significance over more than five decades. Finally, I will say that, at the end of an intense period of dwelling in the "Dollyverse," I am left with a feeling of admiration for how Dolly has carved her own fresh path in this world, and a feeling of inspiration to try and do the same. May it be so for anyone who reads this book.

ABOUT THE AUTHOR

Tracey Laird is a professor of music at Agnes Scott College in Decatur, Georgia. She is the author or editor of four books, including *Austin City Limits: A History* (Oxford University Press, 2014) and *Austin City Limits: A Monument to Music* (Insight Editions, 2015), the latter co-authored with her spouse, who is also a writer. She has contributed a chapter on "Country Music and Television" to the collection *The Oxford Handbook of Country Music* (Oxford University Press, 2017). Her perspective on the twenty-first century is part of the 50th Anniversary edition of Bill Malone's seminal *Country Music, U.S.A.* (University of Texas Press, 2018).

IMAGE CREDITS

Page 5 MediaPunch Inc/Alamy Stock Photo. Page 6 ehrlif/Shutterstock. Page 9 ©ABC/Getty Images. Page 11 Pictorial Press Ltd/Alamy Stock Photo. Page 12 New World Photography 1968/Courtesy of the Country Music Hall of Fame® and Museum Page 14 Nicole Weaver/Alamy Stock Photo. Page 16 Michael Ochs Archives/Stringer/Getty Images. Page 17 Media Punch/Alamy Stock Photo. Page 18 CC wikimedia.org/Shutterstock. Page 20 Pictures Now/Alamy Stock Photo. Page 22 Media Punch/Alamy Stock Photo. Page 25 Samuel A. Tarkington/Country Music Hall of Fame. Page 27 Monument Records/Country Music Hall of Fame. Page 29 Everett Collection/Alamy Stock Photo. Page 32 Michael Ochs Archives/Stringer/Getty Images. Page 33 *Hello I'm Dolly*, Photograph. https://www.loc.gov/item/ihas.200003688. Page 34 Music City News vol. 05, no. 03, Music City News Publishing Co., Inc./Courtesy of the Country Music Hall of Fame® and Museum Page 36 Curtis Hilbun/Alamy Stock Photo Page 37 Country Music Hall of Fame. Page 38 Pictorial Press/Alamy Stock Photo. Page 41 Michael Ochs Archives/Stringer/Getty Images. Page 42 Bettmann/Getty Images. Page 44 Michael Ochs Archives/Stringer/Getty Images. Page 46 Hope Powell/Courtesy of the Country Music Hall of Fame® and Museum. Page 49 Music City News vol. 07, no. 05, Music City News Publishing Co., Inc./Courtesy of the Country Music Hall of Fame® and Museum. Page 50 Michael Ochs Archives/Stringer/Getty Images. Page 52 Hum Images/Alamy Stock Photo. Page 53 Donaldson Collection/Michael Ochs Archives/Getty Images. Page 56 Michael Ochs Archives/Stringer. Page 57 Bill Waterson/Alamy Stock Photo. Page 59 Raeanne Rubenstein/Courtesy of the Country Music Hall of Fame® and Museum. Page 63 Leonard Kamsler/Courtesy of the Country Music Hall of Fame® and Museum. Page 64 Michael Ochs Archives/Stringer/Getty Images. Page 67 Chris Walter/WireImage/Getty Images. Page 68 Paul Natkin/ Archive Photos/Getty Images. Page 71 Richard McCaffrey/Michael Ochs Archives/Getty Images. Page 74 ©Courtesy Everett Collection. Page 76 ©Courtesy Everett Collection Page 78 Tom Hill/WireImage/Getty Images. Page 81 ©ABC/Courtesy Everett Collection. Page 83 ZUMA/Alamy Stock Photo. Page 84 Donaldson Collection/Getty Images. Page 85 Tom Hill/Michael Ochs ArchivesGetty Images. Page 87 Richard McCaffrey/Getty Images. Page 89 Harry Langdon/Archive Photos. Page 91 Kevin Winter/Staff/Getty Images Entertainment. Page 93 Harry Langdon/Archive Photos/Getty Images. Page 95 Media Punch/Alamy Stock Photo. Page 96 CBS Photo Still-Courtesy of CBS Broadcasting Inc. Page 98 The Hollywood Archive/Alamy Stock Photo. Page 99 The Hollywood Archive/Alamy Stock Photo. Page 100 LGI Stock/Corbis Historical. Page 103 ©ABC/Getty Images. Page 105 AJ Pics/Alamy Stock Photo. Page 106 Pictorial Press/Alamy Stock Photo. Page 108 Pete Still/Redferns/Getty Images. Page 109 Records/Alamy Stock Photo. Page 111 Mark Humphrey/Associated Press. Page 113 ©Photoshot/Everett Collection. Page 114 Reuters/Alamy Stock Photo Page 116 William Nation/Sygma/Getty Images. Page 119 Ron Davis/Archive Photos/Getty Images. Page 121 Album/Alamy Stock Photo. Page 124 G. Paul Burnett/Associated Press. Page 126 Lennox McClendon/Associated Press. Page 128 Images-USA/Alamy Stock Photo. Page 131 Ron Davis/Archive Photos/Getty Images. Page 133 The Hollywood Archive/Alamy Stock Photo. Page 136 Media Punch/Alamy Stock Photo. Page 139 Ron Galella, Ltd./Ron Galella Collection. Page 140 Courtesy of the Country Music Hall of Fame® and Museum. Page 143 Paul Natkin/Getty Images Entertainment. Page 144 Paul Natkin/Archive Photos/Getty Images. Page 145 Maximum Film/Alamy Stock Photo. Page 147 Kevin Winter/Staff/Getty Images Entertainment. Page 149 ZUMA Press Alamy Stock Photo. Page 151 ©Disney Channel/Courtesy Everett Collection. Page 153 Ryan Born/WireImage/Getty Images. Page 155 Shannon Finney/Getty Images Entertainment. Page 156 Gareth Davies Getty Images Entertainment. Page 158 Inset Mathieu Polak/SygmaGetty Images. Page 158 The Hollywood Archive/Alamy Stock Photo. Page 160 R. Diamond WireImage/Getty Images. Page 161 Tami Chappell/Alamy Stock Photo. Page 163 Ed Rode/Getty Images Entertainment. Page 164 Paul Harris/Getty Images Entertainment. Page 167 KMazur/WireImage. Page 169 J. P. Aussenard/Staff/WireImage/Getty Images. Page 171 Brian Rasic/Getty Images Entertainment. Page 175 Jon Super/RedfernsGetty Images. Page 179 ABC/Getty Images. Page 180 Mark Wilson/Staff/Getty Images News. Page 183 ZUMA/Alamy Stock Photo. Page 186 Michael Caulfield Archive/WireImage/Getty Images. Page 189 Kevin Winter/Staff/Hulton Archive/Getty Images. Page 191 The White House/Handout/Getty Images Entertainment. Page 193 Michael Buckner/Staff/Getty Images Entertainment. Page 195 Rick Diamond/Staff/Getty Images Entertainment. Page 197 ©ABC/Getty Images. Page 199 Bruce Glikas/FilmMagic/Getty Images. Page 201 Curtis Hilbun/Alamy Stock Photo. Page 202 Curtis Hilbun/Alamy Stock Photo. Page 205 Cinematic Collection/Alamy Stock Photo. Page 206 Valerie Macon/AFP/Getty Images. Page 209 Clynt Garnham Publishing/Alamy Stock Photo. Page 211 Jim Dyson/Getty Images Entertainment. Page 213 Curtis Hilbun/Alamy Stock Photo. Page 215 Rick Diamond/Staff/Getty Images Entertainment. Page 217 Christopher Polk/ACM2016/Getty Images Entertainment. Page 219 Kevork Djansezian/Stringer/Getty Images Entertainment. Page 221 Matt Winkelmeyer/Staff/Getty Images Entertainment. Page 224 Curtis Hilbun/Alamy Stock Photo. Page 226 Lester Cohen/Getty Images Entertainment. Page 228 Jason Kempin/Staff/Getty Images Entertainment. Page 230 Terry Wyatt/Stringer/Getty Images Entertainment. Page 232 Douglas Mason/WireImage/Getty Images. Page 234 Erika Goldring/Getty Images Entertainment. Page 236 Jason Kempin/Staff/Getty Images Entertainment. Page 238 American Pictorial Collection/Alamy Stock Photo. Page 240 Michael Loccisano/Staff/Getty Images Entertainment. Page 242 Tony R. Phipps/Getty Images Entertainment. Page 245 Curtis Hilbun/AFF-USA/Alamy Stock Photo. Page 247 Theo Wargo/Staff/Getty Images Entertainment. Page 251 Kevin Mazur/Getty Images Entertainment.